THE GREEK VIEW OF POETRY

BY

E. E. SIKES, M.A.

PRESIDENT OF ST. JOHN'S COLLEGE, CAMBRIDGE

AUTHOR OF
" ROMAN POETRY" "THE ANTHROPOLOGY OF THE GREEKS" ETC.

HYPERION PRESS, INC.
Westport, Connecticut

HOUSTON PUBLIC LIBRARY

INDEXED IN GK. & Roman a.

Published in 1931 by Methuen & Co., London
Hyperion reprint edition
Library of Congress Number 78-20494
ISBN 0-88355-870-X
Printed in the United States of America

Library of Congress Cataloging in Publication Data
Sikes, Edward Ernest, 1867-1940.
  The Greek view of poetry.

  Reprint of the 1931 ed. published by Methuen, London.
  Includes bibliographical references and index.
  1. Criticism—Greece—History. 2. Poetry—History
and criticism. I. Title.
[PN87.S57 1979]   881'.009   78-20494
ISBN 0-88355-870-X

PREFACE

THE object of this book is to examine the critical theories and—in a broader sense—the popular appreciation of poetry by the Greeks. Incidentally, for the sake of completeness, I have touched on the whole range of Greek critics, in their references to prose as well as poetry, so that the present work may, I hope, be regarded as material for the First Chapter in the History of Criticism. But I have chiefly concentrated on poetic theories for several reasons: firstly, because a full discussion of rhetoric would have swollen this book to an inordinate bulk; secondly, because the classical analysis of poetry for the most part applies to prose, owing to the Greek habit of regarding the Word as a unity, whether expressed " in metre or without it "; and thirdly, because a book—if it is to be even moderately successful—must be a labour of love, and, in my own love of Greek literature, Homer and Aeschylus, Aristophanes and Theocritus are still the first charge on a debt of half a century.

No sane man, of course, denies the supreme value of Greek poetry; but it is sometimes objected that the Greek poets builded better than they, or at least their critics, knew. There is some justification for this warning. As Longinus saw, criticism is " an after-growth of much experience "; and the first and even the last attempts of the Greeks to estimate poetic principles and values are often crude and sometimes wrong-headed. The structure raised by Aristotle needs a continual overhauling, and there are some modern critics who think it radically unsound and indeed beyond repair. With this extreme position I have little sympathy; on the contrary, I believe that the Greek critical foundations were, on the whole, well and truly laid. But, even if the building were ruinous, it would not greatly affect the purpose of this book, which is mainly historical, concerned with the relative value of poetry to the Greeks themselves. It is true that they sometimes gave bad reasons for admiring good poetry. Their passion for Homer, in especial, was frequently marred by qualms of conscience, for which the moderns, with a wider perspective, have no use. We can now take a short cut to poetic appreciation, avoiding the long route strewn with pitfalls of Greek philosophy and theology. But there is still an interest and a profit in retracing the long way. We cannot fully understand Greek thought without viewing it in relation to the poets; and we can only attain this view by an historical examination of their criticism, with its faults as well as its achievements.

There have been numerous treatises on particular Greek critics from Plato to Longinus, but there is still room, I think, for a survey of the whole field in a single compass. I do not, of course, forget the interesting, though sometimes hypothetical work of Egger, to which I owe not a little, although I owe still more to Saintsbury's monumental *History of Criticism* for facts as well as inspiration. But even the ample sweep of his first volume is not comprehensive enough to cover the wide stretch of ground in detail; and, in any case, the more recent work, not only of classical scholarship but of general criticism and æsthetics, seems to warrant a new synthesis. In this direction, I have learnt most, perhaps, from the Aristotelian studies of Butcher and Bywater, supplemented by the Italian scholar Rostagni; but I must not omit acknowledgment to a younger student—Mr. D. W. Lucas, Fellow of King's College, Cambridge—whose critical essay (at present unpublished) on Greek criticism, to the time of Plato, has more than once helped me in correcting or confirming my own conclusions. Finally, the editions of Longinus and other Greek critics, by the late Professor Rhys Roberts, require a very special tribute which I gratefully pay to his memory. For proof-reading, I have to thank two colleagues, the Rev. C. F. Angus (on Plato) and Mr. M. P. Charlesworth (on the rest of the book), who—in the time-honoured, but very necessary disclaimer—are not responsible for statements with which they may well disagree.

A few paragraphs or phrases in this book have been reprinted, by permission, from a lecture on Homer, delivered during a cruise of the Hellenic Travellers' Club in 1929. Otherwise the work has served only as the basis of lectures for Classical students, to whose patience I would dedicate it, if I had not hoped that it might also interest a larger public.

E. E. S.

CAMBRIDGE, *April, 1931*

CONTENTS

vii

THE GREEK VIEW OF POETRY

CHAPTER I

EARLY CRITICISM

§ 1. The Beginnings of Criticism

IN strict logic, a discussion of poetry should begin with a definition of its nature. But the history of criticism has amply proved that poetry is easier to recognise than to define; and early critics, content with assuming that it was a divine gift expressed in song, were more interested in the function than in the nature of the art. What was poetry "for"? Was it to instruct or simply to please, or for both objects combined? As we shall see in detail, the Greeks were too moralistic a nation to divorce the poetic impulse from ethical values, even if there were some who revolted from the theory that the end of poetry is instruction— a theory natural enough when the poet (whatever else he might be) was certainly a teacher. Indeed, the history of Greek criticism is largely occupied, not so much with a denial of the function of art to teach, as with the relation between this teaching and the claim of pleasure to be its immediate end. In this connexion, it is interesting to note that the earliest Greeks, of whom we have any record, seem to have gained, by intuition, the position which their descendants reached after

I

centuries of argument—that poetry, whether instructive
or not, must be delightful.   Homer is here decisive on
his own art ; for nothing is more striking than his
frequent stress on pleasure as the essence of his poetic
appeal.   Demodocus at the court of Alcinous received
from the Muse the gift of " sweet song " in return for
his blindness.[1]   Again, the listener " gazes on a bard
who from the gods has learned to sing words delightful
to men, and they urgently desire to hear him, whenever
he sings." [2] The minstrel's theme might be sad,
as Odysseus and his son had reason to know ; but
Telemachus acknowledged that the bard was not to
be blamed for the sorrow which the gods give, but
rather praised for the pleasure which men take in the
newest song.[3]   It is perhaps a pity that later Greeks
were not content with these sane words of the prudent
Telemachus.

   This " delight " in song is, for the epic bard, not
merely the natural pleasure which modern psychology
has hardly better explained by re-naming it æsthetic
satisfaction.   Hesiod at least, recognises it as a sort of
anodyne : if a man has sorrow and hears a minstrel
singing the glories of the men of old or the blessed gods,
he straightway forgets his pain.[4]   In Homer, we recall
Achilles, soothing his wrath by a song of heroic deeds.[5]
But, in the main, the function of Homeric minstrelsy is
positive rather than negative.   Homer can tell a tale
full of pathos without suggesting that his audience need
consolation ; and, indeed—as Andrew Lang, discussing
the *Adoniazusae* of Theocritus, might well have remembered—a king's court is not the best place to com-
fort those who are " sick and sorry."   The pleasure of
the epic was its own end, and was produced by enchant-

----

[1] *Od.* 8, 63 f., and 487 f.   [2] *Od.* 17, 518.   [3] *Od.* 1, 325 f.
[4] *Theog.* 98 f. ; cf. 55   [5] *Il.* 9, 189.

ment (θέλξις)—a term which survived as a classical definition of the poetic process.

With this word and its cognates, the primitive connexion of poetry with magic is clearly shown. The same word is used to describe the spell of the witch Circe, who enchants the comrades of Odysseus, and only fails with the hero himself, because he is protected by the counter-charm of " moly." [1] That magical plant belongs to Hermes, the arch-wizard, whose wand charms the eyes of men in sleep ; [2] and there can be no doubt that the staff (ῥάβδος, σκῆπτρον), which Hesiod received from the Muses as a token of his poetic mission, is no other than the magician's wand.[3] It is no mere " emblem," but, in its own sphere, has the potency of the cestus, with which Aphrodite holds all the enchantments of love (θελκτήρια).[4]

Had the word θέλξις lost its literal significance by the time of the epic, and already become a metaphor, as " charm " and " enchantment " have become in modern times ? The question is impossible to answer with certainty ; but Homer still lived in the atmosphere of magic, and may fairly have claimed for his own song the power, in kind if not in degree, of Hermes and Circe. Such, in effect, is the " spell " of poetry—whether κηληθμός is a magical term or not—when the Phaeacians listened to Odysseus in the dim-lit halls.[5] For the gods could easily pass on their own efficacy to the human interpreters of their will or knowledge—the ἀοιδοί. Their " singing " covered all poetry, whether recited to the accompaniment of the lyre, as probably in epic, or

---

[1] *Od.* 10, 305.   [2] *Od.* 24, 2.

[3] Hes. *Theog.* 30. See de Waele in Pauly-Wissowa, *s.v.* Stab, and in his *Magic Staff or Rod in Graeco-Italian Antiquity* (1927).

[4] *Il.* 14, 214, an embroidered strap. Later identified with the girdle ; see Leaf, *ad. loc.*

[5] *Od.* 11, 334, κηληθμῷ ἔσχοντο κατὰ μέγαρα σκιόεντα.

" sung," as in the dirge or marriage-song—forms of
poetry too popular to be often mentioned in a royal
palace, although they belong to a stage far earlier than
the epic itself.[1] It was late before the "poet" (ποιητής)
supplanted the " singer," just as the *poeta* of Roman
literature took long to oust the *vates* of pre-Hellenic
Italy.[2]

The object of epic poetry was to sing " the famous
deeds of men " (κλέα ἀνδρῶν), and the singer naturally
claims that these deeds are " true," a record of historic
fact revealed by the Muses or Apollo to ignorant men.[3]
Here, precisely, lay the trouble in later criticism : this
alleged truth was often found to be false, and the teacher
was therefore the more to be condemned for using
delightful speech to conceal his " lies." As a fact, the
Homeric poet nowhere lays emphasis on the instructive
value of his song, being content that it should please.
But Homer suffered for the sins of a rival school which
openly assumed the office of instruction. For it is in
Hesiod that the singer first becomes an inspired teacher,
with a divine message to deliver. The Boeotian school
may be later than the Homeric, but it certainly preserves
a more primitive conception of the poet as a prophet,
whose function is not necessarily to please—a Jeremiah
could have given little pleasure to his original hearers—
but to tell the truth, as revealed by some higher power,
by singing "what is, and shall be, and has been." [4]

[1] For the marriage-song, see *Il.* 18, 493 ; for the pæan or dirge,
Il. 22, 391 ; the Linus-song, *Il.* 18, 570. The " hymn " occurs once
in the *Odyssey* (8, 429).

[2] The first certain uses of ποιητής and its cognates, in the restricted sense, are found in Herodotus and Aristophanes. See p. 74.

[3] *Il.* 2, 484 f. ; cf. *Od.* 8, 44, 62, 488, 498 ; 17, 518 ; 22, 345.

[4] *Theog.* 1-105. It is probable, as T. W. Allen holds (*Homer*,
p. 78), that the *Theogony* and other works belong to the school of
Hesiod, i.e. the author of the *Works and Days*. For the didacticism
of the school see Powell and Barber, *New Chapters* (second series),
p. 189, and Evelyn-White, *Hesiod* (Loeb).

Hesiod indeed, at least in the *Theogony*, is so far Homeric that he insists on the pleasure of his message to men, just as the Muses themselves delight the mind of their father Zeus. But his song, for all its sweetness, is valued because of its utility.

Greek criticism, therefore, when it arose, was confronted with the general belief that the end of poetry was to teach pleasurably. Being unable to discriminate between the poetry of imagination and the verse which really took the place of a prose, as yet unborn, the critics were handicapped at the very start; and the theory of didacticism, however modified, remained an incubus which could never be entirely expelled. In justice to the critics, it must be remembered that they could not have renounced the *right* of the poet to teach, without flagrant violation of the facts. The gnomic and lyric poets were continually quoted for their advice; the great dramatists were, first and foremost, διδάσκαλοι, teachers; and, in the last age of Greek poetry, which coincided with the full development of criticism, the school of Aratus and Nicander was avowedly didactic. The only mistake of the critics—shared by popular opinion—was to confuse the right with the necessity of teaching, so that instruction was expected from poets who were innocent of any desire to " improve." It has taken many centuries to reach the conception that a poet may appeal in spite of his didacticism; the Greek problem was rather to discover how far instruction could be combined with pleasure. The problem, which runs through all ancient criticism from Aristophanes to Quintilian, is implicit not merely in Hesiod's practice but in his own definite words. And, indirectly at least, the different aims of the Homeric and Hesiodean schools seem to have caused the first literary quarrel of antiquity. There is surely a censure of the epic poets implied in the opening lines of the *Theogony*, where the Muses tell the shepherd-poet " we know how to speak many lies like the truth ; and we know how to speak true things when we wish." [1] The passage was destined to be remembered in another connexion ; [2] but, in its original context, it may well have been a claim for Hesiodean " truth," and a rebuke to the Homeric singer, whose imagination is condemned as a " lie." [3] Hesiod will not take refuge in the fiction of the epic, and, in particular, he will not acquiesce in Homer's reticence about the seamier side of Greek religion—a legacy from older and cruder theology—but, at all cost, will speak the truth.

That the two schools were rivals is clear, even if we do not lay stress on Hesiod's line that " beggar is jealous of beggar, bard of bard." This rivalry was no doubt partly due to social class. The Homeric bards seem to have held a position of trust in the royal courts, and must have won more honour than was suggested by Bentley in his famous remark that Homer wrote for small earnings and good cheer. Agamemnon left his wife in charge of his minstrel, who had to be killed before Aegisthus could persuade Clytemnestra to be unfaithful.[4] Hesiod, on the other hand, though living under the rule of petty princes, and a sufferer at their hands, is essentially a poet of the people. The author of the *Works and Days* had little, either politically or poetically, in common with the *Wrath of Achilles*. Cleomenes put the

---

[1] 27-28.   [2] See p. 68 f.

[3] In later times, no doubt, the " lie " was thought due to the fallibility of the human agent who corrupted the divine message ; such, apparently, was Plato's view, if we may judge by the *Laws*, 669c and 700d.

[4] *Od*. 3, 267 f., where εἴρυσθαι means " to watch." Strabo (1, 2, 3) and Athenaeus (1, 14b) explain the passage as implying that the poet was a moral instructor ; this, however, is not Homeric, but Stoic.

matter tersely in observing that Homer was the poet
of Lacedemonians, Hesiod, of Helots; and Alexander
followed in his preference for " the poet of kings." [1]
Of course there might be rivalry between members
of the same school, as perhaps in the "Contests"
in which Hesiod himself took part, when he won an
" eared tripod " at the games held at Chalcis in honour
of Amphidamas. [2] But the legendary contest between
Homer and Hesiod (*Certamen Homericum*) may be taken
as a recollection of the struggle between two schools
personified by their founders. The *Certamen* itself is
a late compilation of the Antonine age ; but it contains
old material, which can be traced with some probability
through Alcidamas, in the fourth century, to Aristophanes
(*Peace* 1280) and, still earlier, to Lesches of Lesbos, who
is credited with a poem of the later epic age itself. [3]

The true epic period closed with the *Homeric Hymns*,
which show no desire to instruct. In the hymn to the
Delian Apollo, the blind singer of Chios asks for recognition as the " sweetest of singers, in whom all take most
pleasure." Although the subject of his hymn is as religious as the *Theogony*, he does not pose as a Hesiodean
prophet, but continues the Homeric tradition of pure
pleasure. The Delian hymn has other points of interest.
It gives us, in a few lines, a clear picture of a πανήγυρις
or *festa*, attended—as similar festivals even now in the
island of Tenos—by pilgrims from all parts of Greece,
who listened not only to professional singers, but to a
chorus of women imitating the various dialects of the
pilgrims, apparently in order to act for the local choirs. [4]

---

[1] *Theog.* 80 f., *Works*, 248, etc. See generally H. M. Chadwick,
Heroic Age, ch. xi. For Cleomenes, cf. Plut. *apophth. Lac.* 223*a* ; for
Alexander, Dio Chrys. *or.* 2, 8 f.

[2] *Works*, 654.

[3] See T. W. Allen, *Homer*, p. 19 f. ; Powell and Barber, p. 36 f.

[4] Allen and Sikes, *Homeric Hymns*, p. 87 (*h. Ap.*, 157) and Append.
309.

And it is not, perhaps, altogether fanciful to regard Delos—the scene of the legendary contest between Homer and Hesiod—as the natural meeting-place for the Ionian and Boeotian schools, where the gay, sceptical, pleasure-loving Homeridae, who delighted in the loves of Ares and Aphrodite, and in the precocity of the thief-god Hermes, fought out the first battle of the bards with their sterner, moralistic rivals, who drew their inspiration from Helicon.[1] However this may be, the Delian hymn is a document of rare value as the first description of the Panegyris, with its poetic Agon, which, throughout Greek history, was to exercise such influence on the conditions of poetic publication.   Times were changing since the bard had sung to an aristocratic audience.   The Homeric singer indeed survived—though much more loosely attached—in the lyric poets, like Pindar, commissioned from time to time to satisfy a king or tyrant with an epinikian ode.   But by the beginning of the sixth century—and the hymn to Apollo cannot be later—the poet has long ceased to be merely, or mainly, the private retainer of the aristocrat. Whether Homeric or Hesiodean, he has become the servant of the public, and the *festa* gives him, in more senses than one, the opportunity of " publication." Ceasing, moreover, to be a paid dependent of the court, he has to look elsewhere for his livelihood.   If Hesiod —a farmer—had other means of subsistence, many rhapsodists, besides the blind bard of Chios, must have lived by popular favour ; and in part, at least, the favour was sought by competition.   In the true Homeric age, the bard, reciting in his patron's hall, had no competitors to fear.[2]   But, by the time of Hesiod, the Agon, with its prize for the successful poet, was already

---

[1] Allen and Sikes. *Homeric Hymns*, p. lv.
[2] See E. Egger, *L'histoire de la critique chez les Grecs*[2], p. 6 f.

established as a feature, not of course peculiar to the Greeks, but so characteristic of their social habits as to have a marked bearing on their views of poetry. The Greek, being a "four-sided man," made no distinction between the virtue of mind and body, and it was not less natural to crown a poet than a winner in the pentathlon.

The singing-match was of immemorial age, and had "won its way to the fabulous" even in Homeric days. If the *Certamen* may rest on historical past, Homer himself throws back its origin to the mythical time when Thamyris competed with the Muses.[1] The *motif*— familiar in the story of Apollo and Marsyas—is repeated in other myths, as when the Sirens challenged the goddesses of song, and were duly punished; or when the daughters of King Pierus committed the same offence, and were changed into birds for their presumption.[2] Even Nature must fall into line: Corinna, according to a newly-discovered fragment, relates that the mountains Cithaeron and Helicon contested in song before a jury of gods.[3] In actual custom, the singing or musical competition, as part of the wider gymnastic Agon, is too well-known to need reference; but, side by side with the public festivals, the private contest must have survived, much as described by Theocritus, whose rustic competitors, even when they nominally belong to the mythical past, are no doubt reflexions of his own experience among the shepherds and goat-herds of Sicily.

There was honour, as Longinus saw, in this rivalry; but the quality had its defect, if not for the poet himself, at least for his critic, with whom we are mainly concerned. The prize-competitions of poets produced the

[1] *Il.* 2, 595.   [2] Anton. Lib. 9; Paus. ix. 34, 3.
[3] Diehl, *Anth. Lyr.* i. p. 477. Edmonds, *Lyra Gr.* iii. p. 26.

theory—never very helpful, and often lamentable—
that poetry was itself competitive, one poet being
classed with another as superior or inferior, according
as he surpassed or fell short of some acknowledged
" rival." The extent to which the Greeks (and still
more the Romans) succumbed to this wrong-headed
principle will be only too patent in the history of later
criticism. It is obvious, too, that the whole idea of the
critic's function was powerfully affected by the theory
and practice of poetic competition. Centuries before
any fixed canons of literature could be evolved, judges
were needed to award the prize ; and later critics took
over the name (κριτής), and the function of " judging "
between the competitors. We know little of the principles which guided the decision of the judges in Attic
drama ; [1] but these judges were in full possession before
the rise of the literary critic, who could not fail to be
influenced by the basic idea of decisions between rival
claims. The Aristophanic Agon between Aeschylus and
Aristophanes, with Dionysius for judge, is in direct line
with the immemorial decisions of the Panegyris.
Hence the Greek critic only too often posed as an
arbitrator, and rarely doffed his judicial robes. This
attitude, in itself, is harmless enough—provided that
the reasons are good, it makes little difference whether
they are written in a study or delivered from the bench—
but the theory of competition was always a danger to
the free criticism of the individual poet without more or
less odious comparisons. Possibly the modern revulsion
from this method goes too far : a poet may be better
understood by reference to other poets ; but even
Croce's isolation of a poem as incomparable, a thing-in-
itself, is sounder than a comparative method which can
only estimate one poet in terms of another.

[1] See Haigh, *Attic Theatre*, p. 144 f.

§ 2. Xenophanes on Homer

The seventh and sixth centuries added new forms of poetry to the hexameter, and immensely widened the field of poetic art by the development of personal expression both in the lyric and elegiac poets. But the appreciation of those who heard the war-songs of Alcaeus, the love-poetry of Sappho, or the gnomic wisdom of Theognis, can hardly have differed in kind from the uncritical delight of the old Panegyris. Sappho, it is true, founded a " school " ; but her teaching must have been mainly the example of her splendid genius, apart from the instruction of her pupils in the musical technique which was so necessary an equipment of all lyric poets. We find—as might be expected—some isolated remarks which may be called " critical," as implying an æsthetic judgment. But when Simonides, for example, defined poetry as vocal painting, painting as silent poetry,[1] or when Corinna gave her pupil Pindar the advice to sow (myths) with the hand, not with the whole sack,[2] these " criticisms " do not of course imply any reasoned or systematic theory of art ; they are simply the deductions which any poet might easily draw from his own experience. In general, the great lyricists of the sixth century were too busy with their own magnificent practice to feel the need for theoretic support.

But, before the end of this century, a serious difficulty had arisen, which, if not strictly critical in a modern sense, at least drew attention to the character of poetry, and so indirectly paved the way for a study of its principles : Homer and Hesiod were discovered to be " immoral." The discovery dates from the rise of the philosophic schools, and is certainly connected with the general attempt to re-examine the origin and nature of

[1] Plut. *de glor. Ath.* 347.   [2] *Ib.* 348.

existence. The gods were part of φύσις, no less than men, and were found to be unworthy of their place in Nature. Herodotus, a century later, was not quite scientific in saying that Homer and Hesiod gave the Greeks their theology ; but the statement was in substance true, since Greek education was so completely based on the two poets that, if the Epic were discredited, the very foundations of the Greek system would be undermined. The earliest attack is associated with the poet-philosopher Xenophanes, and is sweeping enough : " Homer and Hesiod assigned to the gods all that is shame and blame to men—stealing and adultery and deceit towards one another." [1] Xenophanes was the first to point out that men have created gods in their own image just as horses would worship a horse-god. In the same century, Pythagoras is said to have seen in Hades the souls of Homer and Hesiod punished for their calumny of the gods ; [2] while Heracleitus wished that Homer and Archilochus could be thrown out of the lists and beaten, and was contemptuous about Hesiod as a teacher.[3]

There was, however, an easy line of defence. Before the end of the sixth century, Theagenes of Rhegium (who is dated as contemporary with Cambyses, 529-522 B.C.) is said to have " first written on Homer," and to have used the allegorical method—destined to play so large a part in later criticism, when the anachronism of turning Homer into a philosopher was neglected.[4] It is possible that the method may be even older ; for Pherecydes, who belongs to the earlier part of the century, seems also to have allegorised Homeric myth-

----

[1] See Diels, *die fragm. d. Vorsokratiker,*[4] i. p. 59 f. (11B, 11).
[2] Diog. L. viii. 21.   [3] Diog. L. ix. 2.
[4] Diels, ii. p. 205 (schol. Hom. Ven. on *Il.* 20, 67) ; cf. Schol. Aristoph. *Peace,* 928 ; *Birds,* 822 ; Euseb. *præp. evang.* x. 2.

ology.[1] Allegory can be either " physical " or " ethical,"
and it is probable that the allegorists adopted both
kinds impartially. The great stumbling-block of the *Iliad*
—the War in Heaven which many of Milton's readers
long accepted at its face-value — might be explained
away as the poetic account of physical phenomena,
the eternal opposition of " heat " and " cold," " wet-
ness " and " dryness." This explanation was the more
obvious, since the Greeks always recognised their gods
as departmental personifications of Nature. But the
theomachy might equally well represent the conflict of
ethical qualities, Athena being mind or wisdom ; Ares,
brute force ; Aphrodite, desire or passion. Anaxagoras,
in the fifth century, did not neglect either means of
interpretation. He is stated to have been the first to
hold that the Homeric poems are on " virtue and justice "
—a bold counter-attack on the enemy's camp—so that
one of his weapons appears to have been the ethical.[2]
On the other hand, Anaxagoras was primarily a physicist
(his great conception of mind was hardly ethical), and
he certainly had recourse to physics in explaining the
arrows of Apollo as the sun's rays, and so on.

It is easy to dismiss the method of allegory, as applied
to Homer, with the superior contempt of modern
historical knowledge. The epic poet—we are often
and rightly told—is not a Dante or a Spenser, to clothe
the deepest thoughts of theology and morality in human
actions and characters. Homer must be read in the
light of his own age—an age whose simple thoughts
and elemental notions are reflected by the poet in direct
and unsophisticated language. This is the veriest
truism of anthropology ; but, like many truisms, it
need not be all the truth. The case against Homeric

---

[1] See J. Tate in *Class. Rev.*, Dec., 1927, p. 214.
[2] Diog. L. i. 3, 7.

allegory is strong, but it may be overstated. In the first place, Homer is not—as used to be thought—a "primitive." Although his gods are purely anthropomorphic, he does not forget their close connexion with the powers of nature. In matching Hephaestus with the river-god Scamander he certainly allegorised —in the Anaxagorean sense—by opposing Fire and Water. The deadly shafts of Apollo are not merely the weapons of an archer-god: they are real poetic symbols of the sun's burning rays, even if the poet himself may be only half-conscious of their physical origin, or may by no means wish his hearers to remember it. As with physics, so with ethics. Here, again, Homer is no simple child of nature. During the course of the epic age, human morals were growing beyond the static conceptions of divine behaviour. Zeus and Athena are distinctly nobler and "higher" in the *Odyssey* than in the *Iliad*, and Olympus itself has moved from Thessaly to the heaven. The folklore of the *Odyssey* is most probably much older than that poem ; but even if the poet invented such stories as those of Circe and the swine, or Odysseus and the Cyclops, he was quite capable of suggesting a "hidden meaning" or allegory.[1] No doubt the story was (and is) good enough to stand on its own merits ; nevertheless the "morality" of the song of the Sirens or the Circe-myth must have been perfectly plain to the author himself, and there is no reason why his hearers should not have drawn the moral as readily as Cicero or Horace.[2] It is at least certain that Homer does not use a folk-myth merely as a pleasant (or unpleasant) story ; he deepens

---

[1] ὑπόνοια, later ἀλληγορία.

[2] Cic. *de fin.* v. 49 ; Hor. *Ep.* i. 2, 23. As A. Y. Campbell remarks (*Horace*, p. 276), " the ethical interpretation which Horace gives to the cup of Circe can hardly have been quite absent from the mind of the writer."

and spiritualises its meaning. The myth of Bellerophon,
for example, is not related—as a modern folklorist might
relate it—simply for its own sake : it has a real tragic
significance.[1] Such myths, being altogether human,
needed no allegory to explain them ; but many folk-
tales could not be completely humanised, and it is
reasonable to suppose that—whatever their primitive
values—the author of the Odyssey intended them to be
significant, rather than mere excrescences in a human
drama. If the case for a "hidden meaning" is not
proved for the myths of Circe and similar stories, we
might add passages where allegory is even more evident,
such as the well-known description of the Prayers,
lame and wrinkled, who personify a penitent sinner ;
and the reference to Atê, who walks over the heads of
men. Such clear allegories might be explained as later
additions to the *Iliad ;* but they are none the less
genuinely epic, and Plato quotes from the latter passage,
as Homeric, without suspicion.[2]

No one, at the present day, would argue that Homer
is "allegorical" in the sense of the word which might
fit the *Faery Queen* or *Endymion,* or even, perhaps, the
Aeneid ; but some excuse, or at least some explanation,
may be found for the Stoic heresy. Apart from their
lack of historical propriety—the most serious drawback
of ancient criticism—the Stoics suffered from the confusion of poetic values. As has been well said, "there
is a vast deal of difference between a significant story
and an allegorical story."[3] The Wrath of Achilles and
the Voyage of Odysseus are full of significance as inter-
pretations of human life ; but the early epic poet
approaches life in a way diametrically opposite to that

---

[1] See M. P. Nilsson, *Greek Religion* (E.T.), p. 176 f.
[2] *Il.* 9, 502, 19, 91. Plato, *Symp.,* 195d.
[3] L. Abercrombie, *The Epic,* p. 42.

of the allegorist. Homer deals with his characters directly as real examples of life ; his ethical values are secondary, deduced from the behaviour of the persons. The principle of the allegorical poet is exactly the reverse. Starting from ethical and spiritual preconceptions, he embodies these in persons expressly invented to typify these moral qualities or aspirations. Both methods have produced great poetry, but it is, of course, a grave anachronism to credit an epic poet with a process that belongs to the abstract modes of philosophical thought. There is no hidden meaning in the story of Achilles or Odysseus, as there may be in that of Aeneas, if he is the Virgilian prototype of Augustus. Virgil wrote at a time when allegory had become an accepted tradition, developed by the Stoics, from whom he freely borrowed ; but the attempts of Chrysippus and Cornutus to " philosophise " Homer were so plainly absurd that the Epicureans at least (who had some dim notion of historical perspective) protested against a method, which " turned the oldest poets—though they never even suspected such a thing—into Stoics." [1]

Such as it was—and it failed to satisfy Plato—the use of allegory was the only available defence against the charge of immorality. But Homer was exposed to another attack. On the assumption that the poets were teachers, they were, or should be, " wise " ; and the word σοφός had become a stock epithet of poets from an early date. Was the title justified ? The well-known complaint πολλὰ ψεύδονται ἀοιδοί—poets tell many lies—is certainly as old as Solon, and probably much older ; it sums up the attitude of early criticism, which had no conception—or at least no word—for the imagination, and demanded that poetry should

---

[1] Velleius in Cic. *N.D.* i. 14, 41 ; cf. Seneca, *Ep.* 88.

above all things be " true." Part of the mischief was
due to verbal confusion : ψεῦδος is applied alike to
imaginative " fiction " or downright lies, just as its
power in producing illusion (ἀπάτη) might be either good
or bad according to context and circumstance. The
sixth century, in short, could not disabuse itself of the
old belief that a poet's main business was to record
fact, even if it was always tacitly or openly conceded
that he might embroider fact in order to please.

If the poets often lied, their reputation for wisdom
was bound to suffer ; and here the chief attack seems
to have been by Heracleitus—in this respect, as often,
the great forerunner of Plato. The time had not yet
come to deny all wisdom to the poet ; but the sixth-
century philosopher was at least not afraid to discover
feet of clay in poetic idols. No doubt Heracleitus was
largely influenced by his own philosophic system, which
could not be reconciled with the naïve naturalism of
Homer and Hesiod. The " ancient quarrel " of poetry
and philosophy was rooted in metaphysics not less than
in ethics. Heracleitus found the governing principle of
the world in Strife—the balance of opposing forces—
and he therefore criticised the Homeric prayer that
strife might be abolished. So, too, Hesiod—" the
teacher of most men "—is blamed for not knowing that
Day and Night are one.[1] Hence men are fools to trust
in the bards of the people, who may know much, but
are yet but unprofitable teachers.[2] It is clear that the
trend of early Ionic philosophy was towards its logical
conclusion in the *Republic*. The criticism of Homer was
already side-tracked into a path which ended in a blind
alley, and the task of the next generation was to retrace
the path and to start afresh. Homer, as a philosopher,
had been proven incompetent ; but the great majority

[1] Diels, fr. 12B, 57.   [2] Fr. 40, 104.

2

of the Greeks were, after all, not philosophers but
φιλόκαλοι, lovers of beauty, and would not renounce
their love at the bidding of Xenophanes or Heracleitus.

§ 3. The Age of Pindar

By the beginning of the fifth century the lyric impulse
of Greece had flowered in Pindar, whose views on poetry
have a peculiar value, not only because he is quite free
from philosophic bias, but because a poet—unless we
hold, with Plato, that he is incompetent to explain
himself—has the first claim to be heard on his own art.
There is an even more important reason for studying
Pindar's poetic creed : although his lyric genius is
perfectly intelligible to modern experience, his subject
—the epinikian ode—is almost entirely outside the
range of our response. The cult of athletics no doubt
plays as prominent a part in modern life as in ancient
Greece ; but it has no longer the same æsthetic and religious appeal to poetic sympathy. The Pindaric ode
has been called " the most Greek thing in ancient
poetry," [1] precisely because it is most exclusively Greek.
For this reason any light that Pindar can throw on
his own ideals is welcome to ourselves, however superfluous it may have been to his countrymen and contemporaries. And we need not be surprised to find that
Pindar's view of poetry is, in some respects, as " Greek "
—in this exclusive sense—as his subject-matter. Himself an aristocrat, he wrote for aristocratic victors ; and
this fact may well account for his insistence on the
supremacy of genius over art, in the great controversy
which (whenever it started) retained its interest until
the days of Horace and Longinus. Pindar might have
justly claimed to be a great artist ; but he magnified

---

[1] J. B. Bury, *The Nemeans of Pindar* (Intro.).

his office rather than himself, and its honour was due
to a direct gift from heaven. He was in the direct line
of Hesiod as the " prophet of Zeus," and the sanctity of
his inspiration permitted him to offer advice, encourage-
ment and even warning to tyrants and nobles with whom
he mixed on equal terms. His tone has often been
described as priestly ; and, in the absence of a dogmatic
religion and an effective sacerdotal class—the Greek
priests being mainly confined to mere ritual—Pindar
certainly seems to have partly filled the gap. For,
apart from the gnomic character of his " advice "—
a feature shared by most poets of his time—he is the
most oracular of poets. His very obscurity must have
been in part intentional, to be in keeping with Pythian
tradition. It is not without significance that he belonged
to a sacerdotal family, and was probably himself a priest
of Cybele.[1]

With this character and such antecedents, Pindar was
bound to lay stress on the traditional theory of inspiration as the source of poetry. The doctrine—however
spiritualised by later Greeks—is a well-known legacy
from " primitive " thought, and its savage (and more
modern) analogies are too familiar to need discussion.
Strictly, a spirit or god dispossesses the human soul
from its proper tenement ; the poet is " outside " or
" beside " himself in an ecstasy (ἔκστασις), such as was
associated with Cassandra and the Sibyl.[2] The body
of the medium is naturally disturbed by its unwonted
(and often unwanted) occupant, and is thrown into a
state of hysteria or convulsion, which the Greeks called
mania or enthusiasm (μανία, ἐνθουσιασμός). These

---

[1] *Pyth.* 3, 77.

[2] See generally Rohde, *Psyche* (E.T.) p. 255 f. Classical references to inspiration are collected by W. Kroll, *Studien zum Vers-
tändnis der röm. Lit.* p. 24 f.

symptoms, of course, are not confined to the spirit of
poetry or prophecy—they are a regular feature of
ecstatic religion, whether Orphic, Corybantic or Bac-
chanal.   But even the serene Apollo could affect his
Pythian priestess by the direct penetration of his sacred
breath ; and the Delphic oracle preserved, to the last,
the literal meaning of enthusiasm and ecstasy.

The Olympian religion, however, tended to outgrow
this savage conception of mephitic vapours as the
visible manifestation of deity.   Formal prophecy was
protected at Delphi by religious conservatism, but
poetic inspiration did not require the outward and
visible sign of the divine presence.   The ravings of the
Pythia could hardly have been to the taste of an Apolline
worshipper, who, like any eighteenth-century theologian,
prided himself on being " religious without enthusiasm."
Homer and Hesiod acknowledged inspiration ;   but
neither poet would have cared to be thought ecstatic
or " possessed " in the Pythian and Sibylline way.
Their inspiration, it is true, came direct from heaven,
but they sang " well and with understanding," and had
full knowledge of what they sang.   Indeed, an Homeric
bard like Phemius claimed to be self-taught—an expression which at least implies that he made the best
use of his divine gift.   So, in later times, Pindar might
be a " prophet of the Muses," [1] but he was fully conscious
of his message—not, as Plato was to argue, a Medium
for divine outpourings.   In this sense, inspiration ceases
to be thought of as a temporary and abnormal state of
the body, and passes into a more or less regular and
permanent condition of the mind.   Enthusiasm becomes
natural ability or genius.   Of course genius may be at
times dormant ; but it is always potentially active.

The secular quarrel between the champions of Nature

[1] Fr. 90.

and Art was thus closely related to the doctrine of
inspiration ; and Pindar is convinced that the poet
owes his wisdom to natural genius (φυά), whereas training (τέχνη) alone is useless. Again and again, he insists
on the great antithesis between the " man who knows
by nature " and the man who " learns." [1] Such a poet
was not likely to decry his own profession, even if there
were pretenders—" chattering daws that vainly croak
against the eagle of Zeus." [2] Indeed, the whole function
of the epinikian odes may be summed up in his proud
claim of giving the same immortality to the subjects
of his song that Homer gave to Ajax.[3] With these
words, Pindar consciously links himself with tradition.
But the age of Xenophanes was doing its work well ;
and Pindar, for all his admiration of Homer, is no
uncritical follower. His attitude towards the myths
is not the thorough purging of Xenophanes—his own
art depended on the use of myths which neither Xenophanes nor Plato would have allowed ; but he refuses
to acquiesce in certain grosser beliefs which Hesiod
either accepts or would have tolerated. In a famous
passage, he expresses a shocked disbelief in divine
gluttony, since " it is meet for a man to say nothing
disgraceful of the gods." Such stories as that of Tantalus
and Pelops, " decked out with glamorous lies, lead men
astray, beyond the tale of truth." [4] He pointedly draws
a distinction between this " true word " and the myth,
in which the grace of song too often causes what is past
credit to be believed. Still more striking—because he
mentions Homer by name—is his criticism that the poet
gave fame to Odysseus beyond his deserts : " for on his

---

[1] *Ol.* 2, 94, σοφὸς ὁ πολλὰ εἰδὼς φυᾷ ; 9, 100, τὸ δὲ φυᾷ κράτιστον
ἅπαν. So *Nem.* 3, 40, and elsewhere.

[2] *Ol.* 2, 95.   [3] *Isthm.* 4, 37 ; cf. *Nem.* 7, 12.

[4] *Ol.* i. 28 f. ; cf. *Ol.* ix. 29 f., where he rejects the battles of the
gods—such tales are κακὴ σοφία.

fiction (ψεύδεσι) and on his winged device there is a
grandeur ; poetry deceives and leads men astray with
its tales." [1] The passage is both a praise of poetry,
which can so beguile the hearer, and a rebuke to Homer,
who can so misuse his power of " sweet words."

For, beyond all other lyrical poets (except perhaps
Sappho) Pindar is the apostle of sweetness. He has
been called the poet who loves τὰ ἐν Ἑλλάδι τερπνά,
the joys of Greece ; and these joys—of wealth and
youth and athletic success—needed delightful poetry for
their expression. Hence his emphasis on the beauty of
song, personified in the Grace or Graces. They, with
Mnemosyne and the Muses, preside over the poet's art,
but their function is even wider than that of a Muse,
or rather, perhaps, they complete her inspiration. The
Graces are not only concerned with art ; they embody
and idealise the beauty of the human form in action,
when they shed a glory on the runner at the goal.[2]
Whatever their primitive functions may have been in
their ancient home at Orchomenos, the Graces have
become, for Pindar, the giver of " all things pleasant and
sweet for mortals, whether a man be skilled in song or
blessed with beauty or renown." [3] They typify, in fact,
all that wide range of beauty which—mingled and often
confused with much that we should now call notions of
the " good " or " useful " rather than of the " beautiful "
—the Greeks summed up in the term of τὸ καλόν. As
such, they are equally the companions of Aphrodite and
the Muses ; they add beauty to truth, as even Plato

---

[1] *Nem.* vii. 20 f. ; cf. viii. 25. Both odes are for Aeginetan victors,
whose hero (Ajax) was tricked by Odysseus ; but, in any case,
Pindar disliked a " foxy " man ; see Farnell, *Pindar, ad loc.*

[2] *Ol.* vi. 76.

[3] *Ol.* xiv. In *Pyth.* ii. 42, the monstrous Centaur was born
" without the Graces." For other references see Sandys' *Pindar,
Index s.v. Grace.*

acknowledges, in admitting that the poets are often inspired to sing true things in a pleasing way.[1]

We have seen that the great poet of Panhellenism is remote from the common herd by virtue of his poetry as well as his aristocracy ; and he seems to wear his singing-robes as a sacred vestment or even as a prophet's mantle. Horace was impressed by the attitude, and— as *Musarum sacerdos*—even tried to recapture it, although he knew and confessed that he was no Pindar ; while, in more modern times, the priestly rôle of Ronsard, the prophetic singing of William Blake, and the " robe " claimed by Wordsworth in the *Prelude*, remotely carried on the tradition. But Pindar, though perhaps less normal than the soldier Aeschylus or than Sophocles— a typical Athenian citizen and gentleman—made no pretence, in private life, to be other than his fellowmen. He knew himself, as a man, to be " the dream of a shadow." The fifth century did not encourage any feeling of cleavage between the artist and the citizen. As has often been remarked, there was no invidious distinction between the higher and the humbler forms of art—the epithet " fine " has no equivalent either in Greek thought or its terminology. At best, a poet or a sculptor was but a superior $\tau\epsilon\chi\nu\acute{\iota}\tau\eta s$ or craftsman, working for the state, as a potter or carpenter might work.[2] In Athens, the mere profession of a poet was apparently not held in great account, however much his actual poetry might be admired.

Certainly the prophetic side of the poet was kept in the background, since the Athenians (though they might

---

[1] *Laws* 682a.

[2] In Xen. *Mem.* iii. 10, the painter, sculptor and shield-maker are interviewed by Socrates without discrimination. Plato (*Prot.* 312b) despises all professionalism (in medicine, sculpture, music and education) as unfitting a free man.

tolerate Delphi), were suspicious of unofficial prophets, whom Thucydides misliked and Aristophanes ejected, as impostors, from his ideal city of the Birds. In any case, the service of a soldier or statesman ranked far higher ; and in this connexion we may quote the well-known epitaph of Aeschylus, said to have been inscribed on his tomb at Gela.[1] In spite of the fact that the tomb served as a meeting-place for tragic poets, this epitaph contains not a word about the poetry of Aeschylus, who is praised only for his valour at Marathon. The omission is glaring, and must be deliberate. Obviously, a man's fame is thought to rest on his military achievement—the free gift of a citizen to his state, eclipsing his technical and professional ability. It might be thought that such an extreme view belongs to the ages of Plutarch and Lucian rather than to the fifth century : the former remarks that Athens does not celebrate the tragic victories of Aeschylus and Sophocles, but the anniversary of Marathon ; while Lucian goes even further, making his goddess of Culture despise Pheidias and Praxiteles as persons, although their works are admired.[2] Lucian's contempt, it is true, may be partly discounted, as being an argument against following the sculptor's trade instead of " education " ; but it is none the less characteristic of an age which ranked a sophist above a mere artist. If, however, the evidence of a Plutarch or a Lucian is hardly valid for fifth-century opinion, we may quote the words attributed by Thucydides to an Athenian who cannot be accused of any hostility to art. The funeral oration of Pericles is eloquent in preferring the active life to its " imitation " :

---

[1] *Life of Aesch.* 55. According to Pausanias (i. 14, 5), the poet wrote his own epitaph, just before his death.

[2] Plut. *de glor. Ath.* 349 ; Luc. *somn.* 9. Anatole France (*Sur la Pierre Blanche*) makes Galho take the same view.

" we shall not need the praises of Homer or any other panegyrist whose poetry may please for the moment, although his representation of the facts will not bear the light of day." [1]

But, if the Athenians paid too little respect for the status of poet, the Sicilians made ample amends. When we consider the extraordinary honour paid to Empedocles of Agrigentum, we seem to be transported into a different age and among another race. Yet Empedocles was contemporary with Pindar and Aeschylus, nor was Agrigentum less civilised than Athens. It is true that he was not merely a poet. In philosophy, he stood in the forefront of science, as his experiment with the clepsydra (to prove the material nature of air) is sufficient proof, while the imagination of his poem on Nature marks him as one of the greatest among Greek thinkers. Lucretius, who did not agree with his philosophy, had reason for his splendid eulogy of the Sicilian poet as the noblest product of the island. No doubt his popular fame was largely due to the wonders with which he was accredited. The admiring crowds who followed his triumphant progress through Sicily looked on him as the averter of pestilence rather than the exponent of a philosophic system in verse. Empedocles, in fact, was so much more than a poet that he could even claim divinity. None the less, his many-sided activities were grouped round, and followed from, his central position as a poet ; and no one, perhaps, except Aristotle—for very insufficient reasons—has ever doubted his poetic merits. But the interesting point is that Empedocles stands quite outside the normal sphere of the Greek poet. He is a survival from an order of things which Greece had long outlived, although it sometimes reverted to its discredited modes of thought.

1 Thuc. ii. 41, 4 (Jowett).

And no conception seems more primitive than that of
the poet-magician, since there is reason to believe that
he represents the remotest origins of primitive poetry,
as uttered by the witch-doctor, whose inspiration is
a sort of self-hypnotism.[1] Although even Aristotle
allowed that Empedocles was " most Homeric " (which
may be true of his style) he is essentially pre-Homeric,
the last manifestation of the medicine-man, whose
sorceries or " Purifications," delivered in oracular verse,
recall the magic of a savage tribe.   He was born out of
due time, for the serenity of the epic poet had for
centuries repressed the conception of the sorcerer, just
as the Olympian religion had over-shadowed the crude
vestiges of pre-Hellenic barbarism.   Among the tangled
strands which wove the complex character of the Sicilian
philosopher-poet, the main thread (apart from his actual
philosophy) that seems to emerge is the notion of the
Healer.   Empedocles himself founded the Dorian school
of medicine, in which magical spells certainly played
a considerable part.   The school of Hippocrates were
fully justified in their opposition to the methods of the
witch-doctor.[2]   Yet it was no doubt this strain of
wizardry that captured the popular imagination, since
the belief in the poets as healers remained throughout
the classical age—and longer.   Aristophanes, insisting
on the " use " of poetry, names Musaeus as the oracular
healer of diseases, and is followed by Horace in a well-
known line :

avertit morbos, metuenda pericula pellit.[3]

It is significant that, when the Middle Ages could no

----

[1] R. Graves, *On English Poetry*, p. 19 f.   Wyndham Lewis (*Time
and Western Man*, p. 198) calls art the civilised substitute for magic.
[2] Hipp. περὶ ἱερῆς νούσου.
[3] Aristoph. *Frogs* 1033 ; Hor. *Ep*. ii. 1, 136.

longer appreciate Virgil as poet, they could at least admire him as magician.

§ 4. THE SOPHISTS

The age of sophistry coincides with the full develop-ment of Greek poetry and the first period of Attic prose. For at least a century—after the Peisistratids had welcomed Simonides and Lasos and Anacreon—Athens had become the home, if not often the birthplace, of lyric poets. The fact that no member of the " canon " was Athenian is of minor importance, when we remember how many of the greatest lyric poems—the choruses of the *Supplices* and the *Agamemnon*, of the *Antigone*, the *Troades* and the *Birds*—were Attic. Aristophanes had reason in describing the land of Cecrops as a place " where there are holy processions and sacrifice and offerings at all seasons of the year : and, when spring returns, there is the joy of Dionysus and the stirring of choral song and the deep-voiced music of the flute." [1]

But, although the pure lyric of Simonides and Pindar was welcomed at Athens, it was outside the main stream of Attic poetry, except as a comparatively minor part of the drama.[2] A stranger like Gorgias, coming to Athens in 427 B.C., could not fail to be struck by the supreme place of tragedy and comedy in all spheres of Athenian life, social and religious as well as æsthetic and intellectual. Even more than the epic, the drama provided the most obvious subjects for discussion of literary principles ; and here the sophists led the way. It is true that, as far as we can judge from our frag-mentary sources, the sophists were not mainly concerned

---

[1] *Clouds* 299 f.

[2] Plutarch (*de glor. Ath.* 348) remarks on the lack of melic poets at Athens.

with literature, in its developed forms. There is no certain proof that any sophist studied a particular poet or " compared " Aeschylus and Euripides in the Aristophanic way ; but they have at least the credit of studying the preliminaries. They went to the root of the matter by starting with the Word, which is also Reason. We need not here linger over their efforts—often crude and childish—to construct grammatical definitions. The first attempts to discover the working principles of language were, of course, an easy target for ridicule, and Aristophanes in the *Clouds* made excellent use of his opportunity. But Protagoras and Prodicus were no mere grammarians. Their insistence on " correctness of speech "—including such questions as the distinction of apparent synonyms—shows a wide view of language in relation to literature. Protagoras definitely claimed that " skill in words " was a great part of education, since it was necessary for understanding the poets." [1] His own skill in words was not very useful, if we may judge from his censure of Homer for invoking the Muse unbecomingly in the imperative mood—a remark with which Aristotle had no patience.[2] With all its drawbacks, the new philological study was momentous : it not only diverted attention (at least temporarily) from the moral censure of Xenophanes, but opened an avenue for the linguistic approach to poetry which the Greeks were so thoroughly to explore.

Here, however, poetry found a dangerous rival, in the growth of rhetoric. The sophists, as a class, were above all things practical teachers. Athenians might be interested in such theoretical questions as " Can virtue be

---

[1] Plat. *Prot.* 339a. On ὀρθοέπεια, see Plat. *Crat.* 384b, and often. Besides Prodicus, Hippias and Democritus, among others, wrote on the subject.

[2] *Poet.* 1450b, 15.

taught ? " but that litigious people were far more concerned with the art of persuasion, which could bring success in the assembly and the law-courts ; and the chief object of the sophists was to develop this function of the Word. The art of Corax and Tisias satisfied a more pressing need than even the understanding of Homer. It was no doubt an advantage that the nascent study of the Word should be founded on the broadest possible basis ; that poetry and rhetoric should be recognised as equally manifestations of the Logos. The danger lay in the confusion between the two manifestations, and (still worse) in the subordination of poetry to its younger rival. As a fact, the invasion of rhetoric into the province of poetic theory was only too well justified by the change in poetry itself. We have merely to contrast the simple, untechnical arguments of the trial-scene in the *Eumenides* of Aeschylus with the formal speeches of Euripides, to realise that the atmosphere of the court had gravely infected the theatre. Gorgias, a visitor from Sicily, the home of Corax and Tisias, had excuse for regarding the Word, whether uttered by poet or orator, as equally " persuasive." Everywhere it is " a mighty ruler who, with the smallest and most invisible body, does the most divine deeds ; for it can stop fear, remove sorrow, produce joy, increase confidence.[1]

So far, the power of the Word is quite general ; but Gorgias proceeds to distinguish, even although his distinction between prose and poetry is not very decisive —a rhetorician with a strong tendency to use poeticisms

[1] Gorg. *Helena* 8. In the last word, I read θαρσαλέον (Weidner) for ἔλεον, as Pity, being thought akin to Fear, should be removed rather than increased ; see p. 120. Of recent years it has been doubted whether this tract is authentic ; the latest editor (O. Immisch, 1927) defends its authenticity (introd. p. v f.). In any case the document belongs to the fifth century.

could hardly be expected to draw a clear line of demarca-
tion. There are, indeed, " two arts "—of poetry and
rhetoric—but the Word is of equal value in both. Poetry
is differentiated only by its obvious, if unsatisfactory
definition as metrical speech ; its hearers are affected
by " shuddering awe and tearful pity and a yearning
for sorrow (sympathy)." The germ of Aristotle's
theory is here apparent. There follows a sentence
which seems specially, though not exclusively, to define
the " magic " of poetry : " the inspired chants uttered
by means of words become bringers of pleasure, removers
of pain ; the power of the chant, joining with the
opinion of the soul, charms and persuades and changes
it (the soul) by its magic." [1]

Nevertheless, in spite of the formal difference, Gorgias
plainly regards the two arts as even more than akin.
Their *effect*, at all events, is the same : both work by
charm (θέλξις) and persuasion (πειθώ) and by these
agencies change " opinion." Gorgias seems to have no
clear idea on the difference between the two spheres of
the Word—that of persuading the mind by logic and that
of appealing to the emotions. Herein—as has been
noticed by Mr. D. W. Lucas—he is thoroughly Greek :
he imagines Paris to have convinced Helen, not by a
passionate declaration of love, but by sophistries cal-
culated to turn her wavering opinion. As Mr. Lucas
concludes, " the intellectual appeal had, I believe, a
far greater emotional effect than it has with us." It
might be added, in illustration, that the plays of
Euripides, for all their droppings of warm tears, are
certainly examples of logic invading the sphere of the
emotions. But we must remember that, for Gorgias,

---

[1] Gorg. *Helena* 10. ἔνθεοι διὰ λόγων ἐπῳδαὶ ἐπαγωγοὶ ἡδονῆς, ἀπαγωγοὶ
λύπης γίγνονται. συγγιγνομένη γὰρ τῇ δόξῃ τῆς ψυχῆς ἡ δύναμις τῆς
ἐπῳδῆς ἔθελξε καὶ ἔπεισε καὶ μετέστησεν αὐτὴν γοητείᾳ.

the confusion of the two spheres is the more natural
from the fact that persuasion, in modern thought confined to the logical process, expresses a real æsthetic
power in Greek psychology. Peitho is not merely
intellectual. Before Gorgias, Aeschylus had associated
her with Charis.[1] The best proof of this is that they
are both personified as attendants on Aphrodite ; [2] and
—to illustrate Gorgias himself—on a vase in which
(after the capture of Troy) Menelaus lets his sword fall
in attacking his faithless wife, Peitho assists the goddess
of love, by her persuasion.[3] In art she belongs to the
circle of beauty rather than to the realm of Athena and
Hermes—the law-court and the ecclesia—and is a fit
embodiment of the emotional appeal which Gorgias
described as enchantment. That word has surely not
quite lost its literal sense of magic, as when Circe trans-
formed the comrades of Odysseus, and the Sirens sang
their compelling song. The later word to express this
poetic charm is $\psi \nu \chi \alpha \gamma \omega \gamma i \alpha$, itself a magical term—the
raising of spirits. In Aristophanes, Socrates holds a
séance and raises, instead of a real ghost, the lean and
bat-like Chaerephon.[4] We are still in the province of
the wizard or witch-doctor ; and we are reminded that
Gorgias was a pupil of Empedocles, and is said to have
helped his master, being, presumably, a sort of acolyte
in the performance of the magical spells ($\kappa \alpha \theta \alpha \rho \mu o i$),
which the Sicilian wrote in epic verse to ward off disease
and pestilence.[5]

---

[1] *Eum.* 806. ἀλλ' εἰ μὲν ἁγνόν ἐστί μοι πειθοῦς σέβας | γλώσσης ἐμῆς
μείλιγμα καὶ θελκτήριον. See Diès, *Autour de Platon*, i. p. 116.

[2] For Peitho see Ibycus, fr. 5 (Bergk) ; Sappho, 135 ; Pindar,
Pyth. 4, 219 and 9, 43, fr. 122 ; and often in the *Anthology*.

[3] See a red-figured vase in Roscher, *Lex. s.v.* Helena, 1946.

[4] *Birds* 1553.

[5] Satyrus in Diog. L. viii. 58. See generally Burnet, *Early Greek
Phil.*[2] p. 231 f.

In the *Defence of Helen*, Gorgias deals with tragedy only by implication. But there is an interesting fragment from another work which shows that he was directly concerned with the psychology of the drama. He was uneasy about the " fiction " of poetry and its consequent " deceit "—a difficulty illustrated by Plutarch's story that, when Thespis first acted, Solon asked him if he were not ashamed to tell such lies, and refused to accept the poet's ingenuous plea that his tragedy was not serious.[1] The story (like others in Plutarch) is more than a little suspicious as history— it may be no more " true " than the complaint of the Crimean veteran that Tennyson's *Charge of the Light Brigade* was a lie from beginning to end—but it fairly represents a common attitude of the Greek mind. Gorgias defends this " cheating " in his usual euphuistic way : " Tragedy deceives by myths and affections, and the tragic poet who deceives is juster than one who does not ; the deceived is wiser than one who is not deceived." The reason—Plutarch explains—is that " the cheater has kept his promise, and sensibility is easily won by the delight of speech " [2]—or, in Dryden's plainer prose, " we know we are to be deceived and we desire to be so." Butler, who knew his Plutarch, has made this famous in *Hudibras :*

> Doubtless the pleasure is as great
> Of being cheated as to cheat.

We might sum up the views of Gorgias, as far as they are known, in a sort of definition after the Aristotelian manner : Tragedy is a form of metrical composition (poetry), which aims at charming and persuading the audience, who willingly submit to the magic of fiction,

---

[1] Plut. *Solon* 29.   [2] Gorg. *ap*. Plut. *de glor. Ath.* 348.

and feel awe and pity for the fortunes of others represented by the poet. It does not appear from the
fragments whether Gorgias held poetry to be instructive
as well as charming : perhaps he anticipated the position
of the anonymous author of a tract of this period entitled *The Two Arguments*, that poets write not for truth
but pleasure.[1] This Periclean (or Thucydidean) view
was of course traditional, as we see from Herodotus,
who, like Gorgias, defends Helen's character, but at
Homer's expense—the poet wrote falsely about her to
gratify the taste of his audience.[2]

The debt which Greek criticism owes to the forerunner
of Aristotle has hardly been appreciated at its full
value, partly, no doubt, by reason of Plato's hostility
to the sophist. Yet it must be confessed that, however
unsound Plato's own objections to poetry may be, his
criticism of Gorgias is illuminating. The sophist had
found no essential difference between poet and rhetorician : the weapon of both was persuasion ; and Plato
believed that it was the wrong kind of persuasion,
founded not on dialectic, but on an appeal to the
passions. In condemning Gorgias, as rhetorician, Plato
also condemns Gorgias, as critic, out of his own mouth.
If poetry is only persuasive, it must stand or fall with
rhetoric.[3] Later Greeks, however much they disagreed
with Plato, could rarely free themselves from this fatal
alliance of the two arts. And the most mischievous
result of the alliance was due to the predominance of
rhetoric, which—from the age of Gorgias and Euripides
onward—tended more and more to overshadow its

[1] The Δισσοὶ λόγοι is dated about 400 B.C. See Diels⁴, ii. pp. 17
and 340.

[2] Herod. ii. 116.

[3] Plat. *Gorg.* 502d. On Gorgias in poetic criticism, see M. Pohlenz,
die griech. Tragödie (Erläut.) p. 141 ; Rostagni, *Studî ital. d. Fil.
Class.* (N.S.) ii. 721.

less practical partner. There was always the danger
that poetry should be regarded as a species of oratory,
and the verbal analysis of the latter was thought
equally appropriate to the former. Here, both in theory
and practice, Gorgias seems to have been primarily
responsible for a critical method which later critics
pushed to extremes—the evaluation of all literature in
terms of the figures. The style of Gorgias himself is
perhaps the best (or the worst) example of the figurative
manner, and we know that his speech at Athens—full of
antithesis, parallelism and assonance—not only impressed
and delighted the Athenian public, but left its mark on
Thucydides.

Of the figures themselves, little need here be said.
It may be sufficient to point out that few sentences, in
prose or verse, except the simplest statements of bare
fact, were immune from this method of exegesis. The
later rhetoricians recognised two divisions of these
σχήματα : the figures of speech (λέξεως), such as
hendiadys ; and of meaning (διανοίας), such as irony ;
the net—to use the " trope " of metaphor—was double,
and so widely cast that escape was rare.[1] How far
Gorgias theorised on his own practice is uncertain ;
but, as we shall see from Aristophanes, the sophists
had certainly laid the foundations of figurative criticism
before the end of the fifth century.

The close of the sophistic age is marked by the name
of a thinker comparable to that of his great opponent,

---

[1] The trope (τρόπος) was a figure especially found in poetry, to
describe a divagation from the proper or natural use of a word, e.g.
the " spring of life." According to the schol. on Dion. Thrax
(Hilgard, pp. 13, 16) it meant the poet's way, which " turns " from
the expected to the unexpected. For later definitions, cf. Tryphon
in Spengel, *Rhet. Gr.* iii. p. 191 f. Not only metaphor, but cata-
chresis, hypallage and others were τρόποι. See [Plut.] *Life of Homer*,
ii. 15 f.

Plato. Democritus has been badly treated by posterity, which preserved only isolated fragments of his numerous works. With his atomism we are not concerned, except to note, in passing, that his philosophy did not preclude him, as it precluded his follower Epicurus, from a study of literature. So much, at least, we gather from the titles of his lost works—on rhythms and harmony, poetry, the beauty of words, euphonious and cacophonous letters, as well as a treatise on Homer, in which the sub-title—" correctness of speech "—indicates that he worked on the lines of Prodicus and Protagoras.[1] Arguments *ex silentio* are proverbially misleading ; but the lack of ancient reference to his views on literature may lead us to suspect that they were not highly original or important. He seems to have been only one of the many who were endeavouring to discover the magic of poetry on the verbal side ; but he was not merely a student of words : the sole literary pronouncement that struck his successors was his advocacy of poetic inspiration.[2] We know nothing of the reasons which made him " exclude the sane from Helicon," and it is a little curious, in fact, to find the atomist in the company of inspirationists. Did he rationalise inspiration, as only a theological mode of expressing natural ability ? Such rationalism was no doubt in the air, if not explicitly stated before Aristotle.[3] It seems more probable that he really believed in literal inspiration, since he did not deny the existence of spiritual beings whose

---

[1] Diog. L. ix. 7, 13.

[2] Dio Chrys. *or.* 53, 1, Ὅμηρος φύσεως λαχὼν θεαζούσης ; cf. Hor. *A.P.* 295. See generally Clem. *strom.* 6, 168, ποιητὴς δὲ ἄσσα μὲν ἂν γράφῃ μετ' ἐνθουσιασμοῦ καὶ ἱεροῦ πνεύματος, καλὰ κάρτ' ἐστίν. Cic. *de or.* ii. 46, 194 : *de div.* i. 37, 80. Diels⁴, ii. pp. 20, 66. R. Philippson (*Hermes* 64, p. 167) discusses his views on poetry and remarks that he made no use of allegory.

[3] See J. Tate in *Class. Quart.* April, 1928.

influence was felt by men in dreams or waking visions. Epicurus himself acknowledged this influence—the example of the gods, conveyed to men by sense-perception, was a stimulus to their peace of mind, and a justification for public worship—and it is quite likely that here, as usual, Epicurus borrowed from his master.[1]

However much we may regret, on general grounds, the almost total loss of sophistic literature, it seems unlikely that we have lost any critical theories of importance. In the next century, Aristotle's references to the sophists (in the *Rhetoric* and *Poetics*) do not suggest that they developed any principles beyond his own, while his treatment of poetry is certainly an improvement on that of Gorgias, whose work he continues. Perhaps the chief interest in the sophists as critics lies in the fact that they provide a background for the great comic poet, whose views on poetry become more intelligible when seen in their proper setting. With Aristophanes, we are for the first time in touch with a literary criticism which is itself literature.

---

[1] D. W. Lucas holds this view of Democritus, without, however, a mention of Epicurus.

CHAPTER II

ARISTOPHANES

§ 1. CRITICAL FUNCTION OF THE OLD COMEDY

IF Aristophanes had won no higher fame as the greatest of Greek wits, he might still have gained a place in literature as the earliest critic of antiquity, just as Herodotus would be known as the first anthropologist, if he were not more fitly called the Father of History. Aristophanes was the exact contemporary of the great sophists—his first play (the *Banqueters*) belongs to the year in which Gorgias came to Athens. A fast-bound conservative, he was bitterly opposed to their innovations in religion and ethics ; but—as he himself said in another connexion—a man may learn much from his enemy, and Aristophanes was perhaps more imbued with sophistry than he would have willingly confessed. While he shows a more or less good-humoured contempt for the philological key with which Protagoras tried to unlock the secret of poetry, he must have respected that sophist's regard for the poets as educators. Here, at least, the two were on common ground. The fact that poetry was the staple of education throughout the Greek world—even the Spartans made full use of Alcman and Tyrtaeus—is too well known to need illustration ; [1] but we may call Protagoras himself to bear witness : " they put before children the works of good

[1] See e.g. K. J. Freeman, *Schools of Hellas*, ch. ix ; Plat. *Prot.* 325e.

poets to read and learn by heart, containing much advice and many praises and eulogies of great men of old, so that the boy may imitate them in rivalry and desire to be like them."

But in Athens, the field of poetry had been widened by the growth of the drama ; and if its influence at this time may have scarcely penetrated to the schools, the more adult citizen made amends. Tragedy was expected to teach. Indeed, it had almost a monopoly of teaching, since Socrates was at least suspect, and the lectures of the sophists were an expensive luxury. Here, again, evidence is plentiful ; but a single familiar quotation from Aristophanes is decisive : " Boys have a master who teaches *them ;* we men have the poets." [1] It does not appear that any one of the three great tragedians claimed to be a direct teacher, and Sophocles, in particular, would probably have thought the function as unsuitable to a poet as to a sculptor. But both Aeschylus and Euripides, in their different ways, were conscious of a message to deliver, even if they might have resented a suggestion that the message was the only important part of their tragedies. Anyhow we need not wonder at the Greek emphasis on the didacticism of tragedy, when we remember that Mr. Bernard Shaw (so often compared with Euripides) considers the playwright to be " a moralist as well as a dramatist," and boldly calls his own plays " didactic." [2] Failing other means of propaganda in ancient Greece, Aristophanes had still more reason for regarding instruction as the self-evident function of the drama. A tragedy must be judged by its " advice." " Why should we admire the poet ? " asks the Aristophanic Aeschylus ; and Euripides answers : " for cleverness and counsel, and because we make better citizens."

[1] *Frogs* 1055.   [2] *Man and Superman,* Introd.

With these preconceptions, it was inevitable that the criticism of tragedy should be largely moral. The fact that the first critic should be a comic poet is not, of course, surprising to anyone who has studied—even superficially—the place of the comic stage in Athenian life. It is no paradox to say that the comic poets took themselves very seriously. No less than their tragic rivals, they had the privilege and the duty of teaching. A comic chorus was as sacred as the tragic, and must equally advise the citizens. " Comedy, too, knows what is right," says Dicaeopolis, in a speech that for eloquence and—in this case—for wisdom, surely justifies the boast.[1] Dicaeopolis is here concerned with politics in the narrower sense ; but the scope of the Old Comedy included the whole range of intellectual as well as practical life, and (since poetry was moralised) the criticism of tragic drama fell naturally into place with other moral spheres. It is true that, among surviving plays, the *Frogs* is unique in subject, but we know that not only Aristophanes but other writers of the Old Comedy dealt with literary questions. Before Euripides had provided the chief target for criticism, Cratinus had both praised and parodied the epic,[2] and (in the *Bucoli*) he commented on an archon for refusing Sophocles a chorus, in favour of a certain immoral poet who should not have been allowed to sing even at the lascivious feast of Adonis. Phrynichus, too, seems to have made full use of literary comment or parody,[3] and the *Crapatali* of Pherecrates had at least one scene laid in Hades, where Aeschylus was a speaker. Aristophanes himself

---

[1] *Ach.* 496 ; so *Vesp.* 650. See Dion. Hal. *rhet.* 8, 302 ; Quint. x. 1, 65 ; Plut. *de adul.* 68c, *adv. Colot.* 33.

[2] For the praise, cf. Diog. L. *proem.* 12 (the *Archilochi* ; Kock, 2) ; for the parody, Kock, 68 and 315.

[3] In the *Muses*, where his eulogy of Sophocles is remarkable ; cf. p. 114.

repeated the theme of the *Frogs :* in the *Gerylades* the
subject was the decadence of poetry after the deaths
of Sophocles and Euripides—the inclusion of the latter
being rather curious in view of his treatment in the
Frogs—while a poetic contest, in which Euripides took
part, was apparently a feature of his *Proagon.*[1]

So, by the last quarter of the fifth century, the tragic
theatre had offered full scope for comic criticism. The
charge of immorality, once confined to the epic, was
now broadened to include the drama. There was in
fact even greater ground of offence, for Euripides was
nearer home, both in time and place, than Homer. If
the epic poet told unworthy tales of the gods, his views
on human life were (as yet) unchallenged, whereas the
" corruption " of Euripides seemed to old-fashioned
Athenians to have spread over the whole range of city-
life. Tragedy had started as a ritual act, for the glory
of gods and heroes ; the performers were inviolable ;
the spectators purified by sacrifice ; improper conduct
was punished by death ; and now it was ending not
merely in atheism, but in the degradation of other
human ideals. The heroic grandeur of Aeschylus was
being superseded by cheap cleverness and sordid realism.

No phase of Greek thought is more familiar than
this period of the Enlightenment. The issue was grave,
involving not only religion and morality but the whole
system of Athenian education. The conservatives—
although their cause was doomed—were strong enough
to be dangerous. In the early stage of the struggle
Anaxagoras was banished ; in the later, Diogenes of
Apollonia—whose views are satirised in the *Clouds*—
appears to have risked his life at Athens ; at the very
end, the death of Socrates bears witness to the bitter-

[1] Schol. *Vesp.* 61. See Kock, i. p. 510.

ness of the conflict. Euripides himself was a sufferer. According to newly discovered evidence, he was prosecuted for " impiety " by Cleon,[1] although his withdrawal from Athens to the Macedonian court, not long before his death in 406 B.C., does not seem mainly due to political reasons. Finally, it must not be forgotten that this intellectual quarrel largely coincided with the greatest and most disastrous of Greek wars, when the poet was bound to be chiefly valued for his service to the state.

At such a time, Aristophanes might well have been content with purely moral criticism. Had he stopped with this, he would have been within his rights as an ancient critic. But he was a poet, who knew that no poet is exempt from the necessity of giving " immediate pleasure." Consequently his censure of Euripides includes not only moral but æsthetic judgments ; and it is only by virtue of the latter that the comic poet earns the title of critic in the modern sense. This very fact is perhaps the most difficult to appreciate at the present day. We can easily understand the interest of an Athenian audience in the comic criticism of politics and in discussions on social life or morality, including the " morality " of the stage ; but the technique of rival dramatists seems, at first sight, to be an impossible subject for an audience consisting of practically the whole body of adult citizens. It is here that more modern analogies fail. French classical comedy could successfully absorb the spirit of Aristophanes ; but *Les Plaideurs* appealed only to a small and select minority of the nation ; and even this audience (we are told) were afraid that they had not laughed according to the

---

[1] Satyrus gives new evidence for the poet's Anaxagorean tendencies, which some scholars have tried to minimise (*Oxyrh. Pap.* ix. 1176, 37, 3).

rules.[1]   In England, a literary quarrel would seem even
more hopeless as a theme for popular comedy.   Peele's
chaff on Gabriel Harvey's metrical experiments may
occur to the mind ; but the *Old Wives' Tale* is no close
analogy to the *Frogs.*   Hamlet's advice to the actors is
the merest incident in a play within a play.

No doubt, the Athenian audience deserve all that is
often said of their intelligence.   Even after Aristotle's
reminder that there were " two sorts of spectators "—
the warning is hardly needed—we may allow the
" cleverness " of the average member of the audience.
But something more than mere understanding is required for the appeal of a comic *motif.*   A technical
discussion of the drama can only be explained by the
fact that the public was keenly interested in the formal
as well as the moral side of poetry.   We are apt to think
of Athenian education as chiefly based on the ethical
" message " of the poets ; but this poetical training by
no means neglected the form in which the message was
delivered.   As is well known, every Athenian gentleman
learned to sing to his own accompaniment on the lyre ;
and his knowledge of " rhythms and metres " is assumed
in the *Clouds.*   Strepsiades, the typical " Old Man " of
Aristophanes, may object to the new education, but he
has nothing to say against the traditional culture.   The
issue was not between literature and science, but between rival schools of poetry—Strepsiades standing for
Simonides, his son for Euripides.

So, for the first (and probably the last) time in dramatic
history, æsthetic criticism came within the sphere of
comedy.   Granted the universal appeal of tragedy
among an instructed public, the reaction of comedy was
natural and inevitable.   The most obvious form of the

---

[1] Babbitt, *Masters of Modern French Literature,* p. 339.

reaction was by way of parody, and it has often been remarked that the frequency of the mock-tragic (both in language and situation) is the clearest proof of the absorbing interest in the tragic drama. Parody is itself a kind of silent criticism ; and it affords an easy transition to the outspoken criticism of the *Frogs*. And here, as we shall see in more detail, there was ample room for the amusement of groundling and intellectualist alike.[1] The latter could realise the purpose underlying the battle of the two poets ; the former had seen—perhaps too often—the beggar-kings of Euripides ; and it needed no great intellect to laugh at royalty in rags. So, too, a limping hero may have caused " laughter unextinguished " to Aristotle's vulgar spectator, who had at least the support of Homeric gods and modern vaudeville, but there were also serious people among the audience, who must have resented the frequent introduction of a lame Philoctetes or Telephus or Bellerophon as a degradation of tragedy.

§ 2. Aristophanes as Critic

As a critic of literature, Aristophanes shows a marked development during his long career. The two decades between the *Acharnians* and the *Frogs* saw the culmination—for good and evil—of sophistic thought : Athens was definitely parting from the ideals of the men who fought at Marathon, and even Pericles was receding into the past. Meanwhile the genius of Aristophanes was finding itself. His early plays, despite the brilliance of the *Acharnians* and *Knights*, are surpassed, for sheer wit and fancy, by the *Birds* and *Thesmophoriazusae*,

---

[1] On the Athenian audience see G. Ugolini in *Studi Ital. di Filol. Class.* (N.S.) 3, (1923), p. 215 f. (a study of the criticism of Aristophanes which confirms the main conclusions, reached independently in the present chapter).

while his range of subject has broadened. In this connexion, it must of course be remembered that the political situation of Athens had entirely changed between the years 425 and 410. When attacks on Cleon were no longer possible, and even discreet allusion to politics was dangerous, the poet was forced to look elsewhere for a subject, and tragedy or feminism was safer ground. But, whatever the circumstances, there is in fact a real progress in the scope and tone of Aristophanic criticism, as a brief examination of the surviving plays will show. To the end, Euripides remains the head and front of offence; but, while the moral charges have lost nothing of their earlier force, it is not till his later period that Aristophanes becomes a critic in the modern sense.

The *Acharnians* starts the long campaign.[1] Aeschylus was firmly established in the affection of the old conservatives,[2] while Euripides had already earned a reputation for quibbling argument and sophistry, and here offered an easy opening for caricature. But the main reference to the poet in this play is simply comic fun about the rags and beggars. The scene, in which Dicaeopolis pleads for the loan of a disguise like that of Telephus, until Euripides complains that nothing is left of his dramas, is quite justified by its humour; but there seems to be no malice behind, nor even moral censure.[3] In the next year, the *Knights* is so entirely concerned with politics, that no room is left for Euripides, beyond a quotation from the *Hippolytus*, which had won the prize a few years before.[4] The first open attack appears in the *Clouds* [5] (423 B.C.), where Aristophanes

---

[1] There may have been allusions to Euripides in the two earlier plays (*Banqueters* and *Babylonians*).

[2] *Ach.* 10 f.   [3] *Ach.* 294-479.

[4] In 428 B.C., *Knights*, 16-19.

[5] *Clouds* 1361-1377. See Starkie, *ad loc.*

sketches, as a preliminary outline, to be completed in the *Frogs*, a picture of the old and new education, represented by Aeschylus and Euripides. Although the purpose is moral, the main literary distinction between the two poets is cleverly drawn. Aeschylus—the " first of poets " to the older generation—has already become as antiquated as Simonides. To the young Pheidippides, he is " full of sound and fury, chaotic, mouth-filling, a spitter of mountains " ; a set speech of the " clever " Euripides—dealing with incest—is better poetry.

The next few plays do not add any new point of importance,[1] but in the *Thesmophoriazusae* (410 B.C.) Euripides becomes the centre of the argument. He is in danger of his life at the hands of the Athenian women, who resent his imputations on their morality and bring a counter-charge of " atheism." The play itself is certainly one of the wittiest, but it has only a negative value in criticism, as proving how far Aristophanes could still confuse art with morals. It is a pure farce, and its chief humour lies in the concluding scenes where three tragedies—the *Palamedes*, *Helena* and *Andromeda*—are parodied both in language and situation. Of these, the last two had recently been produced (412 B.C.), and were not only fresh to the memory, but must have created some stir at the time of publication. For the *Helena* stands quite apart from the normal spirit of tragedy, and has no counterpart among other extant dramas ; and the *Andromeda*—described by a scholiast as one of the most beautiful works of Euripides [2]—became famous in antiquity. A play, whose theme seems to have been the first example of " romantic love," treated with charm and delicacy, must have caused something of a sensation at the time, if we may judge by its later

[1] *Wasps* 1414 ; *Peace* 146, 532 ; *Lysistr.* 283, 368 f.
[2] Schol. on *Frogs* 53.

popularity, of which Lucian gives a humorous account : [1]
in the days of Lysimachus—a full century after the
poet was dead—the people of Abdera were so much
excited by a performance of this play during a hot
summer, that they caught a tragic fever, and went
about the streets declaiming the lines on Love, the
tyrant of gods and men, until cold weather stopped their
enthusiasm.

Throughout the *Thesmophoriazusae*, it would be hard
to trace any bitterness or hostility.   The tone is frankly
that of a parodist ; and—if we had no further evidence
to the contrary—we might even conclude that Aristophanes admired Euripides.   Such a conclusion could
be amply justified by the history of Greek criticism, since
there are certainly some parodies of the older epic in
the *Odyssey*,[2] and the *Battle of the Frogs and Mice*
carries on the tradition at a later time.[3]   Parody, in
fact, like other forms of imitation, is often the sincerest
flattery.   The most successful travesties have been
written by lovers of their originals or—as Swinburne's
Nephelidia may show—by the originals themselves.
We might even go further, and argue that a parodist
must of necessity be in sympathy with his original :
otherwise he will become a satirist, and his humour will
be lost in the indignation of an Archilochus or a Juvenal.
But in this play, at least, the delightful humour seems
untainted by any undercurrent of satire.

The atmosphere of the *Frogs* is very different.   That
play was produced in 405 B.C.—the year after Euripides
had died—when the occasion of reviewing his whole
tendency seemed appropriate.   Aristophanes, in spite

---

[1] *Quomodo scrib. hist.* 1.

[2] Monro may have seen too many " parodies " in the *Odyssey ;*
but there are passages which can only be explained as mock-heroic.

[3] See Rhys Roberts, *Greek Rhetoric and Literary Criticism*, p. 13.

of his pride in not trampling on a fallen Cleon, was not deterred by respect for the dead. Indeed, he could fairly distinguish between Cleon and Euripides—the influence of the former ceased with his death, whereas that of the poet was still to be feared.[1] All the old charges are now brought together, and their cumulative effect is tremendous. Euripides is a chatterer and a sceptic ; his heroes are cripples or things of rags and tatters,[2] his heroines, love-sick or incestuous ; his gods, new and unorthodox—one of the charges sufficient to condemn Socrates a few years later. He panders to democracy, letting all and sundry—even a woman or a slave—have an equal say. In a word, the whole majesty of the stage has been degraded to the level of common life.

Most of this censure is outside the sphere of strict literary criticism. To-day, the critic is supposed to be concerned only with the æsthetic value of a work of art. As a moralist, he may approve or condemn a play ; but, in so doing he oversteps his proper duty, which is to appraise the work by the canons of art. The *Hippolytus* may be immoral—though here modern judgment does not agree with the ancient—but, anyhow, its morality was a matter for the censor, and the Archon had licensed the play. The critic's business begins where the censor ends.

Such, at least, is a view (still widely held) of the critical function in modern literature. Historically, the view is a legacy of Flaubert in France, and Whistler in England, and was developed in the slogan of " Art for Art's sake," which, however, has lost much of its

---

[1] So Ugolini, p. 223.

[2] There were at least three limping heroes—Philoctetes, Telephus and Bellerophon. The ragged hero was a feature in the *Telephus* and several other plays.

old appeal, since the formula of " Art for Life's sake "
is more satisfying and more comprehensive. The
artist has indeed won his main contention—that art
must be judged by its own laws, which are æsthetic,
not moral. But art, after all, being a human activity,
is not immune from natural instincts of humanity ;
and, even if the artist claims complete freedom both in
subject and treatment, this right can only be exercised
with due respect to these normal feelings. It may be
salutary that certain conventional persons should be
" shocked," but the cause of art is not furthered if all
decent persons are disgusted.

To the Greeks of the fifth century, the formula of
L'art pour l'art would have been either monstrous or
simply unintelligible. Tragedy was a social concern,
to stand or fall by its relation to the whole of life. It
was judged by the canons of existing morality in a
city-state. The Greeks, since the time of Herodotus,
knew perfectly well that morals were " conventional,"
in the sense that the customs of Athens did not hold
good in savage or barbarian lands. But, if a Greek
poet had pleaded that his art should include a subject
not approved by common Greek morality, his public
would have replied that Greeks were not barbarians.
Medea—said Jason—was to be congratulated for having
been taken to a civilised city. However relative morals
might be in the wider range of humanity, the Athenian
code was absolute within its own sphere. Aristophanes
lived to see the first-beginnings of the Cynic school, with
its flouting of convention ; but, even in the fourth
century, the cynic protest was the opposition of a small
minority, and Diogenes himself was chiefly known as a
crank, who delighted to break taboos. In his day, the
Athenians seem to have been tolerant enough of private
divagations from convention ; in the fifth century, the

pressure of standardised custom was at least as strong as that of an English public school. Euripides, however, was not only less fortunate than Diogenes in belonging to a more bigoted age but, as a poet, a servant of the State, he spoke in a public capacity. And one of his main offences was precisely that he broke a moral taboo. The conservatism of Greek drama had excluded sexual love as the dominant theme of a play, although, of course, it could be introduced as a subsidiary interest when required by the myth. As is well known, a romantic view of courtship and marriage—itself very largely a creation of medieval Christianity—was outside the range of a society almost entirely organised on a masculine basis. The contemporaries of Aeschylus found all the romance they needed in the *Myrmidons* of that poet—a play which seems to have given no offence to those who objected to the *Hippolytus*. In the *Frogs*, the Aristophanic Aeschylus prides himself on having never presented a woman in love, much less a Phaedra or Stheneboea, who loved disgracefully. The claim seems to be warranted ; for the *Agamemnon* is no real exception : Clytemnestra's adultery is merely part of the argument, which is concerned with an avenging rather than a faithless wife. In the *Antigone*, again, Sophocles had an opportunity which no modern would have missed ; but the relation between Antigone and Haemon is barely mentioned : it is the status of marriage, not the lover himself, whose loss the heroine deplores. The enormous advance made by Euripides in the treatment of either " romantic " or " lawless " love, need not here be discussed, except in so far as it bears directly on the criticism of the *Hippolytus*. Even at the present day, the subject—the passion of Phaedra for her stepson— might fairly be called " dangerous," though the treatment of the drama is so splendid as to redeem it—like

4

the *Cenci*—from the class of " unpleasant " plays.   In
the fifth century, however, it was the subject that
mattered, and no delicacy of treatment could save
Euripides.   Theoretically, no doubt, he could plead
that the passion of a Phaedra was as much inspired by
Aphrodite as the madness of an Ajax by Athena.   Both
passions were diseases, sent by the gods to destroy their
innocent victims ; and madness was a traditional motive
freely used by dramatists.   Such a view was very much
in the air, when the *Hippolytus* was first produced.
Gorgias (whether before or after the play) defended
Helen with the argument that " if love is a god, he is
too strong ; if it is a human disease, it is not to be blamed
as a sin, but considered a misfortune."[1]   Nevertheless,
even normal and innocent love between the sexes was
a force to be regretted, and perhaps condemned, until
Euripides—in a series of great dramas—explored every
phase of love, from the devotion of Alcestis to the
romance of Andromeda and the lawlessness of Phaedra.

The sin of Phaedra is thus the most striking example
of τὸ πονηρόν, the " badness " which Aristophanes holds
that the poet, as a teacher, should conceal : tragedy
should only " say what is good."[2]   The obvious defence
that " bad " characters may often teach an excellent
moral, is not raised by his Euripides—indeed, the
validity of this defence seems hardly to have struck the
Greeks (as it certainly struck the Romans), owing to
their habit of regarding poetry as positive rather than
negative in its educational effect.[3]   How then, we may
well ask, did Aristophanes defend the " bad characters "
of Aeschylus himself ?   We need not of course expect a

---

[1] Gorg. *Hel.* 19.   [2] *Frogs* 1056.

[3] Later critics admit " bad " characters as necessary to the action,
and as foils to the good, which can thus be more easily chosen ;
see [Plut.], *Life of Homer*, 5.

comic playwright to be strictly logical ; but Aristophanes
and his audience would no doubt have drawn Aristotle's
distinction between necessary and unnecessary badness.
Although they were always a little uncertain on the
point, the Greeks, consciously or unconsciously, accepted the crime of a Clytemnestra. Like ourselves,
they must have felt that her sinning was heroic, on the
grand scale, just as Lady Macbeth has the redeeming
quality of magnificence. So Creon may have all the
faults of a typical tyrant ; but, in the *Antigone*, he
stands for law and order. Even Odysseus, whose
character so much deteriorated in the course of Greek
tragedy, has virtues—if only the virtue of worldly
prudence, which no Greek was apt to undervalue.

All these characters could at least teach some positive
lesson, whereas Phaedra was condemned as beyond the
pale. Here, as so often, the trouble was ultimately due
to the confusion of æsthetic pleasure with the moral
end. The Greeks could hardly grasp the fact, to us so
elementary, that great poetic creations, such as Iago or
Milton's Satan, have been translated into a sphere
beyond good and evil, so as not to be weighed in the
common scale of human values, but judged by our
æsthetic feelings alone. No doubt the Greek critics—
including Aristotle—were sound in their protest against
unnecessary badness. This is inartistic, the means being
disproportionate to the end, with the result that the
poet defeats his own object. In this sense, the moralist
has really the last word, at least for his own times.
Old-fashioned Athenians were honestly repelled by the
subject of the *Hippolytus*, and Aristophanes had a
perfect right, as a critic, to voice their opinion. The
fact that, with this play, Euripides gained one of his
rare victories, only proved that the judges, or the bulk
of the spectators, had already ceased to sympathise
with traditional views.

But, if this attack on the theme of the *Hippolytus* is intelligible, there is less excuse for the critic's censure of the play on other grounds. Euripides had placed in the mouth of his hero the famous words :

My tongue hath sworn, yet is my mind unsworn.

—a line destined to become a byword of reproach in later Greek literature.[1] It was a matter of no consequence that, as a fact, Hippolytus did not break his oath ; it was sufficient that Euripides had apparently condoned perjury—perhaps, after parricide, the deadliest of Greek sins. The Greeks conveniently forgot that characters in Sophocles had made allowance for the breaking of an oath, in certain circumstances.[2] Sophocles however, had always passed muster as moral, and, in any case, his characters had not discussed perjury in an epigrammatic line.

To assume that a writer necessarily holds opinions spoken " in character " is an absurdity which needs no comment, beyond a reminder to ourselves that an average modern spectator is still capable of the confusion. The fault may sometimes be that of the dramatist himself, by his failure to produce the true dramatic illusion. It is indeed often difficult to decide whether a Greek chorus is speaking wholly in character or as the mouthpiece of the poet. The Greek critics themselves were ready to condemn τὸ ἀπρεπές—the lack of proper characterisation—but the general tendency was to hold the author as much responsible for the sentiments of his characters as a modern editor— if he does not make an express disclaimer—is often

---

[1] *Hipp.* 612. See *Thesm.* 275 ; *Frogs*, 101, 1471 ; Plat. *Theaet.* 154d ; *Symp.* 199a ; Arist. *Rhet.* iii. 94, and often elsewhere (e.g. Max. Tyr. xl. 6).

[2] Soph. *O.C.*, 228 f. ; *El.* 47.

held responsible for the opinions of his correspondents.[1]
The poet " created " the characters no less than the
action of a play, and was therefore the creator of their
sentiments. Aristophanes himself, being a poet, must
have known better ; but his business was to discredit
Euripides by all means, and this piece of mud-slinging
was a good comic point.

But, though scurrility may be legitimate in raising
a laugh, it must not be confused with criticism ; and
we have still to decide whether any views of pure literary
importance can be extracted from the *Frogs*, if we
deduct the moral issue as irrelevant. Conduct, according to Matthew Arnold, is three-quarters of life ; and
Aristophanes, to judge from this play, would certainly
have allowed that conduct is three-parts of drama, the
" mirror " of life. There remains the fourth quarter, in
virtue of which the comic poet may be counted as a
genuine critic. By what standard (apart from the
ethical) did Aristophanes appraise the tragic drama ?
Here, we must remember, criticism was musical as well
as literary. Aristotle, it is true, treated music as a
minor part of tragedy ; but in this respect, at least, he
is no safe guide to fifth-century opinion which, as we
see from Aristophanes, judged a dramatist by his music
as much as by his poetry. And both he and his contemporaries, like Pherecrates, condemned the " modern "
music which they attributed to the increase in the strings
of the lyre.[2] The dithyrambist Timotheus was the
chief offender, but he was abetted by Euripides.[3] The

---

[1] Decharme (*Euripides*, tr. Loeb, p. 20 f.) quotes Dionys. Hal.
Rhet. viii. 10 ; Lucian, *Jup. Trag.* 41, for a rare recognition of
sentiments expressed in character : when Euripides speaks καθ'
ἑαυτόν, he uses very different language from that spoken for
dramatic needs.

[2] Plut. *de mus.* 30.

[3] Plut. *an seni* 23, after Satyrus, *Life of Euripides* in *Oxyrh. Pap.*
1176, 39, 22.

latter, at least in his late period, " wrote for the music,"
by neglecting the time-value of syllables, and also by
disregarding the pitch-accent, and his innovations are
of course abominable to the conservative poets.[1]

So far, Aristophanes may be regarded as a musical
critic, in the modern sense ; but in general the comic
allusions to music are not so much technical as moral.
This is not surprising when we remember how largely
Greek music bulked in education, and how completely
it was judged by its ethical effect. Here, again, it is
enough to quote the *Protagoras*, where boys are said to
be taught singing " in order that they may become more
civilised, more rhythmical and balanced ; for the whole
life of a man needs eurhythmy and balance." [2] Greek
melodic modes or " harmonies " were distinguished by
opposite qualities ; and if Plato and Aristotle discuss
music in terms of the emotions, the emotions themselves
are entirely moralised. In the same way, the lyrical
criticism of Aristophanes on Agathon or Euripides is
nearly always confused and entangled with moral im-
plications, not only about the words, but about the
character of the music.[3] We need not suppose that the
average Athenian followed Pythagoras in holding music
as the purgation of the soul, which can only be attuned
to the music of the universe by the " harmony " of the
octave ; but this Pythagorean view, however extreme,
could not have existed in a race unprepared to attach a
value—both mystical and ethical—which few moderns,
perhaps, can appreciate.

From musical to metrical rhythm there is but a short

---

[1] *Frogs* 1314; see generally Edmonds, *Lyr. Graeca* iii. p. 626 f.
[2] Plat. *Prot.* 326b.
[3] See *Thesm.* 67, 130 f. ; *Frogs* 1301. On the relation of Aristophanes to Agathon, see Rhys Roberts in *Journ. Hell. Studies*, 20,
p. 144 f.

step, and here we are on safer ground. If we miss some
of the niceties of Greek metre, we are familiar with its
general effect. Here Aristophanes is at least on the
threshold of literary criticism. As we have seen, the
sophists, including Hippias, who lectured on "metric,"
had prepared the way.[1] Indeed, a people who delighted
in the most intricate rhythms could not fail to be interested in the theory of verse-structure. Aristophanes
of course could only deal with a highly technical subject
in comic terms; but one result of his criticism is clear :
Euripides and Agathon are charged with secularising
the solemn choral metres appropriate to Aeschylean
tragedy.[2]

If we must be suspicious of ancient musical criticism
as rarely æsthetic, we may turn with more confidence
to the formal construction and dramatic value of the
Euripidean tragedy. Aristophanes had the authority of
the tragedians themselves for regarding their rivals
with some jealousy. Only faint echoes of this professional criticism have survived ; notably in the famous
remark of Sophocles that he portrayed men as they
should be, Euripides, as they were. Again, there is the
Sophoclean reproach on Aeschylus that, if he wrote
proper poetry, it was in ignorance—a charge unkindly
interpreted by an ancient critic (Chamaeleon) as implying
drunkenness.[3] Euripides himself more than once used
his own plays as a vehicle for dramatic criticism. In
the *Phoenissae*, he comments, with scarcely concealed
sarcasm, on the lack of probability shown by Aeschylus
in his long-drawn descriptions of the Argive and Theban
champions, "when the enemy is under the very walls."
No less pungent is his rebuke of the recognition scene

---

[1] See p. 28. For Hippias see Plat. *Hipp. maj.* 285*d* ; *Hipp. min.*
368*d*.

[2] See Rogers, Intro. to the *Frogs*.   [3] Athen. i. 22.

in the *Choephori*, which partly depended on the cruel assumption that Electra's feet were as big as her brother's.[1] Aristophanes, in his turn, chooses a purely technical point—the use of the prologue—in his general attack on Euripides. This device was fair game to comedy for more than one reason ; it was an innovation not used by Aeschylus or Sophocles, and it was essentially undramatic—at best, perhaps, a convenient substitute for a modern programme. To judge from the *Life of Euripides*, his prologues were commonly regarded as a bore.[2] Aristophanes himself does not lay stress on the boredom, but (which perhaps comes to much the same thing) he smashes the prologues with the famous ληκύθιον ἀπώλεσεν, interrupting the flow of eloquence at the same place in speech after speech. So far, we may be reminded of Hunt's objection to the monotony of Popian verses :

> On her white breast—a sparkling cross she wore
> Which Jews might kiss—and infidels adore,

with the same pause in a dozen successive lines.   But, in Aristophanes, the joke does not merely turn (as is sometimes thought) on the monotony of this pause, but on the whole grammatical structure : the formula " lost his oil-flask " completes the sense as well as the metre. The whole scene of course is sheer buffoonery, and Aristophanes is simply playing to the gallery ; yet here, as often, the humour was perhaps as effective as any serious criticism on a stiff and awkward device.[3]

---

[1] *Phoen.* 749 ; *Suppl.* 846 ; *Electra* 527 f.   Various attempts have been made (e.g. by Verrall) to defend Aeschylus here ; Euripides, at least, understood him in the obvious sense, and naturally protested that a man's foot was bigger.

[2] *vit. Eur.* 3 ἐν δὲ τοῖς προλόγοις ὀχληρός.

[3] See generally Haigh, *Tragic Drama*, p. 247 f.

The prologue, however, is only a minor detail of dramatic technique; but in his discussion of tragic language Aristophanes approaches a literary question of permanent value. It was here that the antithesis between Aeschylus and Euripides was most striking— between the poet who " built up a wall of grand phrases," as big as Lycabettus or Parnassus,[1] and his rival, who " took over a style bloated with bombast and ponderous words, and reduced its bulk with a treatment of verselets and light exercise and beetroot.[2] Both poets, in their great Agon, defend their own diction : Euripides urging that his style must conform to the situations of common life,[3] while Aeschylus replies that great persons, situations and ideas demand grand language, or—in comic phrase—that heroes must utter fine words to match their fine dresses.

In a comic debate, some confusion as to the real point is pardonable. Ultimately, of course, the issue is not so much between two styles of diction as between two opposing schools of drama which we may conveniently call idealistic and realistic. Since Euripides intended to " introduce familiar affairs, among which we live and move," he could only use familiar language. This point was naturally seen by later critics ; both Aristotle and Longinus defend the new style, with the timely reminder that the innovations were less drastic than they appear—Euripides " concealed his art " by using the language of poetic tradition in a popular way.[4] The real charge, therefore, is that the diction of Euripides is unsuited to characters who are still nominally heroic.

---

[1] *Frogs* 1004, 1056, etc.

[2] *Ib.* 939 ἐπύλλια may be either " little words " or " light verse " ; περίπατοι seems to mean " subjects of discussion " with a play on " exercise."

[3] 959 f. οἰκεῖα πράγματ' εἰσάγων οἷς χρώμεθ', οἷς σύνεσμεν.

[4] See pp. 155, 219.

In other words, Euripides is accused of degrading the dignity of the stage by turning the heroes into ordinary men.   A further—and, to our minds, a more cogent cause of blame—is that the heroes, not content with being ordinary men, have now become sophists and lawyers.   Euripides in the *Frogs*, like Socrates in the *Clouds*—and with more justice—has to bear the odium of the new rhetoric.[1]   Even his warmest admirers have always recognised the truth of this accusation, which has a direct bearing not only in connexion with Euripides, but on all later criticism.   It is in Aristophanes that we may first trace the beginnings of that technical vocabulary which became the incubus of later critics.   Grammar and rhetoric were still in their infancy, but the work of Gorgias and Protagoras was sufficiently advanced to be ridiculed in the *Clouds*, the date of which (423 B.C.)— four years after the arrival of Gorgias—is significant.

By the end of the century the figures were becoming the standard of rhetoric, although their deadening influence was as yet hardly felt.   It is more than probable that many terms, which afterwards became highly technical, had already taken their place in critical equipment.[2]   Some literary faults, such as " ambiguity " and " pleonasm," are familiar enough to play a part in the comic altercation of the *Frogs*.[3]   The literary sin of the " false-sublime " or " frigidity " (ψυχρότης)— a term so often discussed from Aristotle to the latest critic—had perhaps acquired its professional sense in Aristophanes : when the tragic poet Theognis produced a play at Athens, the Thracian rivers felt the " frost." [4]

---

[1] *Frogs* 775 and often.

[2] See generally J. D. Denniston in *Class. Quart.* 21 (1927), p. 113 f.

[3] ἀμφιβολία, παραπλήρωμα in later terminology ; see Rutherford, *Hist. Ann.* p. 186 f.   For both faults cf. *Frogs* 1128-1169.

[4] *Ach.* 139 ; cf. *Thesm.* 170.

But, granted that the figures were already becoming important in serious criticism, they hardly lent themselves to comic fun. Aristophanes had better weapons for his attack on the new school. Even if we discount the value of his moral approach to poetry, as beyond his proper province, there remains a very solid residue of literary criticism to his credit. Stated in modern terms, his position is of course rigidly conservative ; but the conservatism which admired an Aeschylus is not lightly to be condemned. Scholars have often suggested that his praise of Aeschylus is half-hearted : that, although the older poet wins in his duel, he is almost as much battered as his adversary.[1] Such a view seems to neglect the requirements of the comic Agon, which is a genuine fight, not a one-sided quarrel—" if," as Juvenal says, " you can call it a quarrel where *you* beat and *I* am only beaten." Euripides, on his part, deals some shrewd blows, which Aeschylus can only counter with abuse for argument. Aristophanes, in fact, was bound to make out a case against his favourite, and he does this by admitting the force of popular criticisms. Aeschylus may be an inferior craftsman— for he is hardly allowed to defend himself against the charge that his characters sit veiled and in solemn silence, not uttering a monosyllable until the play is nearly finished.[2] The silence was perhaps originally due to technical difficulties of stage-craft ; but Aeschylus was apparently ridiculed for its over-use, and here Euripides scores a palpable hit, which, however, might have been less effective, if Aristophanes had remembered that silence may sometimes be more eloquent than

---

[1] See e.g. A. Croiset, *Aristophane*[3], p. 351 f.
[2] In the *Niobe* and *Phygians*. Compare the beginning of the *Prometheus*.

words.   Again, the Aeschylean pomp and magniloquence were too obvious to be denied : these faults of style and diction were inseparable from any criticism of Aeschylus ; but they probably seemed more glaring to his immediate successors, brought up in the school of Sophocles and still further alienated by the realism of Euripides.   None the less, there can be little doubt that the chorus of the *Clouds* represents the real opinion of the comic poet in calling Aeschylus the Bacchic King —the maker of the finest lyric that Greece had ever known.[1]   Even on the negative side, the poet of Marathon wins along all the line : he does not " sit and chatter by the side of Socrates, having thrown away the art of the Muses and laid aside the chief aims of tragedy." [2]

Such is the end of the bitterest attack which any member of the *genus irritabile* has ever made on a colleague.   Much has been written to qualify or deny the bitterness.   It is often urged that Socrates and Euripides are merely butts for more or less good-natured humour. We may well regard the tale of personal antipathy as unproved ; but it is impossible to believe that the comic poet treats his victims as mere food for laughter. Aristophanes is no worse a critic because—like Horace —he masks his views with ridicule.   The value of his criticism may be disputed.   He can be regarded as prejudiced and reactionary—as one who, however praiseworthy for his love of a great poet, was too narrow to praise another, in his different way as great.   To the majority of his own countrymen, perhaps, his views counted for little, for the next generation reversed his estimate of the rival poets.   Aeschylus, though honoured in his life and immediately after his death, was more and

---

[1] *Frogs* 1252 f.   [2] *Frogs* 1491 f.

more eclipsed by the growing popularity of Euripides.[1]
No Greek, indeed, would have been likely to quote
Aristophanes as a critic at all. Yet the comic poet has
at least one claim to which Aristotle himself is hardly
entitled. The latter—splendid as he is in the demon-
stration of poetic principles—neglects the chief business
of the critic, which is to deal with the document. Even
the " father of induction " is here too apt to be deductive,
using the text only in confirmation of his preconceived
notions on literature. But Aristophanes has the supreme
merit of " keeping his eye on the object," which, for
a critic, means the poem, and nothing but the poem.
He convicts the poet out of his own mouth. His judgments may or may not be warped ; but at least they
are based on the actual evidence. And here, in Greek
criticism, he is unique. We have to wait till the age
of Dio before we can find a parallel to the method of the
Thermophoriazusae and the *Frogs ;* and even Dio, in
his comparison of the three tragic poets, is but a pale
reflection of Aristophanes.[2]

From this point of view, it does not much matter
that the comic poet misjudged the verdict of his own
posterity. A critic is not a prophet, and Aristophanes
had at all events a good case for his own contemporaries.
He was prejudiced ; but even prejudice is more venial
than the calm detachment and indifference which is
sometimes thought proper to a critic. He could not be

[1] See p. 114. According to the *Life of Aeschylus,* a decree was
passed after his death granting the right of obtaining a chorus to
anyone who wished to revive his plays. His son, Euphorion,
gained several prizes in this way. See Quint. 10, 1, 66.

[2] It is true that discussions about the three dramatists must have
been familiar from Alexandrine times onwards ; see e.g. Dion. Hal.
de imit. 422 f. But there his treatment is purely general—on style
and characterisation ; not a single play is mentioned by name, nor
is there a single quotation.

expected to foresee a time when his own Battle of the
Books would be obsolete, and tragedy would be viewed
with the cool analysis of Aristotle and the clear perspective of Longinus. Still less can we blame him for
failing to realise the place of Euripides as the lineal
precursor of modern drama. Least of all, perhaps,
could he appreciate the curious irony of his own position
in the history of the theatre. He lived to see (and take
part in) the breakdown of the old political comedy, but
he could not have foretold the full development of
Menander, whose model, in language, dramatic construction and outlook on life, was not Aristophanes
but Euripides himself.[1]

[1] Quint. 10, 1, 69. Diphilus called Euripides " golden " (Athen.
p. 422 ; 60 Kock). Menander freely quotes or parodies Euripides
(348 and 366 Kock) ; so Philemon, 79. Satyrus discusses several
forms of the Reversal, which are " the backbone of the New Comedy,
and were perfected by Euripides." See *Oxyrh. Pap.* ix. 1176, 39.

CHAPTER III

PLATO

§ 1. The Wisdom of the Poet

AT the beginning of the fourth century the great
wave of Greek poetry was spent. While the Greek
mind had not ceased to be creative, it was now the
historians and philosophers, and (above all) the orators
who were expressing the intellectual life of Athens. The
age of Aristophanes, who could criticise tragic poets as
their contemporary, was yielding to a time when these
masters (especially Aeschylus) had become Old Masters.
In tragedy, the new movement of Euripides and Agathon
was no further developed, and became stereotyped after
their death. Comedy was more fortunate, since even in
the lifetime of Aristophanes it was taking a fresh form,
which by the middle of the century was to pass into the
New Comedy.

It might be expected that the years between Aristophanes and Aristotle would have produced an outburst
of criticism suggested by the comic poet as well as by
the sophists and Socrates. Some of the Socratics,
including Simmias, Crito and Glauco, were certainly
interested in various aspects of poetry, music and the
meaning of beauty ; but only the titles of their works
are recorded.[1] Practically all the critical work of the

[1] See Egger, p. 131.

half century is represented for us by a single great writer whose attitude towards poetry was so hostile that it may be curtly but not unfairly summed up in his own words—the poets must go.

Plato's verdict (which, however, he qualified) is not a mere gesture, nor a hasty exclamation, but a considered judgment to which—as he says—his argument had been leading. At the present day, few, if any, would prefer in this matter to be wrong with Plato rather than right with the rest. But at the time of the Republic, no conclusion reached by his wonderful dialectic could have caused more searchings of heart. Even among his sincerest admirers, there must have been some who made mental reservations, when Glauco agreed with the Platonic Socrates, and optimistically believed that " everyone else would do the same." The poets might be bad theologians and doubtful teachers ; but, after all, they were the glory of Greece. If Aristophanes tried to expel a single poet, he left Homer and Aeschylus untarnished and even, by contrast with Euripides, more magnificent.

It need scarcely be pointed out that Plato's attack on the poets implied a radical change in Greek education. From earliest boyhood the Greeks had been taught to revere Homer as the fountain-head of all knowledge, not only in theology, but also in the conduct of affairs. They may have paid less reverence than the Romans to the *exempla maiorum ;* but they were justified in believing that the aspirations and achievements of their race were typified in Achilles and Odysseus, and we know from Xenophon that the young Athenian was recommended to imitate the Homeric heroes in practical life.[1]   Achilles, in particular, represented the ideal of

---

[1] Xen. *Symp.* 4, 6.

the warrior, materialised at Marathon. When Aristophanes gave the popular conception of Homer as a teacher of war—τάξεις, ἀρετάς, ὁπλίσεις ἀνδρῶν—any Greek would think first of Achilles. But that hero was not merely the Sigurd of Greece; he was the pattern of friendship—the most romantic, if also the most abused feature of classical life; and he had all the qualities and virtues on which the historic Greek laid store—youth, nobility, high intellect, and (that nothing should be wanting) he was both musical and swift of foot.

The hero of the *Odyssey* was perhaps not so blameless; but he, too, had virtues which counted high among his later countrymen. Versatility is the keynote of his character, and this quality—for good and evil—was always the sign-manual of the Greek, surviving even in Juvenal's contempt of the hungry Greekling—*in caelum iusseris, ibit.* The Stoics themselves, no lenient judges, could choose him, in the company of Heracles, as a type of courage and endurance. On the other hand, Pindar, as we have seen, did not admire him, and his " wiliness " certainly needed excuse by those who laid store on the virtue of Truth.

Antisthenes got over the difficulty by understanding πολύτροπος as versatile in speech—Odysseus was a master in all kinds of rhetoric; and Socrates also regarded him as the perfect orator.[1] But the hero's character was certainly changed for the worse during the sophistic age, as is clear from his treatment in tragedy. In the *Ajax*, Odysseus is still dignified and magnanimous, and his rebuke to Agamemnon, who would have denied burial to his enemy, is worthy of the Homeric Odysseus, speaking well to Ajax among the dead.[2] But Odysseus

---

[1] Xen. *Mem.* iv. 6, 15 ; cf. Dion. Hal. *rhet.* 8, 304 f.
[2] Soph. *Aj.* 1365 ; cf. *Od.* 11, 553 f.

deteriorates at the hands of Sophocles himself, who—in
the late *Philoctetes*—represents him as anxious to gain
his end by fair means or foul ; and even so (according
to Dio), the Sophoclean hero was " far gentler and
simpler " than his counterpart in the *Philoctetes* of
Euripides.[1]

The study of Homer in the fifth century was thus
obscured by two radical errors : the poet was made
personally responsible for the morality of his created
characters ; and his poems were judged as good or bad
according to their morality.   Plato himself is a striking
instance of the confusion.   In one of his dialogues—
the *Hippias Minor*—Socrates discusses a statement that
the *Iliad* is a "better" poem (κάλλιον) than the *Odyssey ;*
and the sophist Hippias argues that this is due to the
characters :   Achilles is true and simple, Odysseus
versatile and false.[2]   We need not concern ourselves
with the Socratic conclusion that both heroes are conscious or unconscious liars ;   the point of interest is
that Plato, speaking through the mouth of Socrates,
can only approach the epic in terms of morality.   Here,
as elsewhere, the relation of the pupil to his teacher
is difficult to estimate.   The Socrates of Xenophon's
Memorabilia is fond of quoting Homer and Hesiod, and
plainly regards them as at least popular teachers.[3]   This
view is hardly consistent with the well-known passage
in the Platonic *Apology*, where Socrates complains that
poets are quite unable to explain the meaning of their
own works.[4]   As will shortly appear, this is exactly
the pupil's position, and its statement in the most
" Socratic " of all his writings would seem to imply

[1] Dio *Or.* 52.   [2] *Hipp. Min.* 309, b3.
[3] Xen. *Mem.* i. 2, 56 f. ; i. 3, 3 and 7 ; ii. 1, 20 ; ii. 6, 11 ; iii. 1, 4 ;
iii. 2, 1.
[4] *Apol.* 22b.

that his master was responsible. But, even then, there is a further inconsistency : the Socrates of the *Republic* uses very different language from that of the *Apology*, when he speaks of death as a boon that will allow him to converse with Orpheus and Musaeus, Hesiod and Homer.[1]

Plato's own attack on the poets, in its developed form, is both ethical and metaphysical, and it would be interesting to speculate whether these two lines of thought were independently evolved, or whether he found that the ideal theory—worked out as a complete explanation of the universe—was simply the confirmation of an argument originally advanced on moral grounds alone. There can be little doubt, at all events, that his protest, in its inception, was mainly ethical. It is the legacy of the sixth and fifth centuries. The assaults of Xenophanes and Heracleitus, the invective of Aristophanes, all unite in the early part of the *Republic*, where intense moral indignation is partly concealed by the dangerous calmness of dialectic. None the less, if the protest continued the ethical tradition, Plato approached the problem on broader lines even in his earliest work. The *Ion* is certainly older than the *Republic*, and is to be regarded as the first Platonic dialogue concerning the poets. Here, however, there is no discussion of morals ; the subject is not the *effect* of poetry, but the prior question of its nature. Plato starts his long campaign at its proper beginning—the credentials of poetry. We have seen that the nature of poetry had been debated since, at least, the age of Pindar ; and, in this controversy, Plato sides with the inspirationists against the technicians. In later dialogues, it is true, his advocacy of inspiration turns out to be more damaging to friend than to foe ; but the conclusion of the *Ion*

[1] *Apol.* 41a.

is the argument, repeated in the *Phaedrus*, that "whoever knocks at the door of poetry without the Muses' frenzy, persuaded that by Art alone he will be a sufficient poet, fails of perfection, and the work of the sober is forthwith eclipsed by that of the frenzied." [1] But, if the *Ion* abates the pretensions of Art, it is also a miserable comforter to the "wise" poets who, like Pindar, prided themselves on their consciousness of inspiration in the "steep paths of poetry." [2] To Plato this vaunted wisdom turns out to be not wisdom at all. He reverts to the primitive idea of ecstasy, in which the prophet-poet is merely the unwitting channel of a divine message. The poet himself is "a thing light, winged and sacred, and cannot make poetry until he is inspired and out of his mind." [3] He is like the Corybantes, who lose all self-control, or the Bacchants, who find, on coming to their senses, that their milk and honey are nothing but plain water. [4] The same idea is put into the mouth of Socrates in the *Apology*, where "the makers of tragedies and dithyrambs and the rest" are classed with seers and oracle-mongers as speaking much that is good, but not knowing that it *is* good—a conclusion which annoyed Meletus as the champion of religion. [5] If the poet is ignorant, the rhapsodist is a degree further removed from consciousness of the truth, since he merely repeats his original. Homer, as we have just seen, was thought to be a teacher of war; but, on the assumption that the rhapsodist Ion, his interpreter, "knew" the art of war, why was he not himself a great general?

---

[1] *Phædr.* 245a. See *Ion* 542.

[2] Pind. *Ol.* ix. 115 σοφίαι αἰπειναί. See above, p. 19.

[3] *Ion* 534b πρὶν ἂν ἔνθεός τε γένηται καὶ ἔκφρων καὶ ὁ νοῦς μηκέτι ἐν αὐτῷ ἐνῇ.

[4] *Ib.* 534a.   [5] *Apol.* 22b-23e.

But this is not the whole conclusion. A poet might be ignorant of his message, and yet the message itself might be valuable. After all, the Muses *could* speak the truth, and even the sceptic Thucydides generously allowed that one oracle was justified by the event. This loophole allowed Plato, throughout his life, to admire many " opinions " of the poets.[1] The *Ion* is not directly concerned to refute the popular belief that the function of poetry is didactic. What the author seeks to prove is that we cannot be sure of its value. It may be right by accident, i.e. the poet, being delirious, may or may not have corrupted his message in transmission.[2] In the same way dreams might be either significant or meaningless—the old Homeric belief which the philosopher adopted, distinguishing between the dreams due to man's passionate appetite and those that spring from his reason and so may well convey the truth.[3] If the poet cannot say whether his message is true or false, how can his hearers judge ? The Muses of Hesiod, with disarming frankness, had confessed their ability to speak falsehood. It was not only in the Hebrew tongue that a lying spirit might be put in the mouth of the prophets. But Plato could not take this easy way. The gods could neither deceive themselves nor mankind. Immorality cannot be inspired. A poet's opinion may be right, but it must be checked by Reason. Even if the poet happens on the truth, he cannot do more than remind the philosopher; for " written speech is like painting, where the characters stand up as if alive ; but, if you ask them a question, they preserve a solemn silence." [4] In fine, a poet—as we might put it—does not argue ; he " tells " you, and

---

[1] *Rep.* 383a.
[2] See J. Tate in *Class. Quart.* 23 (1929), p. 148.
[3] *Rep.* 571c-572a ; cf. *Charm.* 173a.   [4] *Phaedr.* 275d.

often tells you wrong. Only dialectic can verify or
disprove the " dusty answers "—the Meredithian phrase
might well be Platonic—which are all that poetry can
offer to explain the uncertainties of things.

To the close of his life—as we see from the *Laws*—
Plato never saw fit to modify his early disbelief in the
" wisdom " of the poet,[1] whose ignorance has been held
to explain a celebrated but disputed passage in the
Symposium. By the end of the banquet, when the cock
crew, Socrates had forced Aristophanes and Agathon
(the only members of the party who were still awake) to
admit that the same person can compose both tragedy
and comedy.[2] At this point, unfortunately, both his
hearers were drowsy, " not very well understanding the
argument," and, as the reporter of the conversation did
not hear its beginning, we are as completely ignorant
as any Platonic poet about its drift. There have been
many who would restore the argument as an anticipa-
tion of Shakespeare's tragi-comedies; and this view
does not perhaps deserve the scorn with which it has
been treated. The serious political purpose of the Old
Comedy, and, on the other side, the occasional humour
of the Tragedy might have suggested the possibility
of a further *rapprochement* of the Kinds. Euripides, in
the *Alcestis* (which took the place of a Satyric play),
had already done something to break down the party-
wall of the drama. Plato might at least have anticipated the medieval moralities, even if Shakespeare was
beyond his prophecy.

But the real objection to this theory is that Plato is
not talking about any fusion of the two kinds of drama.
He is simply arguing that the same poet could write
either kind. So far, this had never been done: as

[1] *Laws* 719c, 801b.   [2] *Symp.* 223d.

Socrates remarks in the *Republic* " the same persons are not successful even in two forms of imitation that seem very closely allied, tragedy and comedy, for example." [1] As a matter of fact, there appears to be no instance of a fifth-century poet who wrote in both forms, although Ion is said, on doubtful authority, to have composed comedies.[2] Plato's argument, therefore, may well be that, since neither tragic nor comic poet is a conscious artist, either could in theory become the mouthpiece of both Muses, with a double inspiration, of which he could give no account.[3] Homer had set the example : the *Iliad* was analogous to tragedy, the *Margites*, to comedy ; [4] and poetry, like history, might repeat itself.

But it must be confessed that, although this line of reasoning seems Platonic enough, another explanation would be equally possible. The two *genres* were very " closely allied " from one point of view ; but, from another, they were " opposites," in their attitude towards life. Remembering the influence of Heracleitus on Plato, we might find the clue in the theory of opposites, which a poet could understand, if he contemplated the idea of abstract beauty, instead of sensible objects. In more prosaic language, Plato himself suggests this explanation, when he allows that the serious tragedy cannot be understood apart from its opposite, the comedy.[5]

§ 2. " THE REPUBLIC " AND " THE LAWS "

It appears, both from the *Apology* and the *Ion*, that Plato's philosophic quarrel with the poets was fixed, in essentials, long before his full statement of the case

---

[1] *Rep.* 395*a*. [2] Schol. on Arist. *Peace* 835.
[3] So A. E. Taylor, *Plato* p. 234. [4] Arist. *Poet.* 1448*b*, 38.
[5] *Laws* 816*d*. See below p. 80. This explanation is suggested by W. C. Greene, *Harvard Studies in Class. Phil.* 29 (1918), p. 31 n.

in the *Republic*.   His objections were not merely ethical
but metaphysical.   What seems to be a development in
the course of the *Republic* itself is due, not to any change
in his settled opinions, but to the exigency of the argument in the handling of that great artistic work.   He
begins with the moral effect of poetry, leaving its nature
for later consideration, simply because, in the early
books, he is dealing with the education of the Guardians,
and his first care is to see that this education is sound.
It cannot be based on Homer and Hesiod, since they
misrepresent the character of the gods, and tell dis-
creditable tales of heroes, who received divine honours
by reason not only of their birth but their example ;
and they even suggest that the wicked prosper, while
the just are miserable—the old difficulty which the
gnomic poets like Theognis had seen and had failed to
solve.[1]

Of course these tales could be explained by allegory.
That method was by this time firmly established, and
had become fashionable among the Cynics, who held it
in trust (to be paid with full interest) for their followers,
the Stoics.[2]   But Plato did not like allegory, calling it
the method of one who is " too clever and laborious and
by no means happy." [3]   He does not deny that the
myths may contain true allegories ; but—as we have
seen—their interpretation is uncertain ;   and, at best,
allegory is only " opinion " which, if immoral, must
be rejected.[4]   In any case, it was useless in education :
" the young cannot discriminate between truth and
allegory," and beliefs adopted in childhood tend to
become fixed.[5]   Even if most adults outgrew childish

---

[1] See especially *Rep.* 377e-392.
[2] Xen. *Symp.* 3, 6.   [3] *Phaedr.* 229d.
[4] On allegory in Plato see J. Tate, *Class. Quart.* 23 (1929), p. 142 f.
[5] *Rep.* 378d.

beliefs—and Socrates in the *Euthyphro* is as incredulous
about Uranos and Cronos as Aristophanes—there remained fundamentalists like the pious Euthyphro
himself, who *did* believe, with the distressing result
that he felt bound to prosecute his own father as a
murderer.

Up to this point, Plato followed the tradition of
Xenophanes. Homer and Hesiod bear the brunt of
attack, but the tragedy is now involved. The stories
of Niobe, of Pelops and his house, and the whole tale
of Troy are immoral: "we cannot suffer the poets to
say that a god was the author of a punishment which
makes the punished miserable." Less kind than Aristophanes, he even singles out Aeschylus, as the head
of tragic poets—and of bad moralists. This special
censure is remarkable, for more than one reason. It
proves that Aeschylus was regarded by Plato no less
than by Aristophanes as the " first of (Athenian) poets " ;
but it also proves that Plato gives no support to the
modern opinion (still widely held) that Aeschylus was
thought to be " orthodox," even as far as that word
can apply to the undogmatic religion of Greece.[1]

From the ethical consequence of poetry he turns to
the prior question of its nature.[2] And here we first
meet with the theory of Imitation, which—with shifting
and subtle changes of meaning—plays the predominant
part in all Greek criticism. Although, as a literary
term, Mimesis is first found in Plato, it must have been
used, in popular speech, from the earliest time when
the Greeks began to speculate about their poetry, for
it is, of course, the most obvious explanation of any
art which we call " representative." But Mimesis had
a far wider connotation. The ritual dance of the Greeks

---

[1] Both points are made by A. E. Taylor (*Plato*, p. 279).
[2] *Rep.* 392c.

was often purely mimetic. Like the savage, they
"imitated," not only by dress, but by appropriate
gestures and music, the animal whose nature they
represented. A Greek girl "was a bear" at the
Brauronian festival ; a bird-dance depicted on an Attic
vase is a prototype of the comic chorus that so often
impersonates an animal. Plutarch quotes three *hypor-
chemata*—he attributes them to Simonides, but they are
more probably by Pindar—which are highly mimetic.
In one, the dancer is bidden to imitate a horse or hound ;
the second apparently describes a deer-hunt, and the
third alludes to the mimic dances for which Crete was
celebrated. It is not surprising that Plutarch, in his
comment, suggests that "poetry is a vocal dance, the
dance is silent poetry," as more apt than the original
definition of Simonides that poetry is vocal painting,
painting is silent poetry.[1]

The poet was mimetic simply because he "made" an
imitation Wrath of Achilles or Return of Odysseus.
To Herodotus, works of silver and gold were ποιήματα—
a word which most naturally applied to the representative
art of sculpture, from the humble frogs "made" by
a child out of pomegranates [2] to the creations of a
Pheidias. The Greeks did not regard the poet as an
imaginative creator—as many moderns interpret the
Maker—but rather as a specialised workman in metrical
language, who makes verse, with or without music.[3]
With these humbler associations, it was easy for Plato

[1] Plut. *Symp.* 9, 15, 2 ; for the definition of Simonides see Plut.
de glor. Ath. 346 f.

[2] Aristoph. *Clouds*, 881.

[3] The connotation of ποιητής has been discussed by H. Weil in
Etudes sur l'antiquité grecque (1900), p. 237 f. The modern view of
poetic creation is not earlier than Dryden, and was popularised by
the Romantics, but the term εὕρεσις (*inventio*) to some extent filled
the gap.

to disparage the poet as a mere imitator of sensible things, which in themselves are only copies of the eternal Idea. At best he was only a professional, who —as we have already seen—ranked with other craftsmen.[1] Plato's whole view of æsthetics was vitiated by this preconception, itself no little due to the Spartan military ideal.

His first objection to the poet is based on Mimesis as impersonation. He starts with the assumption that art impersonates life ; but, as life is itself teleological, the artist should have a moral purpose. It turns out, however, that art is very far from being moral. Briefly, his argument is that the soul assimilates all with which it is in contact. A drama impersonates various characters, good or bad, and this leads to uncertainty in the attitude of the soul. But Plato, unlike Shakespeare, will not allow a man, in his ideal city, to play many parts. His Guardians must imitate only the virtuous ; and they must not be assimilated to those who themselves imitate a number of characters. These limitations exclude both tragedy and comedy, but leave room for the epic, as far as it is purely narrative and shorn of the speeches, which are a form of impersonation.[2] Having reached this conclusion in the Third book, Plato leaves the subject until the Tenth. We there find that Mimesis has changed its meaning. At first applied to impersonation, it now becomes the copying of sensible objects. With the development of the Ideal doctrine, moral arguments are superseded by metaphysical. The poet "imitates" (that is, copies) created things, which are themselves only copies of Ideas, and therefore —in Greek notation—he is third removed from truth.

[1] See above, p. 23.
[2] 392-398. See generally E. Barker, *Greek Political Theory*, p. 192 f.

This metaphysical argument is reinforced by Plato's psychology : the soul is tripartite, and poetry appeals to the irrational part—to the passions, which it feeds and waters, instead of drying them up.[1] So, with the single exception of hymns to the gods and panegyrics on good men, poetry must be banished from the ideal state.[2] We are in the region of the Puritans who anticipated the hymns of the New Jerusalem by songs of praise on earth.

It may be argued that this admission of hymns and panegyrics implies an inconsistency. For, however morally sound, even this kind of poetry is an imitation ; it represents the actions and characters of gods and men. Even if such imitations are allowed in the Third book,[3] they should logically be condemned in the Tenth, where all Mimesis is excluded. We are often rightly warned against an attempt to make the philosopher, groping after truth, too rigidly consistent.[4] But, in this particular instance, it is very possible (as has lately been suggested) that he consciously or unconsciously distinguished between a true and false imitation, just as the inspiration of the poet might be true or false.[5] If so, the true imitation is that of the poet who, while formally imitating the characters and actions of the good, really imitates these in his own life. On this supposition Plato would fall in line with those who, with Strabo and Milton, have argued that only a good man can write " good " poetry.[6] Aristophanes—it may be added—had already given a comic version of some such theory, when he made Agathon remark that Phrynichus composed beautiful dramas because his

---

[1] 606d.   [2] 607a.   [3] 398b.   [4] So Greene, p. 73.
[5] See J. Tate in *Class. Quart.* 22 (Jan. 1928), p. 16, and Finsler, *Platon und die Arist. Poetik*, p. 22.
[6] See p. 210.

own person and dress were beautiful, while the chilly
Theognis could only write frigidly.[1]

It must be acknowledged that, if Plato consciously
drew this distinction, he did not emphasise his meaning ;
but such a view certainly accords with his conception
of authorship in the *Phaedrus*. In that dialogue, the
philosopher is urged not to commit himself rashly or
prematurely to writing his inmost convictions, like a
gardener forcing flowers ; he should rather sow the
seeds of philosophy to be cultivated and slowly developed
in his own mind. In other words, a written book
is final—*litera scripta manet*—allowing the author no
opportunity for correction, and is at best a " pastime,"
or an aid to his memory in old age. The author should
be greater than his published works.[2] So, perhaps,
Plato meant that the true poet, like the philosopher,
may be able to express his personality by a continuous
development of his character. The possibility of " true "
imitation would not only relieve Plato from the charge
of inconsistency, but would make him a constructive,
and not merely a destructive critic. In his view,
practically all extant poetry is imitation of the wrong
sort ; it is the product of ignorance.[3] But the ideal
state might produce ideal poetry, uniting truth and
beauty. The poet would still imitate, but his imitation
would not come within the scope of the " ancient quarrel"
between sensation and knowledge ; it would be based on
the only true knowledge, of Ideas. He would, in fact,
be himself a philosopher, whose special function was to
instil into the minds of all, but chiefly of the young,
a love of those beautiful objects which partake in the
nature of essential beauty, and which lead to the con-

[1] *Thesm.* 149 f.
[2] See *Phaedrus*, 274-278 ; and Taylor, p. 316 f.
[3] See *Rep.* 598d.

templation of that beauty in itself.   Unlike Homer, who
had no more than right opinion, the poet-philosopher
would belong to the class of those whose souls perceived
most of the Truth, before falling to earth—the lovers of
knowledge and beauty and culture.[1]

Whatever the precise line of reasoning may be, it
is clear that, even in the ideal state, the poet is not
banished unconditionally.   He may remain, if he can
show that his inspiration is true, that is, if his imitation
bears the stamp of good character.   This " ikon,"
though inferior to philosophic knowledge, is of value in
education, like any other form of art.   All the arts must
be moralised ;   and, though we may resent any view
of Art as the handmaid of Philosophy or Religion, we
must at all events allow that Plato, far more than the
Puritans, found a worthy function for the artist.   That
the writer of the *Phaedrus* and *Symposium*—a Greek of
Periclean traditions—admired the beautiful " copies "
of Calamis and Pheidias, needs no proof ; that he could
sometimes reconcile this admiration of art with the
supreme demand of reason, is best shown in his claim
for the artistic expression of " the fair and the graceful,
that our young men, dwelling as it were in a healthful
region, may drink in good from every quarter, whence
any emanation from noble works may strike upon their
eye or their ear, like a gale wafting health from salubrious
lands, and win them imperceptibly into resemblance,
love and harmony with the true beauty of reason." [2]

Plato, however, did not live in his ideal city.   So, in
the *Laws*—the work of his old age—he re-examined the
ancient quarrel, in the light of personal experience,
tempered by a certain disillusionment, as Greek politics
were far removed from the eternal pattern.   He did

[1] *Phaedr.* 248d.   See Tate, p. 22.
[2] *Rep.* 401c (tr. Davies and Vaughan).

not depart, in any essential, from his position in the *Republic*. In fact, he simply restated, with more detail and circumstance, the views expressed in the earlier books of that work. But, instead of expelling the poets, he allowed them to remain—on their good behaviour. In practice, this censorship is as drastic as excommunication, since the behaviour which he requires means almost the total disappearance of Greek poetry as he (and we) know it. All that remains is hymns and laudations of the dead (it is not " safe " to praise the living) with music and dances to match, approved by elderly examiners.[1] The drama, of course, fares badly. It had always been a bugbear to Plato, not only in the *Republic*, but in the *Gorgias*, where the tragic poet is described as a kind of mob-orator, whose aim is to please his audience by flattery, instead of giving them salutary truths whether they like it or not.[2] Still even tragedy is to be retained, provided that it submits to censorship, presumably not less strict than that of the *Republic*.[3]

Comedy shared this toleration. Along with tragedy, it was to be expelled from the ideal city, but might be retained in the practical state, if duly expurgated ; it was an entertainment that pleased older children— grown beyond the appreciation of marionettes—although adults would prefer tragedy. There were no doubt special grounds for objection. The comic poet, as Aristotle puts it, makes men " worse than they are," and this form of imitation is therefore obviously inferior to that of tragedy. Moreover comedy is undignified : the Guardians should not be taught that the gods have " laughter unquenchable," and should not be allowed to laugh immoderately themselves.[4] We may remember

[1] *Laws*, 801b.
[2] *Gorg.* 502b.
[3] *Laws*, 658b, 817a.
[4] *Rep.* 388d.

Prynne's disgust (in the *Histrio-mastix*) at " excessive cachinnations of dissolute gracelesse persons." But Plato rather grudgingly admits that the comic satisfaction is natural : the spectator *does* take pleasure in hearing jests on the stage which he would be ashamed to make in his own person.[1] In the *Philebus* he attempts to analyse this pleasure, and concludes that it is a mixed feeling—a reaction to the self-ignorance of others. We laugh at our friends' conceit, so long as this is harmless ; but the pleasure is contaminated by a painful feeling of envy.[2] This psychology, if not exhaustive, is acute. As Mr. Cornford points out, the old comedy is largely concerned with various types of impostors, whose temporary success we vicariously enjoy, while we take pleasure in their eventual fall, which we escape.[3] If this is Plato's own meaning, we may agree with Mr. Cornford that the vicarious indulgence has a real value. Comedy may be a natural outlet for passions which, when inhibited, are likely to be vented in other channels, more harmful to the character. The Old Comedy, however gross, is perhaps a better " purge " than its immediate successor, the comedy of innuendo. But Plato, like all Puritans, had no belief in the outlet of passions, vicarious or firsthand ; and he had to satisfy his conscience otherwise. His justification, in the *Laws*, is that serious things cannot be understood without their opposites. Hence a man should learn both, if only to prevent being ridiculous himself. In other words, comedy is a warning—an argument which, however inadequate to explain its pleasure, might have been useful to Aristophanes when he condemned " bad characters " in the drama.

---

[1] *Rep.* 606b.   [2] *Phil.* 48.

[3] F. M. Cornford, in *New Adelphi*, Sept., 1927. See generally Lane Cooper, *An Aristotelian Theory of Comedy* (1924), p. 98 f.

In admitting comedy, the reformer tries to make
things as difficult as possible. Only slaves and hired
strangers may imitate the ridiculous—we are in the
familiar region of " strolling players and vagabonds,"
and far from the toleration of Plato's own countrymen,
at least in the previous generation, since they could still
remember that it was the poet's original function to
act in his own plays—a custom that survived until
the time of Sophocles, who took minor parts in his
Thamyris and *Nausicaa,* to show his skill as a harpist
and ball-player.[1] Plato no doubt considered any form
of acting as below the dignity of a gentleman ; but it
is significant that he chose the comedian for his special
censure. Again, the comic poet must not ridicule a
citizen either in anger or without anger, whether by
word or likeness, except in pleasantry.[2] This is an
implicit condemnation of the Old Comedy, and the
" ridicule of citizens " is no doubt the chief scandal in
Plato's eyes. It is remarkable, at least, that he lays
no stress on the indecency which has offended many
modern admirers of Aristophanes. Perhaps it would be
more remarkable if he *had* protested ; for the attitude of
to-day (or at least yesterday) is largely due to a change
of manners rather than of morals. Aristophanes of
course is Rabelaisian ; but here the last word was said
by Coleridge on Rabelais : " the morality of his work
is of the most refined and exalted kind ; as for his
manners, to be sure, I cannot say much." Plato could
not have " said much " for the vulgarity ($\tau\grave{o}$ $\phi o \rho \tau \iota \kappa \acute{o} \nu$)
which Aristotle also condemned ; but it must be re-
membered that the criterion of Greek vulgarity differs
from our own, and that what is now regarded as " in-
decent " was actually sanctioned by Greek religion.
Anyhow, there is little in Plato to suggest that his

---

[1] See Haigh, *Attic Theatre,* p. 204.   [2] *Laws,* 816d, 935e.

6

strictures on the Comedy were moralistic, except in the immorality which it shared with tragedy.

Nevertheless, the personal relations between the philosopher and Aristophanes are by no means free from doubt. It is difficult to reconcile Plato's half-hearted, rather contemptuous tolerance of comedy in the *Laws* with the Plato whom we know from other sources. We recall the well-known epigram :

> The Graces, seeking to have a sanctuary that shall never fall, found the soul of Aristophanes.

There is no reason to question its authenticity, and we might be content to regard it (like the poems to Aster) as belonging to the philosopher's " unregenerate " youth ; but, even so, there is a contrast, hardly explained, between the *Laws* and the *Symposium*—itself the work of his mature life—in which Aristophanes appears in no unfriendly light.[1] Indeed, if Plato really thought that the poet's attack on Socrates in the *Clouds* was influential at his trial, Aristophanes is surely treated with the greatest leniency. It has been supposed that, although he pardoned the comic poet, he showed his disdain for one who was " devoted to pleasure and laughter " ; yet, in the context, the disdain is not apparent.[2] But need we labour to explain the inconsistency—if it exists ? Plato is not only a philosopher ; he is also a great dramatist and—which is still more to the point—a great humorist. In one phase of his many-sided genius, his art is more than a little akin to the spirit of Aristophanes.[3] When all is said, the humour

---

[1] *Symp.* 177e, 189b.

[2] A. Croiset (*Aristoph.* p. 311). L. Robin (in *Le Banquet*) also lays too much stress on the odium of the *Clouds*.

[3] See W. C. Greene, *The Spirit of Comedy in Plato* (*Harvard Studies in Class. Phil.* 31, 1920), where possibly more than justice is done to this aspect of Plato.

of the *Euthydemus* and the *Symposium* cannot be harmonised with the sobriety of the *Laws ;* and Plato is
himself the best example of his own suggestion that
the same man could write comedy and tragedy. His
" inconsistency," in refuting this very same suggestion
elsewhere, is a proof—if proof were needed—that Platonism is not a rigid system, but an enquiry by a genius of
many moods and diverse gropings after the truth. He
could at times forget to judge poetry as a philosopher,
if credence may be placed in his own pupil Heracleides
Ponticus—himself a writer on the subject of poets and
poetry—that his master so far preferred the poems of
Antimachus to those of Choerilus that he despatched
Heracleides to collect the verse of the Colophonian poet
in his own city.[1] After this, we need not be too hasty
in discrediting the story that Plato took so much delight
in the comedies of Aristophanes and the mimes of
Sophron that their poems were discovered in his death-
bed.[2] His own dialogues, as has often been observed,
may be understood as philosophical mimes ; and though
his references to comic poets—notably Epicharmus—
are few, he is at least as favourable to the writers of
comedy as to those of tragedy.[3] He knew that the
comic spirit is the bitterest foe of pretence.[4]

But, besides this external evidence, it is clear from his
own works that, in the secular struggle between sense
and reason, Myth and Truth, his loyalty was divided.
He had been brought up in the traditions of aristocratic
education, with its almost exclusive staple of music
and poetry ; and he was by nature a poet. We need
not rely too much on the trustworthiness of Diogenes
Laertius, who records Plato's early essays in various
forms of poetry, nor on the literal truth of the statement

[1] Egger, p. 166.
[2] Greene, *op. cit.,* p. 121.
[3] See *Theaet.* 152e ; *Gorg.* 505e.
[4] *Phileb.* 48.

that he burnt his poems after hearing Socrates.[1]   A more convincing proof lies in Plato himself—not only in his own confession of love for poetry, but in the dramatic form which he freely uses, and—most of all—in his love for the myth.   For, to a Greek, poetry and myth were terms almost interchangeable.   Myth was something more than the subject-matter—the " business " or " stuff " of the poet, as Corinna had called it [2];   it seemed to be the very essence of poetry, requiring only metrical expression to become a pure poem.[3].   And Plato fell back on the Myth, because, being a poet, he knew that philosophy itself required the aid of poetic intuition, where the proof of reason failed.   In one of his moods, he could say hard things of a poet, as a charlatan, a mob-orator, a speaker of untruths.   Yet, if poetry is fiction, it might still be a " noble lie," such as the philosopher could use in re-writing mythology for his State,[4] as well as in the great series of myths in which he satisfied his own imperious need of poetry. It was surely from his own personal experience that the priestess Diotima speaks : a poem is due to the desire of parenthood that springs from the natural yearning for immortality ;   Homer and Hesiod and other great poets have created a progeny whose fame is far more illustrious than that of any children in human shape.[5]

Philosophy must be supreme, but at a cost which Plato does not disguise.   The struggle, and its final issue, is revealed by the Socrates of the *Republic :* " I must speak my mind, although I confess I am checked by a kind of affectionate respect for Homer, of which

---

[1] See generally D. Tarrant in *Class. Rev.* 40, 3, p. 104 f.

[2] Plut. *de glor. Ath.* 348.   [3] See *Phaedo,* 61b.

[4] *Rep.* 414b.

[5] *Symp.* 209d.   Aristotle followed (*Eth. N.* ix. 7, 1168a) : Poets, more than other craftsmen, dote on their poems as if they were their children.

I have been conscious since I was a child. For, of
all those beautiful tragic poets, he seems to have been
the original master and guide." [1] And later: " we are
conscious of being enchanted by such poetry ourselves,
though it would be a sin to betray what seems to us the
cause of truth "; and therefore " we must take a lesson
from those persons who, after becoming enamoured of
an object, deny their passion at any cost, if they think
it injurious. [2]

§ 3. ART AND MORALITY

Plato has been called a fanatic, in respect of poetry
and art.   The term is surely misapplied to one who
took into account both reason and emotion, and who
—having, as he thought, to make a choice—preferred
reason.   Even then, as we have seen, the choice was not
rigidly exclusive.   If he denied that art was the whole
of wisdom, he allowed that it might be the beginning
of wisdom. [3]   The way is not barred to reconciliation,
and the legislators in the *Laws* hold out this hope to the
tragic poets : " We are ourselves poets of the finest
drama in the world, for our state is an imitation of the
finest life.   If you can show that your poems are as
good as ours, or better, we will give you a chorus." [4]
It is easy to find fault with Plato's conclusions on
the ground that his premiss is obviously inadequate.
Mimesis—at least in the sense of copying—is not the
end of art ; and (which is more important) the charge
was hardly less absurd in the days of Plato than in our
own.   Popular opinion, of course, then as now awarded
the palm to the most flagrant copyist—hence the stories

---

[1] *Rep.* 595*b* (Davies and Vaughan).   [2] *Rep.* 607*e*.
[3] W. P. Ker (*Collected Essays,* ii. ch. 33) is here in point.
[4] 817*a-d.*

of painted grapes which the birds pecked, and the painted curtain which deceived even a fellow-artist. But we know enough about Greek painting to be sure that Zeuxis and Apelles were no more illusionists than Pheidias or Sophocles. Educated people always understood that it was the duty of any artist to improve on the model—unless, as in comedy, he exaggerated its defects. Viewed in this light, the doctrine of Imitation can be restated in modern terms as the idealisation of nature, and as such, is still thought worthy of defence —and attack—even if it competes with some fifteen rivals as the foundation of æsthetics.[1]

We have seen that Plato's chief objection to Mimesis lay, not in the process of copying (though this, too, had its dangers) but in the thing copied, since $\tau\grave{a}$ $a\grave{i}\sigma\theta\eta\tau\acute{a}$, *sensibilia*, could not disclose Reality. He did not foresee the answer of the neo-Platonists, that an artist may seek, through phenomena, the beauty which nature only in part reveals ; though, in the *Symposium*, he had himself pointed out that ideal beauty could only be apprehended through the particulars of sense. Why, it may be asked, did he fail to make it plainer that Art, being concerned with beauty, might be at least a valuable means to knowledge ? His answer would have been that Art cannot be *the* means, which is the sphere of philosophy. Art could not be an end in itself, because the artist's vision is emotional, and the emotions, if not actually suppressed, must be subordinated to Reason. But he does, in effect, allow that art may be *a* means to knowledge, as a training for the soul not yet prepared for the more rigorous treatment of philosophy, though he does not develop this doctrine with the depressing thoroughness of Plutarch and the Stoics.

[1] I borrow the number from *The Foundations of Æsthethics* (2nd ed. 1925), by C. K. Ogden, I. A. Richards and J. Wood.

As long as Art is confused with morals and judged by
extraneous canons, Plato's error, in one form or another,
is bound to recur, as a few examples (taken from various
ages) will sufficiently prove. Early Christianity had,
of course, its own reasons for protest, when Augustine
or Boethius could not reconcile the old literature with
the new dispensation. The story of Virgil in the Middle
Ages is too familiar to recapitulate ; but, as a random
illustration, we may note the spirit of Plato in the
avatar of Alcuin who, " watching the devils nip the toes
of the other monks in the dormitory, called anxiously
to mind that he had scamped the Psalms to read the
Aeneid." [1] Plato had at least more excuse than Tolstoy,
who deliberately sinned against the light, in denying
the claim of art to be appraised by its own laws. No
doubt his rejection of the (then) new slogan *l'art pour
l'art* was called for—" if you spoke nowadays of the
necessity of morality in literature, no one would understand you " [2]—but his remedy was worse than the
disease. He differed from Plato, by holding that " art
is an organ co-equally important with science for the
life and progress of mankind, its function being to
transmute the reason of science into feeling " ; [3] but,
here agreeing with Plato, he was obsessed by the moral
criterion of literature. His aim was to create a " world-
art " which should establish brotherly union among men
—the last words and the sum of his book. No more
than Plato could he realise that art is an independent
activity, and that the sole business of the artist is to
express himself in terms of beauty. To him, art is not
disinterested ; it must serve mankind, and Tolstoy is
a thorough Platonist, or even outvies Plato, by his

[1] H. Waddell, *The Wandering Scholar*, p. xxiii.
[2] Tolstoy's Diary (E.T.) under date of entry 1853.
[3] See *What is Art ?* tr. A. Maude.

insistence that few examples of living art—he does not spare most of his own works—could stand the moral test. But, with unconscious irony, he cites the *Iliad* and *Odyssey* in the list of exceptions. Homer transmits " very elevated feelings "—a warning, surely, to the shades of both Russian and Greek, that to pass ethical judgments on works of art is not always " the part of a fortunate man."

If we sum up our conclusions, it will be evident that, from a strictly modern point of view, Plato can hardly be called a critic at all, since he never comes to close quarters with the actual documents. His many references to poetry deal only with isolated passages, and are almost wholly confined to the moral issue. He has no sympathy with Pleasure, as the End of art, which Aristotle was to place in the forefront of criticism. While recognising the æsthetic fact—it could not be overlooked—he deprecates its existence. His views on Pleasure range from bare toleration to contempt or censure, but pure æsthetic satisfaction is not of their number. There is always the suggestion, if not the open charge, that the " Muse of tragedy " is meretricious.

Nevertheless, Plato must always be reckoned as one of the incentives for the literary criticism of others. It is true that his direct influence was largely negative— such prejudice, from its very intransigence, demanded refutation, and all the later Greek critics were vitally concerned to disown or at least to pass over this inconvenient heresy. But his positive value must not be overlooked. His view of the subordination of art to morals was painfully one-sided ; but, now that the pendulum has swung violently to the other extreme, we are none the worse for his reminder that " Life is the best and most beautiful drama," and we, its " poets " or actors, must not tolerate an unworthy representation.

Nor is it superfluous, even now, to be warned against
the tyranny of mere technique, although the warning
may have been far more needed in certain "Alexandrine" periods of literature. Plato's emphasis on the
limitations of τέχνη is the more impressive in that, with
Sophocles, he is himself supreme in combining genius
with art. He was the first to state in precise terms—
what Sophocles had already shown in practice—the
law that a composition should be put together like a
living creature with organic unity.[1] After so many hard
things said elsewhere against the poets, it is pleasant
to find the philosopher calling Sophocles and Euripides
to bear witness on dramatic construction : Sophocles
would say to one who could write single speeches, without fusing these into an artistic whole, " you possess
the preliminaries of tragedy, but not tragedy itself." [2]
This tribute to poetic art may seem slender enough ;
but it proves that even in the *Phaedrus*—where poetry
is called a mere " holiday-production," if it is not
written with a knowledge of philosophic truth—Plato
could remember that he belonged to a company of
fellow-artists. It is the more a pity that he could not
bring himself to compose the ancient—and needless—
quarrel : that he could not recognise the error of any
antithesis between two methods of approach to Reality,
which are never rivals, and which—as indeed he knew—
may often be partners and co-workers.

This line of argument, however, touches only the
fringe of the whole matter. The Ideal theory, as initi-
ated by its author, was a foe to poetry ; but the foe
could easily be turned into a friend. No great poet,
after all, can entirely dispense with Plato's idealism, in
whatever terms he may interpret the conception ; and,

[1] *Phaedr.* 264e. See S. H. Butcher, *Harvard Lectures*, ch. 4 and 5.
[2] *Phaedr.* 269a.

if this is true of the poet, it is equally true of the critic, who can only hope to play the part of an Ion, with perhaps rather more success than Plato allows that rhapsodist. For, as Mr. Saintsbury reminds us, some form of Idealism is necessary to the critic : " the beauty of literature is hardly accessible except to one who is more or less a Platonist." Aristotle himself—though he excludes any Platonic enthusiasm from his extant works—must have owed a far greater debt to his master than he seems willing to confess. And, if Aristotle was only too successful in repressing this enthusiasm, it was destined to find a full outlet in the noble passion for great literature that marks Longinus as a Platonist, who showed his master's own spirit in rejecting his heresy.

CHAPTER IV

ARISTOTLE

§ 1. General Principles of Poetry

PLATO, theoretically, had banished the poets; but poetry is a natural instinct, and the Greeks knew (as well as Horace) that Nature, even if expelled with a pitchfork, will return. Here, at least, it is not surprising that Plato's pupil deserted his master. But there is an apparent paradox in the fact that the earliest Apology for Poetry came, not from a poet—Aristotle's ode to Virtue can hardly entitle him to that name—but from a philosopher, a traitor in the Platonic camp.[1] To Aristotle, however, there could be no question of treachery—the ancient quarrel was meaningless. The truth of philosophy—including what we should call science—was not antagonistic to the truth of poetry. His defence was no less effective because he showed so little of the poet in his own attitude. If he felt the devotion of a Sidney or Shelley, he was at pains to conceal it. At the time, the cause of poetry was best served by meeting Plato on his own ground; and Aristotle's

---

[1] Our direct knowledge of Aristotle's critical position is of course mainly drawn from the *Poetics* and a few incidental allusions in the *Rhetoric*. His lost work (*On the Poets*) seems to have defended poetry and discussed the ideal poet, besides dealing with the theory of inspiration. See generally A. Rostagni, *Aristotele in Studî Ital. di Filol. Class.* (N.S.), 2 f.

poetic position was the direct outcome of his main
metaphysical departure from Platonism.   In his model
of the universe he had rejected the theory of Ideas,
substituting the formula of Becoming in place of abstract
Being ;   and this principle not merely explained the
existence of poetry, but gave it a high philosophic
value.   As knowledge of the universal could only be
attained by a study of particulars, it followed that all
processes of Becoming must be observed, whether in the
physical world or in the spiritual life of man.   In the
latter sphere, both history and poetry had their proper
place, and, as between the two, Aristotle's well-known
preference for poetry is of course perfectly logical :
history is less " universal," since what *has* happened is
particular, what *may* happen is universal.   Such universals have a real existence, but not in the supra-
mundane sense of the Platonic Ideas.   They exist as
concrete and objective things in our own world.   They
are common to many individuals, and are therefore more
worthy of philosophic study than the character of a
single individual.[1]   If we apply this premiss in con-
sidering the relative values of history and poetry, it is
evident that Alcibiades is less " universal " and " necessary " than Achilles.   " History describes events in
which the necessary sequence of effect on cause is obscured by a thousand casual interventions ;   poetry,
and particularly tragedy, depict the inevitable depend-
ence of destiny on character." [2]   Aristotle allows that
a historical subject can be treated by a poet.[3]   He could
have said no less, in view of the general belief that the
persons in the Trojan or Theban myths were historical.
But his philosophic reason is that " there is nothing to
prevent some events which have actually happened from

[1] W. D. Ross, *Aristotle*, p. 158.
[2] *Ib.* p. 278.   [3] *Poet.* 1451b, 29.

conforming to probability and inevitability "—a statement, or understatement, of (no doubt) unconscious
humour. Agamemnon was a real person; the poet,
however, does not report his words on a given occasion
—" if so " (Aristotle might have said) " the less poet
he "—but gives the words and actions typical of the
person. The type, in fact, is essential to poetry.
Herein, Aristotle not only draws the logical conclusion
from his general theory of universals, but correctly
interprets the genius of Greek epic and drama—the
two Forms which are his main standards of poetry,
since they show " universality " in the highest degree.
As applied to poetry, the universal is concerned only
with human action—a broad term, indeed, as " action "
includes the passions which lead to, or are consequent
on action—but still exclusive of mere moods or passive
frames of mind.[1]

The particular stress on " men in action " is thoroughly
Greek. Gorgias had already defined poetry as concerned with πράγματα, and Plato's theory of mimetic
referred specially to the epic and drama as dealing
with human action, whether narrated or represented.[2]
Aristotle starts with the Platonic definition, and, as
usual, finds it unsatisfactory. For his master had spared
the narrative part of epic, reserving his chief censure
for the imitation of tragedy, whereas Aristotle sees equal
poetic value in both Forms. This broad-mindedness is
not extended, apparently, to lyric, or at least to the
lyrical parts of tragedy. His silence, in the *Poetics*,
about this branch of art has been variously explained.
He probably regarded lyric as bound up with the music,

---

[1] 1447b, 23. The universal in poetry is further defined in 1451b,
8 " how a person will speak or act according to probability or
necessity."

[2] Gorgias, *Hel.* 9 ; Plat. *Rep.* 603c.

a mere "accessory" to the drama, in which only the action and the story mattered.[1] But, besides this practical reason, in the special sphere of drama, Aristotle's definition of poetry in general would hardly have allowed him to rate lyrism at its full value, in modern estimation. Pindar's epinikian odes might possibly conform to his theory of action ; but how could Sappho satisfy his formula ? Being both a Greek and himself a lyrist (of a sort) Aristotle would not have denied that her love-songs were beautiful, but he probably regarded them as trifles, unworthy to be classed with the serious Forms of the art. Later critics made ample amends for this neglect ; but no Greek approached the modern attitude towards the " personal " lyric—so often regarded as the fittest expression of a poet. To the ancients, of course, the need of " self-expression " would have seemed almost meaningless. Still less would the Greeks have understood a modern extension of that theory, in which a poet believes himself, or is believed by others, to be content with self-expression without an audience. As an historical fact, the sixth century, often called the great age of lyric, might equally well be called the age of poetic personality. Before Sappho, Alcman had already gloried in revealing his personal experience, even putting into the mouths of a feminine chorus his defence against a charge of low birth, or—in other " maiden-songs "— boasting of his gluttony, or complaining that old age excluded him from the dance.[2] But the natural Greek habit of thought was to regard the poet—even when most personal—as having a message to communicate, and

---

[1] 1450a, 21 τὰ πράγματα καὶ ὁ μῦθος τέλος τῆς τραγῳδίας. For Aristotle's classification of lyric under μελοποιΐα, see Bywater, p. 97. So the Aristophanic Euripides, criticising the choruses of Aeschylus, calls him κακὸς μελοποιός (*Frogs* 1250).

[2] See fragments 26, 46 (Edmonds) ; Diehl, *Anth. Lyr.* i. p. 34.

hence his work was almost entirely viewed in relation to its effect on the audience. Indeed, the most serious defect of the theory of Imitation is that it led the critics to regard poetry as external to the poet, not as the expression of his personality.[1] It can hardly be denied that the Aristotelian definition of poetry leaves Sappho out of account; and, as we have no evidence that Aristotle broadened it to include her, we are forced to assume that he classed love-poetry as of no philosophic importance, or, at any rate, as far below the Epic and dramatic Forms.

Poetry, then, deals with universals by imitation. Here, again, Aristotle is working on Platonic lines— while he turns Mimesis from an antagonist into an ally of philosophy. Art imitates characters, emotions and actions, and music is the most imitative of all the arts— a thoroughly Greek conception, which should have itself dispelled any false view of Mimesis as mere copying.[2] Plato had already held that music is an imitation of character, and indeed this view was unchallenged until the Epicureans denied the moral influence of that art.[3] In poetry, as in other arts, it is the " likeness " that gives pleasure, but this likeness may represent men either as better than they are (in Homer and Sophocles) or worse, or as they are.[4] As to the nature of æsthetic satisfaction, Aristotle brings it heavily to earth from the heaven in which Plato had placed his architypal Beauty. The pleasure lies simply in observing the likeness—" that is he." This explanation at least accounted for the

---

[1] So R. K. Hack in *Harvard Studies in Class. Phil.* 27 (1916), p. 55.

[2] *Pol.* 1340a, 18.

[3] *Rep.* 398 f. See p. 172. For the Epicureans see Philodemus, *de musica*, iv. col. 3, 23 (p. 65K) οὐδὲ γὰρ μιμητικὸν ἡ μουσική, καθάπερ τινὲς ὀνειρώττουσιν.

[4] *Poet.* 1448a, 4.

fact that objects (such as corpses), which we see with pain, give pleasure when represented by art. The cause of the pleasure is purely intellectual, depending on the recognition of the likeness, although Aristotle seems dimly to feel that this philosophic satisfaction is not quite adequate, so that he is forced to add that, if you have not seen the original, the pleasure will be due to the execution, or the colour, or some such cause.[1] But this is merely a passing suggestion ; as far as possible, æsthetic pleasure must be rooted in the intellect.

If poetry is a form of intellectual pleasure, it follows that the poet must be fully conscious of his own meaning. Aristotle implicitly throws over the whole Platonic theory of the poet's ignorance and his transient " possession." The doctrine of inspiration—it is true—had become so traditional, that Aristotle himself appears to accept it, without qualification, in one passage of the *Rhetoric*.[2] But, in the *Poetics*, his more considered judgment is that poetry is the product of natural ability (εὐφυΐα) *or* ecstasy,[3] and the whole treatise really rests on the former alternative. The " mania " is no temporary enthusiasm, but permanent and conscious ability. Dryden was no doubt unscholarly—according to modern canons of scholarship—in correcting Aristotle's *or* to *not* (ἢ to οὐ) ;[4] but he probably did the philosopher no injustice, for the " wit " of English Augustans is exactly what Aristotle demanded as the manifestation of natural ability, wholly removed from enthusiasm.

Poetry, then, is the art of evoking the emotions (or certain emotions) which must be checked by reason.

---

[1] 1448 *b*17.

[2] *Rhet.* 1408*b*, ἔνθεον ἡ ποίησις. So *Probl.* (xxx.), 954*a*, 34. (Maracus was a better poet ὅτ' ἐκσταίη.)

[3] 1455 *a*, 32 εὐφυοῦς ἡ ποιητικὴ ἢ μανικοῦ.

[4] Pref. to *Troilus and Cressida*.

The tragic poet *knows* what he feels, putting the scene before his eyes, and even acting the story with his own gestures—advice which had become a commonplace by the time of Horace.[1] He is an imitative artist in the medium of words. But, as all arts are imitative, in different ways and degrees, it remained for Aristotle to define the specific character of poetry. It springs from two causes, of which one (imitation) is an instinct shared by the whole class, while the other (common also to the allied arts of music and dancing) is the instinct for rhythm.[2] In stressing this second cause, he agrees with Plato, who had held that the perception of rhythm and harmony was a divine gift, not shared by lower animals, for the pleasure of man alone.[3] Metres (he goes on to say) are clearly parts of rhythms, and men gradually developed improvisations into poems—an evolutionary view of which the Epicureans made full use. It has sometimes been argued from this passage that Aristotle would at least consistently have admitted Free Verse as a legitimate form of poetry. As we shall see, the later Greeks very nearly realised this view.[4] But Aristotle himself would certainly have regarded a prose-poem as a confusion of the Forms, and indeed as a contradiction in terms.[5] The prose of Gorgias is highly rhythmical, but his *Praise of Helen* was no more a " poem " than the mimes or Socratic dialogues, which Aristotle, recognising their semi-dramatic character, seems to have placed in

---

[1] 1455a, 22 f. ; Hor. *A.P.* 102, *si vis me flere dolendum est primum ipsi tibi.*

[2] *Poet.* 1448b, 20, τῆς ἁρμονίας καὶ τοῦ ῥυθμοῦ where " harmony " (" tune ") refers to poetry in its close connexion with the two other arts in the group. I follow Butcher (p. 140) in taking the second cause of poetry to be rhythm, not the pleasure of imitation, which can hardly be an independent αἰτία.

[3] *Laws* 653e.   [4] See p. 190.

[5] So Bywater on *Poet.* 1447a, 28.

7

an anonymous class of their own.[1]   Nor can we neglect
the Aristotelian emphasis on Becoming—or, in modern
language, Evolution.   Just as Tragedy—one of the
specific forms of poetry—" went through various changes
before it found its (proper) nature," so poetry in general
developed from the germs of merely rhythmical im-
provisation.   Poetry is an art as well as a natural gift,
and the art requires metre for its full expression.[2]   We
need not rely on passages such as a casual remark that
" prose composition must have rhythm but not metre ;
otherwise it will be a poem,"[3] since this is too loosely
expressed to be conclusive.   But Gorgias, Plato and other
previous thinkers had regarded metre as a necessary part
of poetry, if not as one of its " causes " ; and if Aristotle
had been combating this received opinion, he would
surely have made his objection more evident.   No Greek,
in fact, could wholly emancipate himself from Homeric
preconceptions, even in defiance of Greek logic : Homer's
own art was metrical, and he was the greatest of poets ;
therefore, every poet must use metre.

On the other hand, although a poem requires metre,
Aristotle definitely states that metrical form does not
in itself make a poem.   Homer and Empedocles wrote
in the same metre, but Empedocles should be called
a physicist rather than a poet, and if the work of Herodotus were versified, it would still be a kind of history.[4]
Both science and history are excluded by his law of the
universal, although the two culprits break it in different

---

[1] *Poet.* 1447b, 10 ; cf. Diog. L. iii. 25, where Aristotle is said to
have placed the λόγοι of Plato between a poem and a prose composition.

[2] I cannot here follow Bywater (on 1447b, 11), who holds that
" metre, in Aristotle's view, is only one of the accidents of poetry."

[3] *Rhet.* iii. 8, 1408b, 30 ; so Plato, *Phaedr.* 258d ; *Gorg.* 502c.   For
Isocrates see p. 161.

[4] 1447b, 18 ; 1451b, 1.

ways. History, as we have noted, is a record of particular action, and is condemned on this ground; physics—which seems " universal " to us, does not imitate " *men* in action," and is therefore out of court. It may well have caused Aristotle a pang to deny Empedocles the name of poet, since the fragments of his work *On Nature* so clearly prove his right to the title, even if his kindred spirit, Lucretius, had not named him as the most glorious product of Sicily. Aristotle, indeed, seems to have been of two minds; for elsewhere he calls Empedocles Homeric in his use of metaphors and other poetic devices.[1] But in the *Poetics*, at least, the system is everything, and the poet must conform.

The inadequacy of an attempt to restrict the freedom of poetry has never been more painfully illustrated than by this formula of the Universal in human action. As it stands, it would remove from the list a considerable number of the greatest poets, including Lucretius and Wordsworth. Yet, if the law of Universality is too rigid, it contains an important truth. Even Lucretius failed to subdue the details of atomism; large masses of his work are intractable—no less " prose," as Aristotle would have said, because they are written in verse. Lucretius, of course, is a great poet by his power of bringing the Nature of Things into close relation with the hopes and fears of humanity. We read *De Rerum Natura* not merely, or perhaps not mainly, because it grasps the " majesty of things," but because it exhibits the Universe as the framework and setting of human life. But, for Aristotle, no human sympathy can redeem the subject. Wordsworth, too, would be condemned, since mere static and reflective poetry, whether based on man or nature, is obviously not dreamed

---

[1] Diog. L. viii. 57 (περὶ ποιητῶν fr. 70).

of, in Peripatetic philosophy. His modern follower—
Matthew Arnold—was only too consistent ; for, in
order to carry out the theory that " the eternal objects
of poetry are human actions," he even suppressed his
Empedocles, as a poem " in which there is everything to
be endured, nothing to be done," although his present
reputation rests far more securely on *Empedocles* or
Dover Beach than on his *Merope*, for all the action of
that second-rate play. If Aristotle had widened his
law, so as to include not only " men in action " but all
spheres of human interest, his doctrine of universality
might at least have a pragmatic value. Those who
require poetry to be the unique intuition of the individual seem to forget that this self-expression, however
personal, can have no permanent value unless it is also
universal. A particular experience must touch some
chord to which common humanity can respond. The
abnormal, in itself, is not the proper study of a poet,
though it may interest a pathologist. But abnormal
poetry (though it certainly exists) may be neglected.
What here concerns us is the expression of rare, but
perfectly normal states of mind, which many critics
claim to be the fittest province for modern art,[1] but
which are plainly not contemplated by Aristotle. His
exclusion of these states is partly due to historical causes.
Greek poetry was essentially typical, although we shall
have to make important reservations in this broad
statement.[2] Modern poetry has developed the individual personality not only because of the great extension of psychological interest, but because the Greeks
have already exploited, to the full, the potentiality of
the Type. It may, therefore, be perfectly true that, for

---

[1] J. Benda, *Belphégor*, p. 60, notes this modern demand : *l'art
doit ne présenter que des âmes particulières.*

[2] See p. 136.

us, the expression of rare lyrical moods has become the fittest sphere of poetic art, though there are many who would dissent from this narrow claim. Aristotle himself —even with Sappho before him—could not have agreed, for the simple reason that the rare lyrical mood is not the rule, but the exception, in the poetry which he knew. It was not till Roman times that Sappho found her true reincarnation in Catullus. The only important point, therefore, is to decide whether his definition of poetry can be widened to include non-Greek poems without stretching this definition to the breaking-point. Here opinions will differ according to different views as to the exact meaning of which the " universal " is capable.[1] But this much is clear, that, on the whole, Aristotle correctly interpreted the character of the poetry of his own race—that his limitations faithfully reproduce the actual limitations of that great literature.

There remain only Epic and Drama as deserving philosophic study ; and, although the concluding part of the *Poetics* is lost, we have good reason for believing that the work was practically confined to these two. An Athenian of the fourth century—and Aristotle, in all but birth, was Athenian—could hardly fail to regard the two forms as together covering the whole field of poetry, in its essence and function alike. No Hellenic (or modern) sentiment could omit the Epic ; while Drama, serious or comic, was at the time the most vital force in Athenian life. But, even here, Aristotle is true to his instinct for classification. Unable to regard these two forms as twin peaks of Parnassus, he must needs measure their height, and Tragedy turns out to be the topmost peak. Some people, he admits, " prefer " Epic ; but, on philosophical grounds, he gives the palm

---

[1] There are many who deny that poetry has anything to do with universals ; see Hack, *loc. cit.*, p. 55.

to Tragedy, as the completer form of Imitation. It has
all the elements of Epic, with music and spectacle in
addition ; it has vividness when read as well as when
acted (an interesting proof that a reading public was
now developed) ; it achieves its end within a smaller
compass, and concentration gives more pleasure ; and
it has more unity than the Epic, as is shown by the fact
that many tragedies can be carved out of any one of the
Epic poems.[1]

It is indeed a matter of regret that Aristotle approached
poetry by way of the *genre* or Form. As a systematic
convenience the method may have its advantages ;
but it was really a trap into which later critics fell.
In their eagerness to classify, they neglected what should
be the first—and, perhaps, the last rule of criticism—
to understand the author, whatever his means of communication may be. The Greek habit of dissecting
poetry into classes was the more dangerous when the
classes were thus invidiously compared. It is as futile
to draw up a table of precedence for poetic Forms as it
is to arrange the poets themselves in an order of merit.
In this respect, at all events, Croce is right in warning
us that every real poem is incomparable.[2] There is only
a historical interest in recalling that Dryden differed
from Aristotle—" a heroic Poem, truly such, is undoubtedly the greatest work which the soul of man
is capable to perform." [3] Leigh Hunt also gave the
highest honours to the Epic, as including the drama with
narrative besides ; and Leopardi relegated the poetic
play to a low, or even the lowest place, since it is furthest
removed from lyrical or " pure " form—a " peripety "
of Aristotle's judgment which may ironically remind us
of his own favourite reversal in a Greek play. Even so,

[1] 1461b, 26 f.   [2] Croce, *Ariosto*, etc. (E.T.), p. 221.
[3] *Dedication of the Aeneis.*

an Aristotelian could retort that Leopardi's own lyrics (beautiful as they are) do not eclipse the Form in which Shakespeare wrote. To a modern, however, it makes no difference whether a poem is epic or dramatic or lyrical; his only concern is to discover whether the work is poetry.[1] On the other hand, if questions about absolute merit are valueless, there is a pertinent theme which fairly comes within the proper sphere of historical criticism—the relative importance of any one Form in a particular place or period. Poetry cannot be graded by a class-list of Forms, but its expression certainly depends on the environment of time and place. Aristotle, with his slight grasp of historical development, hardly realised this (to us) very obvious fact. Otherwise he might have replaced his absolute order of merit by a more relative list. He knew that, in the Athens of his own time, the drama had no rival as the form of poetic expression to which there was the most natural response. But it did not occur to him (or to many more recent critics) that the gist of the matter is here. No poetic form can be placed first, absolutely and for all time, precisely because the spirit of poetry follows those channels which the spirit of the age marks out as the most appropriate.

Here and elsewhere, it is quite easy to find specks in the sun of Aristotle, and modern critics, perhaps tired of his once unquestioned authority, seem willing enough to examine them with the microscope. But they are of small moment in the scale of his service to criticism. Instead of the didactic prejudices of Aristophanes and the puritanism of Plato he substituted a poetic theory which, however modified, has survived: poetry is an art, and all arts have " their own pleasure."

[1] So J. Middleton Murry, *Discoveries*, p. 156.

This is not the place to analyse in any detail his doctrine of the end of art ; [1] what here matters is the broad fact that Aristotle puts aside the more odious suggestions of Pleasure, realising that it is a natural appetite not to be thwarted but properly encouraged. And this delight is not merely intellectual—although as we have seen, it seems based on the intellect—but emotional. Of course poetry could not be entirely divorced from morals. Aristotle tacitly assumes that art is for the service of man, the political animal : and the *Politics* has much to say on the allied art of music in the educational system of the state. But, in the *Poetics*, he is quite free from the Greek fault of regarding poetry as didactic, or of emphasising its moral function. He assumes that the poet must speak the " truth " ; but what is truth ? There is not the same kind of " correctness " (ὀρθότης) in poetry as in politics.[2] Poetic truth should not run counter to fact, " for every kind of error should be avoided " ; but even the impossible is justified by the end of art, if it heightens the effect.[3] Mimesis has room for both idealism and realism : " Sophocles said that he drew men as they ought to be, while Euripides drew them as they are." The old trouble of Homeric immorality is quietly shelved. Poets have a right to " represent " stories which they do not themselves believe. Xenophanes may be morally sound in his censure, but " this is what they say " ; i.e. Homer is not to be blamed, as a poet, for recording opinion, however mistaken. This solution—Aristotle may have felt—might not satisfy the moralists, who

---

[1] See e.g. Butcher, ch. 4.   [2] 1460b, 13.

[3] 1460b, 25 εἰ οὕτως ἐκπληκτικώτερον ἢ αὐτὸν ἢ ἄλλο ποιεῖ μέρος. The term ἔκπληξις is regularly used for the means by which a poet excites and pleasurably surprises his hearers. Johnson (*Life of Waller*) follows : " the essence of poetry is invention ; such invention as, by producing something unexpected, surprises and delights."

could ask *why* Homer told these stories. He therefore
adds that we must bear in mind the persons concerned,
the circumstances and the end, which may justify the
means " to secure a greater good, or to prevent a greater
evil."

Such are Aristotle's answers to the old moralistic
censure of the poets. His own love for the epic is clear
not only from the internal evidence of the *Poetics*, but
from the testimony of Isocrates, who contemptuously
mentions the interest of the Lyceum in Homer and
other poets.[1] But the detractors had now become
a formidable body; and, as we have seen, their objections were by no means confined to the moral issue.
These were collected in a work entitled ἀπορήματα or
προβλήματα Ὁμηρικά—" Difficulties " or " Problems "
of Homer—which exists in fragments.[2] There has been
much discussion as to the authorship; but it is admitted
that the work is Peripatetic if not Aristotelian. However, for our present purpose, we need go no further
than the chapter in the *Poetics* mainly concerned with
such problems and their solutions,[3] from which quotations have already been drawn. Among the general
charges against poetry the most damning—to a Greek
—was that poetic statements were often " impossible "
or at least " irrational." For example, the pursuit of
Hector round the walls of Troy was an impossibility;
Aristotle replies that a thing may be impossible but yet
credible, judged by the standard of poetic correctness.
In his famous phrase, a probable impossibility is to be
preferred to an improbable possibility. So the charm
of poetry can conceal the irrational, although he quite

---

[1] Isocr. *Panath.* 18 and 30 f. ; cf. Dio, *Or.* 53, 1.
[2] Arist. *fragm.*, ed. Rose. The tradition lasted until Porphyry,
whose ζητήματα was indebted to the older work.
[3] Ch. 25.

rightly notes that such improbabilities pass muster more easily in epic than in tragedy, where they should at least be excluded from the main action as distinct from narrated incidents.[1]

In dealing with such difficulties Aristotle lets fall almost casually, a solution which, if it had been consistently applied, would have spared the Greek critics much searching of heart. Defending Homer from the charge of improbability, he quotes a line that had caused offence :

> Their spears stood upright on the butts.

Such, he explains, was the fact in the time of Homer, " as it still is in Illyria." [2] It is tantalising to see how narrowly Aristotle missed the development of a historical method in dealing with the ancient form of the Homeric Question. Thucydides had taught him the theory of " survivals in culture," and the *Politics* shows (at least in theory) a grasp of anthropological perspective.[3] But it did not occur to him that this Homeric evidence for a past stage of civilisation was equally cogent for earlier religion and morality. We cannot indeed expect a Greek to view Epic religion with the detachment of Andrew Lang or Frazer ; but it is none the less regrettable that even Aristotle could not see, in the *Iliad* and (still more) in the *Theogony*, the many relics of primitive belief and practice which later education had long discarded. In that case, Homer would have needed neither attack nor defence—least of all by means of Allegory, which the Peripatetic seems to have disliked no less than Plato. But such a method, if applied to

---

[1] 1454*b*, 8.

[2] *Il.* 10, 152 ; *Poet.* 1461*a*, 3. So the barbarous treatment of Hector's body is excused in ἀπορήματα Ὁμηρικά fr. 166 (Rose).

[3] See the author's *Anthropology of the Greeks*, p. 10 f.

the Epic, was of course impossible, without a radical revaluation of Homer, for which no Greek was ready. The " Bible " of the Greeks could not be so drastically brought up-to-date. Homer might nod, or even lie— so much could be conceded ; but poetry was a form of knowledge, and it was incredible to any Greek that the greatest of poets should know less than his imitators.

There are some whose criticism of Aristotle goes deeper than dissent from certain of his conclusions. It is often argued—especially by followers of Croce—that his whole psychological conception of the poetic process is mistaken, and therefore that his conclusions are, at best, no more than brilliant guesses, flashes of light which show up the darkness.[1] But Croce's own æsthetic position is—to say the least—precarious ; and even if we accept his psychology of intuition, we cannot on this account logically reject the judgments of Aristotle, without also rejecting all the theories of his successors, from Longinus to Dryden, and again to Coleridge, Sainte Beuve and Arnold, since these great critics were no less ignorant of Crocean æsthetics. In any case, the Greek service to criticism does not depend, in any great measure, on the psychology of the poetic process. We may grant that Aristotle's view of poetry is too intellectual. His æsthetic satisfaction turns out to be derived from the pleasure of learning, and its highest intensity appears in the use of metaphors which gratify by suggestions of unexpected resemblance.[2] In his system, poetry must stand by the ultimate appeal to the mind rather than to the emotions. Nevertheless, the champion of Pity and Fear cannot be accused of neglecting, in practice, the emotional end—the ψυχαγωγία—of poetry.

[1] Rostagni, *op. cit.*, p. 100 f.
[2] *Rhet.* iii. 10, 2 ; cf. Cic. *orator*, 39, 134 ; *de orat.* iii. 155.

Again, it is true that he does not wholly free himself
from the intrusion of morality ; but his insistence of
the " proper pleasure " of tragedy—and of poetry in
general—was far more than of historical importance,
as a counterblast to Plato ; it pointed out, once for all,
the way on which all sound literary criticism was to
travel.   Instinctively, he discovered the real place of
ethics in literature by turning to Sophocles, the impersonal artist who neither taught religion, like Aeschylus,
nor corrected it, like Euripides.

Some of the flaws which have been found in Aristotle
belong to the general nature of Greek criticism, and
indeed to the specific character of Greek poetry itself.
His view of Art is no doubt too circumscribed and an-
thropocentric.   With his insistence on the formula of
" representing men in action," he seems to exclude all
external nature from the province of poetry.   Here he
is not only Socratic and Platonic but is justified by the
actual trend of Greek poetry, which—like the sister
arts of sculpture and painting—was rarely concerned
with Nature, except as subsidiary to the human drama,
until its last phase in Alexandria.   Moreover, he limited
even the proper study of mankind, as a poetic motive,
to " universal " man, so dismissing—at least in theory—
the personal impulse of lyric poetry, except as far as
this experience was social.

Beyond all this, Aristotle has two defects belonging
to his own personality rather than to the national
character.   In the first place, his genius was so entirely
systematic and comprehensive, that he could not confine
himself to the examination of a particular author or
a single poem.   Even his marked preference for the
Œdipus did not lead him to analyse Sophocles, as
Aristophanes had analysed Euripides.   Still more serious
is the lack of that enthusiasm which must inspire the

critic as well as the poet. Longinus, as a thinker, ranks far behind the "Master of those who know"; but criticism, like poetry itself, is not born of knowledge alone, and we must turn to the lesser man for that passionate love of great poetry which it was no part of Aristotle's method to exhibit, unless, indeed, we follow a distinguished modern writer in holding that the real critic must be an Aristotle—intellectual and not emotional. His argument is that the enjoyment of poetry is a pure contemplation, free from all accidents of personal emotion. It is the critic's duty to see the object as it really is, whereas the ordinary reader may often indulge in an accidental stimulus, being unable to distinguish the poetry from an emotional state aroused in himself by the poetry.[1] This intellectualist view seems to neglect the truth that, as poetry itself is emotional, the critic cannot detach himself from the emotions, although it is plainly his business to see these "universally," without preoccupation in any accidental or personal stimulus. However this may be, it is better, ultimately, that knowledge should precede enthusiasm rather than the converse. Criticism should be something of a science as well as an art; and, in the long run, it was perhaps a gain to the study of literature that its first great critic laid down general principles instead of enlarging on particular works of art. There was, indeed, the drawback that these principles were destined to be narrowed into positive laws, with grievous damage to future criticism. But Aristotle cannot be held responsible for the extravagance of those who—like other followers of other great men—have misunderstood his teaching. And now that the error of idolatry and the equal error of iconoclasm have been cleared away, we

---

[1] T. S. Eliot, *The Sacred Wood*, p. 13.

can at last observe him in a fairer perspective. Criticism has passed through the long age of viewing art as a moral teacher, and it has also outlived the short reaction of viewing art as of no moral significance at all. We have returned to the sane outlook of the Greek critic, who knew that an art must be judged by its own inherent principles, and that its function is to give its proper pleasure ; but that this pleasure is part of the heightening of human life, and cannot be divorced from the morality of life. To Aristotle, man is a political animal, and ethics is a branch of politics. Art, therefore, is regarded, not so much as the expression of a rare individuality as a form of giving delight to the whole community. Art must be universal in its range, because only the universal can find a response in the whole body-politic, to which it should appeal. It must therefore shun the bizarre, the outrageous and excessive, and cling to the Mean, which is perfect sanity. And, if Aristotle had been asked whether this Mean can best express that intensity which we regard as essential to poetic creation, he would have pointed to Homer and Sophocles, asking, in his turn, whether the finest Greek poets lacked enthusiasm, for all the Moderation of their genius.

§ 2. TRAGEDY

When Aristotle wrote the *Poetics* the great age of Tragedy had passed away. Aeschylus had already become a Classic, and the two other members of the triad had been dead for about half a century. But their works were still performed,[1] and younger poets were continuing the tradition, even although, in Aristotle's words, " after many changes Tragedy stopped (in its

---

[1] E.g. The *Antigone* was often reproduced (Dem. *F.L.* 246).

development), since it had attained its proper nature.[1]
As a fact, one of the greatest " changes," which was to
affect modern drama, had been tried but apparently
found wanting : Agathon attempted to widen the scope
of tragedy by taking names outside traditional mythology
and Aristotle admits that, although both the actions
and names of this play—the *Antheus*—are fictitious, they
give no less pleasure.[2]   But the innovation was not
followed up—the myth was too firmly based to be
overthrown in serious poetry—and the tragic drama,
in essentials, remained true to the classical type of the
fifth century. Aristotle was therefore placed in an
excellent position for reviewing the whole achievement
of Attic tragedy, with an horizon stretching from
Aeschylus to his own pupil Theodectes, although he was,
perhaps happily, spared from seeing the aftermath of
tragedy in the dramas of Lycophron and other members
of the Alexandrine Pleiad.

He shows little sympathy with Aeschylus. His few
references to that poet are either purely historical, or
rather faint praise, or even censure.[3]   In this neglect
Aristotle has at least the support of his contemporaries,
who seem to have almost completely shelved Aeschylus
in favour of his two rivals.   It is curious that Athenians,
never backward in their admiration of Pindar, should
have failed to understand their even greater country-
man.   The critics, from Aristophanes to Dio, were not
niggardly in their appreciation of his " sublimity," in
the Longinian sense ; but even Longinus sees this
quality at its highest in Sophocles. We can hardly

---

[1] *Poet.* 1449*a*, 15 πολλὰς μεταβολὰς μεταβαλοῦσα ἡ τραγῳδία ἐπαύσατο
ἐπεὶ ἔσχε τὴν αὐτῆς φύσιν.

[2] *Poet.* 1451*b*, 21.   The correction of ἄνθει (The Flower) to Ἀνθεῖ
is now generally accepted.

[3] The references are given by Haigh, *Tragic Drama,* p. 123.

resist the conclusion that the " Hebraic majesty " of
ideas and language was something beyond the poetic
experience of any later Greek, except perhaps Longinus
himself. To the average critic elevation of thought
needed impeccable style for its communication ; and
Aeschylus failed to please the later Greek ear, trained
by long practice to respond to the polished " maxim."
As has often been noted, the comparative scarcity of
his fragments is a proof that the old master was the
least quotable of the three dramatists. Greeks could
not easily forgive a poet who was neither rhetorical
nor sententious.

If Aeschylus was undervalued as a poet, he became still
further eclipsed as a playwright ; and here we must not
forget that Aristotle is less concerned with " pure "
poetry than with dramatic construction. His brilliant
definitions and generalisations are apt to obscure his
main interest—the making of a good drama. He is,
first and foremost, a critic of plays as plays, and so the
high poetry of an Aeschylus is of small importance except in as far as it furthers the action or produces the
proper End of the drama. But, in technique, Aeschylus
was plainly out of date.[1] It might be thought that
the author of the *Agamemnon* would have satisfied the
Aristotelian desire for pity and fear. But, when the
writer of his *Life*—a sympathetic piece of criticism—
remarks that Aeschylus has " few devices for drawing
tears," and " uses the spectacle and plot more to strike
by the marvellous than to effect (artistic) illusion,[2] we
are no longer surprised that Aristotle himself had no
great affection for hippocamps and tragelaphi.

His own canonic artist alone fulfilled the law of the
Mean, which is so conspicuously Aristotelian that we

---

[1] See p. 129.

[2] *Vit. Aesch.* πρὸς ἔκπληξιν τερατώδη μᾶλλον ἢ πρὸς ἀπάτην.

are apt to forget its universality in Greek thought. Although Aristotle does not, in so many words, apply his favourite doctrine to Sophocles, the application is implicit. In diction, that poet was always recognised as standing midway between the " pomp " of Aeschylus and the σοφία or " quibbling " of Euripides.[1] Again, in technical construction, Aristotle prefers his use of the chorus to that of Euripides, and of course to that of Aeschylus, who in this respect was quite out of fashion : the part played by the chorus in his *Supplices* or even in the *Eumenides* was far too overpowering. Still more important, it was Sophocles who provided the perfect Plot, and the critic's well-known preference for the *Oedipus Tyrannus* is on this score fully justified. There were other reasons : the Theban story is a fine example for drawing out pity and fear ; for its " Reversal " (whether this term is to be understood as meaning a simple reversal of fortune, or as the effect of a blinded human action ironically recoiling on the agent's head) ; for the type of its hero, and for the skill with which the " irrational " element is kept outside the action.[2] In fine, it is clear that the *Œdipus* gives Aristotle the standard to which neither of the others can attain. Modern judgment—backed by the experience of frequent reproduction—so completely bears out this claim that here, at least, we may congratulate ourselves in being able to agree with the great critic for his own reasons. It is the more astonishing that these reasons did not appeal to the judges on the production of the play, which formed one of the trilogy defeated by Philocles, the nephew of Aeschylus, although the writer

[1] Plut. *de glor. Ath.* 5.
[2] 1453b, 1452a, 1453a, 1454b, and 1460a. On the Reversal see F. L. Lucas, *Tragedy*, p. 91, and Butcher, p. 328.

8

of the *Argument* properly adds that it was conspicuous
among the works of Sophocles.   Whatever the cause of
this verdict, it was certainly not due to any unpopularity
of the poet during his lifetime, since more than half his
plays must have won the prize,[1] thus justifying Xenophon
in naming him, as the representative of tragedy, with
Homer as representing the epic.[2]   It was only a step
for Polemo to bring the two into even closer relation,
by calling Homer an epic Sophocles, Sophocles a tragic
Homer—the finest compliment that a Greek could pay
to any successor of the poet who, in his own person,
seemed to represent the full achievement of the race.[3]
As a pure poet, again, Sophocles was not undervalued
by his contemporaries.   In the *Frogs*, Aristophanes had
dismissed him with a courteous line of praise, because
the moral antithesis of Euripides was Aeschylus alone ;
but, in another play, the comic poet refers to the " honey"
of his lyrics, which had earned him the title of the Bee.[4]
In the actual year of the *Frogs*, Phrynichus, the rival
of Aristophanes, made the Muses sit in judgment on the
tragic poets, and paid a special tribute to Sophocles—
" happy in his long and unclouded life, the maker of
many beautiful tragedies." [5]

But Sophocles himself was not allowed to occupy
the vacant throne of Aeschylus without challenge from
the candidate defeated in the *Frogs*.   During the half-
century (or more) between that play and the *Poetics*,
Euripides had been steadily gaining ground in public
estimation.   His fame was secure, before his own death,
in the whole Hellenic world, if we may judge by
the familiar stories that the Syracusans spared many

---

[1] See Haigh, *Attic Theatre*, p. 48.
[2] Xen. *Mem.* i. 4, 3.   [3] Diog. L. iv. 20.
[4] Aristoph. *fr. inc.* 2.   Other reff. in Haigh, *Tragic Drama*, p. 161.
[5] *Arg. Oed. Col.* (Kock 51).

Athenian captives, owing to their ability to recite his verses, and that

> the repeated air
> Of sad Electra's poet had the power
> To save the Athenian walls from ruin bare.[1]

Such tales, if not historically true, are good examples of Aristotle's own reminder that truth is not always fact. It is indeed clear that the death of Euripides was regarded not merely as a loss to his own country—the fine tribute of Sophocles, who appeared in mourning, with his actors and chorus ungarlanded, is proof of this—but as a panhellenic disaster : " all Greece was his tomb." [2] In Aristotle's own time, Euripides had reached the height of a fame that was not merely " popular," since the orators, the comic poets and Alexander himself shared in the general enthusiasm, which may be summed up in the often-quoted exclamation of a character in Philemon " if the dead were conscious, I would hang myself to see Euripides." [3]

Aristotle is not to be found in this company. On some counts, he even agrees with the censure of Aristophanes, although his reasons are not so openly moralistic. Nevertheless it is surely the old ethical bias that leads him to demand that dramatic characters should be " good " ($\chi\rho\eta\sigma\tau\acute{a}$) beyond the standard of Euripides. He may be pardoned for a confusion that survived to the nineteenth century, when even Shelley (in the *Defence of Poetry*) was perturbed by the fact that great poets could draw the most villainous characters, with pleasure to their readers and themselves. The author of the *Cenci* took refuge in a kind of mystic Platonism

---

[1] Plut. *Nic.* 29 ; *Lys.* 15.   [2] *Vit. Eur.* 42 f. (Dindorf).
[3] *Ib.* 82. Alexander recited a considerable part of the *Andromeda* from memory, Plut. *Alex.* 53 ; *Athenæus*, p. 537. Other references in Haigh, *Tragic Drama*, p. 318.

to excuse the villainy ; it is the more to Aristotle's credit that he dropped Plato, in essentials, even if a little of his moral criticism survived. So he objects to the character of Menelaus as needlessly bad, while Melanippe is too sophistic, and Iphigeneia (*in Aulis*) is inconsistent—the last, by the way, being a less happy judgment than the others.[1] On grounds of construction, he finds several faults in the Euripidean chorus,[2] and objects to the misuse of the *deus ex machina* (in the *Medea*) and to the handling of the " irrational " in the same play, where the appearance of Aegeus has neither probability nor dramatic use.[3] The *Medea* was rightly held to be a masterpiece, and the Stoic Chrysippus paid it the tribute of continual quotation ; [4] so that these criticisms of technique, in which Euripides " manages badly," have a special interest. On the other hand, Aristotle freely allows that the *Cresphontes* and *Iphigenia in Tauris* are well-made plays, and no one who has seen a representation of the latter is likely to dissent.

The broader issues involved in the Euripidean drama are hardly mentioned. Although Aristotle is still so far under the influence of morals as to prefer the " nobler " types of Sophoclean character, he nowhere blames Euripides for realism. Provided that the characters are not needlessly bad, he seems to regard tragedy as having no less right to imitate " men as they are " than to aim at portraying them " as they should be "— whether the word " should " ($\delta\epsilon\hat{\iota}$) is to be explained as æsthetic or moral obligation. Nor does he express any opinion on other innovations which Aristophanes had

---

[1] *Poet.* 1454*a*, 28 and 1461*b*, 20. See above, on *Aristophanes*, p. 50. Aristophanes of Byzantium (*Argum. Eur. Or.*) followed, in complaining that in the *Orestes* all the characters except Pylades are ignoble (φαῦλοι) and the play is χείριστον τοῖς ἤθεσι.

[2] See below p. 129.   [3] 1454*b*, 1, 1461*b*, 21.

[4] Diog. L. vii. 180. For the fame of the *Medea* see p. 180.

noticed and condemned, such as his beggar-kings, his women in love, and—above all—the questioning and argumentative spirit of the new school, which was turning the drama of heroic action into a debate analogous to a modern " discussion-play." To Aristotle, Euripides has faults, but they are almost entirely the faults of the playwright ; and he has one great redeeming merit : he is " the most tragic of poets," [1] which definition of course refers to his doctrine of pity and fear. The estimate is fully borne out by such a play as the *Hecuba*, or *Troades* or *Hercules Furens*. But there are others, in which " nobody kills anybody " ; and these do not satisfy Aristotle : " they give, not the true tragic pleasure, but that of comedy."

That, indeed, is the root of the matter. If we agree with Aristotle, that Pity and Fear are the emotions purged by tragedy, it follows that these emotions must not be weakened by a happy ending. If, on the other hand, we discount their value in producing the " pleasure " of tragedy, we must still admit that sentimentality —the " weakness of the audience "—is the ruin of the really tragic play, just as it has been the ruin of countless novels. The essence of the tragic hero lies not in his death (which happens to the most unheroic), but in the fact that, after a certain crisis in his life, we cannot imagine its continuance to be tolerable or thinkable. This principle holds good even if the play does not end in actual death—Aristotle is content with " a change from good to evil fortune," and his favourite *Oedipus Tyrannus* does not require the hero to die. What the play *does* require is that Oedipus should henceforth be dead in the sense that tragically matters—dead not merely to the world (that, perhaps may be of no great

---

[1] 1435*a*, 30 ; cf. Quintil. x. 1, 68.

moment), but to himself. His true life is done. He
may still be the cause of pity and fear in his physical
death (as shown in the later play *Oedipus at Colonus*);
but that drama is not so much a true tragedy as a
religious mystery. It may prove that there was purpose in his life, but it starts from the point at which
that life is really finished.[1] The truth of Aristotle's
great pronouncement on the tragic ending is perhaps
too obvious to need illustration, beyond a bare reference to *Hamlet*, or *Macbeth* or *St. Joan*. On the negative
side, it may be sufficient to recall an extreme instance,
where the most " tragic " of Shakespeare's plays was
ruined by Nahum Tate's egregious adaptation, in which
Lear regained his kingdom and Cordelia was safely
married—

That Truth and Vertue shall at last succeed.

§ 3. THE FUNCTION OF TRAGEDY

No critical judgment relating to poetry has been more
quoted and debated than the passage in which Aristotle
defines the function of tragic art. " Tragedy represents an action, serious, complete and of a certain
magnitude, in language adorned with each kind of
artistic decoration . . . through pity and fear producing the right catharsis of these emotions." [2] Here
almost every word could be (and has often been) discussed ; but, in a book which cannot treat Aristotle's
æsthetic with any fulness, only the last sentence need
be briefly examined. Its general meaning—after some
centuries of criticism—has been fairly well established.[3]
The basic idea of *catharsis* is certainly borrowed from

---

[1] See J. T. Sheppard, *Aeschylus and Sophocles*, p. 81.

[2] *Poet.* 1449b, 24 f.

[3] For the extensive literature see Bywater on *Poet.* 1449b. 27.
Sandys, *Hist. of Schol.* i. p. 62.

medicine—purgation, not purification (as was long assumed) is primarily intended. At the same time, the
latter process is not to be excluded. A purge is also a
means of purification—in ancient medicine, when blood
was drawn, the rest was thereby purified.[1] Behind all
this, there lies the primitive conception of homœopathy
which has left so many traces in medicinal folklore. The Greek formula—ὁ τρώσας καὶ ἰάσεται—
is familiar in its English equivalent "the hair of the dog
that bit you." Tragedy is viewed as arousing certain
emotions (which would be deleterious if allowed to
remain dormant) in order to quell these disturbing
elements in the soul by their violent discharge. Aristotle's general meaning is made clear by his analogy
from music. This, he says, is to be studied for education,
purgation, intellectual enjoyment, and relaxation. He
adds " some persons fall into a religious frenzy, whom we
see disenthralled by the use of mystic melodies, which
bring healing and purgation to the soul. Those who are
influenced by pity or fear and every emotional nature
have a like experience . . . and all are in a manner
purged and their souls lightened and delighted." [2]
Here Plato had already shown the way. In the *Laws*
he remarked that, just as nurses rock their restless
children to sleep, "employing motion, not rest," [3] so
Bacchanals are cured of their frenzy by the use of the
dance and music : external motion cures the agitation
of the soul. The children and the Bacchanals—Plato
adds—suffer equally from the emotion of *fear*—a psychological explanation of very doubtful correctness, which,
however, may throw light on Aristotle's insistence on
fear in tragedy. His own reference to the function of

---

[1] Butcher, p. 269. K. Svoboda, *L'Esthétique d'Aristote* (1927), p. 95.

[2] *Pol.* 1342a (Jowett's tr.).   [3] 790 f.

music goes far to explain his view of the tragic pleasure produced by Catharsis.

In naming the two passions of Pity and Fear Aristotle, as usual, is developing or correcting earlier views. If Gorgias did not bracket them as both awakened by (poetic) speech, Plato had more than once spoken of their influence in tragedy.[1] Aristotle himself co-ordinated the two by holding that " what we fear for ourselves, we pity in others," [2] and, though (in one passage) he regards fear as " for the hero," he also insists that the hero is like ourselves.[3] The two emotions, then, are closely related in his psychology ; and both have equally to be modified by purgation. Nevertheless it is not clear how Aristotle thought that this process could be applied with equal force and propriety to both. For they are not really homogeneous. Pity is no doubt a " good " characteristic ; [4] but how can Fear be " good," unless the emotion is watered down to the rather unheroic measure of the Caution that permits a man to fight another day ? The two emotions are not a pair. Aristotle, however, seems to treat them as if reducible to a single psychological unit, so that the same purgation can be applied with equal effect to unhomogeneous parts. However this may be, he had clearly to meet Plato's difficulty that the satisfaction of tragedy is mixed with pain—people " weep " when they are taking pleasure " [5]—and the pressing problem was therefore to explain how this pain is only apparent. His solution seems to be that, in tragic pleasure, the element of pain (which we should feel in real life) is expelled by purging. On the stage, calamities are

---

[1] For Gorgias, see p. 29.   For Plato, *Ion*, 535*c* ; *Rep.* 387*b* ; *Phaedr.* 268*c*.

[2] *Rhet.* 1382*b*, 27, 1386*a*, 27.   [3] *Poet.* 1453*a*, 5.

[4] *Rhet.* 1386*b*, 12.   [5] Plat. *Phil.* 48*a*, 50*b*.

viewed without *excess* of either pity or fear, so that the
Peripatetic doctrine of the Mean is preserved.[1]

Historically, then, Aristotle's position is clear enough.
Pity and Fear had been accepted by his predecessors
as the chief emotions concerned, in some way, with
the effect of tragedy ; and his own business was to explain how their working could be harmonised with the
" pleasure " of dramatic art. With regard to the two
emotions, in themselves, we may agree that, in different
ways and proportions, both have their place in any
analysis of tragic satisfaction. It is sometimes urged
(after Hegel) that Pity plays a minor part in our reaction to characters nobler or loftier than our own :
" we do not sympathise with Othello because Othello
is a force beyond our ken." [2] We may reply that,
although such a character may be inspired by a force
beyond our own experience, Othello is himself a man,
and *mentem mortalia tangunt.*

But what of Fear ? Can this impulse be pleasurably
evoked by the poet ? In the ordinary, non-æsthetic
sense, fear can only be an unfortunate intrusion. No
doubt the Southern temperament was (and is) more apt
to break down the party-wall between the two states
of æsthetic and " real " fear. There may be truth in
the story that, on the production of the *Eumenides*,
boys fainted and women miscarried.[3] But—if he knew
the tale—Aristotle would have protested that the
tragedy defeated its own end by causing excessive
emotion. His defenders interpret this " fear " with
various shades of meaning and different modes of

----

[1] Diog. L. v. 31 (the wise man should be μετριοπαθής). See
generally A. Rostagni in *Studî Ital. di phil. class.* (N.S.), 2, p. 1 f.
for the æsthetics of the Aristotelians.

[2] See A. Nicoll, *Introduction to Dramatic Theory*, p. 73 f.

[3] *Vit. Aesch.* 4 (Dindorf), Pollux 4, 110.

action, ranging from Milton's "Terrour"—which is surely too strong—to the "sympathetic shudder" and "almost impersonal awe," which Butcher believed to be the true tragic fear intended by Aristotle and actually experienced by ourselves.[1] But the philosopher does not really explain *how* fear is purged, either by music or the drama. It would appear that the poet is to administer "doses" of emotional excitement, to cure the soul of excessive passion. But at best—one might think—such a dose could only relieve pain—a definition of pleasure which would no doubt satisfy an Epicurean, but which cannot have been really intended by Aristotle himself, since his own definition of pleasure, as a concomitant of activity, is far more positive.

A further question arises. If pity and fear have actually a place in causing tragic satisfaction, was Aristotle right in limiting the cause to the two? There may be room for both impulses in such a play as the *Oedipus* or *King Lear ;* but is such a limited Catharsis sufficient to explain our interest in either play? The formula is surely too narrow, if we regard the whole history of the drama, which Aristotle knew only in its first chapter, confined to a single manifestation of the tragic spirit. We have now to take into account not merely the wide extension of tragedy from Shakespeare and Goethe to Ibsen and Shaw, but also the corresponding difference of the spectators in taste and sympathy, in religion and civilisation, during the centuries which have passed since the Athenians first assisted at the ritual act of primitive drama. It is true that Aristotle (after Plato) made allowance for the broad distinction between the "vulgar" and the "educated" spectator ; [2] but he is rather optimistic in believing, apparently, that

---

[1] *Aristotle's Theory of Poetry,* p. 258 f.
[2] Plat. *Gorg.* 502a ; *Laws,* 658d ; Arist. *Pol.* viii. 7, 1342a, 18.

the two classes could have much the same psychological responses. There can be no doubt that, in an Elizabethan play, like *King Lear*, the " levels of enjoyment " are very numerous. They include, at one end of the scale, the subtle pleasure of the most refined appreciation and, at the other, the crude satisfaction of the groundling in bloodshed or brutality.[1] The Greeks of course mitigated some of the horrors in the stage of Marlowe and Shakespeare by the rule of excluding bloodshed from the eye—*ne coram populo pueros Medea trucidet*—but still it is difficult to believe that their vulgar and refined spectators were equally affected by one and the same purgation. The fact may well be that Aristotle—in spite of his divergence from Plato—was still influenced by Platonic morality ; and, as the same code of morals applied to the whole body of citizens, he unconsciously assumed that all members of the audience were equally responsive to the same æsthetic stimulus.

We may therefore conclude that, if there is truth in Aristotle's definition of the tragic function, it is not the whole truth. Modern critics, even when they start with his pair of impulses, can hardly end with them. A recent psychologist bases his partial defence of Aristotle on the view—derived from Coleridge—that tragedy is a reconciliation of opposite or discordant qualities. " Pity, the impulse to approach, and Terror, the impulse to retreat, are brought in Tragedy to a reconciliation which they find nowhere else, and *with them who knows what other allied groups of equally discordant impulses.* Their union in an ordered single response is the Catharsis by which Tragedy is recognised, whether Aristotle meant anything of this kind or not."[2] It may be mentioned,

---

[1] See I. A. Richards, *Principles of Literary Criticism*, ch. 27.

[2] I. A. Richards, *op. cit.*, p. 243. The italics are mine ; see also F. L. Lucas, *Tragedy*, p. 48, who criticises this theory.

in passing, that Aristotle could hardly have meant
" anything of this kind," as he nowhere suggests the
reconciliation of pity and fear, which, as we have seen,
he regards as allied, not antithetic forces.   In any case,
two points of interest seem to emerge : firstly that pity
and terror are *not* adequate to produce the æsthetic
satisfaction peculiar to tragedy ; and secondly that,
whatever impulses there may be, their balance and
harmony is imperative.   For the appeal of tragedy is
clearly by a synthesis, not by a conflict, of emotions.
We need not agree with the theological views of Milton
in the last magnificent lines of *Samson ;* nor are we
obliged to feel that " justice has been done " in many
tragedies.   But great tragedy does teach us—and, so
far, we may acquiesce in the ancient view of poetic
teaching—that there are lives which, however marred
and broken, are in the end worth living, so that, like
Milton's Chorus, we may leave the theatre with all
passion spent.   Such an attitude can result only from
an adjustment, a synthesis, a harmony.   The discord
must be resolved.

But modern criticism of the Aristotelian end does
not stop here.   It may be a matter of small importance
whether pity and fear, or some other impulses, are
concerned with tragic pleasure ; the more serious objection lies in their purgation.   To treat the function
of tragedy as a purge may serve as a metaphor, but this
cannot be elevated to the dignity of a *vera causa.*   In
modern equivalence, it has been called a " vaccination-
theory," and there is no pleasure in the process of
inoculation.   The pleasure that we expect from tragedy
is both immediate and positive, something more than
simply prudential and medicinal.   As a writer on the
drama has remarked, Aristotle " would have this
medicine restore us to the normal, to health, but surely
it is an elixir, not a remedy, and the function of tragic

drama is to exalt, not to cure us." [1]   In fact, if a medical
metaphor is to serve at all, tragedy must be more than
a sedative ; it should be a tonic and a stimulant.   Its
value is certainly as an enlargement of our experience ;
the learning that our workaday philosophies do not
always dream of all things in heaven and earth ; the
recognition that character may triumph over circumstance, so that " O the pity—or the terror—of it " is
not the sole or final word.   In seeing a great tragedy, we
can perhaps find a stimulus that may produce exultation
—a sense of triumph in realising that pain and death
may have more than a physical bearing, even in a world
that may seem unintelligible.   Tragedy may not lessen
—it often deepens—the mystery of human life ; but it
can at least show that the mystery, if insoluble to the
philosopher, is significant to the artist, who may appre-
hend some aspect of existence that philosophy cannot
comprehend.

Like all Greek critics, Aristotle was confronted with
the difficulty of explaining the pleasure derived from the
contemplation of the Ugly : pain and death are obviously
ugly, and yet their " imitation " is a source of pleasure.
Was he content to suppose that the negative purgation
of pity and fear was sufficient to effect this positive
pleasure ?   If so, the Athenian spectator would have
taken his pleasure as sadly as the proverbial English-
man.   The difficulty was real, as we see, if not from
Aristotle himself, at least from Timocles—a writer of
the Middle comedy—who suggests that the spectator
forgets his own troubles, in contemplating the far sadder
fate of a Tantalus or Niobe, and so, " thrilled by
another's misfortune, he goes away with both pleasure
and instruction." [2]   The theory is crude enough, but

[1] W. M. Dixon, *Tragedy*, p. 127.   C. E. Montague in *A Writer's
Notes on his Trade* (1929), p. 221 f. is interesting on this point.
[2] *Athen.* 6, 223 (6 Kock).

it is at least an honest attempt to turn pity and terror into some sort of æsthetic value. It remained for Longinus to note that, even if tragedy has its "own" pleasure, this specific pleasure belongs to the more comprehensive satisfaction of all great poetry, and indeed of all great creative literature. The stimulus of poetry is indeed more varied than Aristotle conceived; but the philosopher was not altogether beside the mark in emphasising its æsthetic value as based on recognition. The poet, like any other artist, expresses his intuition of life, and the audience recognises the "likeness," the semblance of reality. Even if we leave the theatre without the exultation that a great tragedy may produce, there still remains the feeling that we have been sharers in a presentation of life, not otherwise revealed to our normal existence. The tragic poet has imitated, that is, has *shown* us life, as exhibited to his consciousness, and our own perceptions have been broadened thereby.[1] In the end it is precisely this poetic experience that gives the highest value to the great tragedies of the world. The argument of the *Agamemnon* or *Macbeth* is, in itself, a sordid matter for the newspaper and the law-court. It remains for the poet to describe not only the ugliness of the particular facts in their relation to human life, but their deeper, more universal significance in the art of living. Here, after all, the dramatist has the same function as any other poet, as Aristotle well knew, in drawing no strict line of cleavage between epic and tragic expression. And so we may perhaps be content with laying stress, not on the special impulse of pity or fear, but rather on the general power of the poet to increase our limited awareness of life, by the communication of his own keener perception and more abundant vitality.

[1] See R. A. Scott-James, *The Making of Literature*, p. 338 f.

CHAPTER V

ARISTOTLE (*Continued*)

§ I. THE PARTS OF TRAGEDY

A HISTORY of criticism is not very nearly concerned with the formal analysis of tragedy, which Aristotle divided into six parts—plot, character, diction, thought, spectacle and song. But, in the course of this analysis, the philosopher, sometimes casually, sometimes with emphasis, lets fall certain ideas not only of historical interest but of permanent importance. As we have seen, he approaches the drama from an evolutionary standpoint, although the process of evolution stops with Sophocles. He holds the view (which has hardly been refuted by certain modern scholars) that Attic tragedy was Dionysiac from the outset, starting with " the leaders of the dithyrambs." [1] Otherwise, he does not discuss the religious origins of the drama. For example, he misses the ritual significance of the mask, and shows little recognition of the vast influence of tradition in moulding dramatic form. Nevertheless, he is sound on the main point—that the chorus is the germ of tragedy, and that its treatment by later poets—Aristotle ignores Thespis—was vital in the evolution of a purely ritual act ($\delta\rho\hat{a}\mu a$) into an action ($\pi\rho\hat{a}\xi\iota\varsigma$) of æsthetic value.

Logically, the first question to be settled is whether

---

[1] *Poet.* 1449a, 9 f.

this chorus was a help or a hindrance in the fully developed theatre.   The hindrance is beyond question—the mere presence of a group, more or less remote from the main action, which may often require secrecy, is a severe strain both on the ingenuity of the dramatist and the credulity of the audience.   On the other hand, the help—in the hands of a master—is perhaps as real, even when it may seem most suspicious.   During the major pauses of the plot (afterwards marked by the " Acts ") the " relief " of choric odes is patent enough ; but this relief is no less needed in these places where the plot is being developed at its most tense and emotional stages.   A Greek chorus, uttering the tritest sentiments in a couple of lines between the passionate or closely-reasoned speeches of the chief persons, often strikes the reader as a tiresome interruption.   But on the stage the effect is very different.   A continuous flow of essential dialogue cannot be followed without some mental pause of less tension.   Failing comic " relaxation," the chorus gives this breathing-space, with a break which, so far from being trivial or fatuous, is welcome and indeed necessary.

Aristotle himself, being mainly interested in the actors, and especially in the hero, does not deal with these psychological or technical problems.   The chorus was in effective occupation, and his object was simply to determine its proper place in the economy of the play.   Obviously, its members performed a double function, firstly as dancers and singers, and secondly as participants in the action, and they had to be considered in both capacities.   He does not minimise the " pleasure " of music ; but, in this aspect, he regards the chorus as an accessory (like scenic effects) rather than as a vital part of tragedy.[1]   What really mattered

[1] 1449b, 28 ;   1450a, 10 (where music comes last in order), and 1462a, 16.

was to consider their relation to the plot, as managed by the actors technically so-called. Here his opinion is quite definite : " the chorus should be regarded as one of the actors and as a part of the whole, and should share in the action, not in the manner of Euripides but of Sophocles.[1] That Aeschylus does not come under comparison is not surprising ; Aristotle clearly regards the great poet, at least in dramatic construction, as a mere stepping-stone towards the goal of Sophoclean perfection. So far, indeed, he had reason : the earliest extant play of Aeschylus (the *Supplices*), in which the chorus is really the protagonist, discloses the dramatic restrictions involved in the use of only two actors ; and the introduction of a third, in his later plays, was borrowed from Sophocles himself. It is probable that Aristotle would have held that a play like the *Eumenides* laid too much stress on the chorus of Furies, who may be said to divide with Orestes the honours of the protagonist. But, if Aeschylus here shows the excess of the Mean, Euripides is no less an example of its defect. So much Aristotle at least seems to imply ; but it is not easy to understand his definite preference for Sophocles in this respect. The two poets, as far as we can judge from their surviving works, give much the same importance to the chorus, both in the proportion of lines assigned to their part, and in their relation to the plot.[2] Both equally satisfy the requirement of " participation," as needed to preserve the unity and coherence of the drama ; and, as a fact, the typical chorus of Euripides is not more separated from the action than (for example) the chorus of the *Ajax*. On the other

---

[1] 1456a, 25.

[2] See A. E. Phoutrides (*Harvard Studies in Class. Phil.* 27, 1916) who strongly dissents from Aristotle's criticism of the Euripidean chorus, as in any sense " decadent."

hand, it is often argued that the choral *odes* of Sophocles
are more relevant to the plot than are many Euripidean
lyrics, which seem to anticipate the " interludes " of
Agathon. Aristotle, however, does not expressly distinguish between the two functions of the chorus.   He
probably thought that Euripides degraded its part, both
in acting and singing, if we may judge from a *scholium*
on the *Acharnians* which may well be Peripatetic.[1]
Aristophanes there accuses Euripides of letting his
chorus stand by in futile passivity, while every one else
is allowed to chatter.   The scholiast adds that Euripides
makes his choruses " say things not arising out of the
plot, as in the *Phoenissae*, and as not sympathising
with the wronged." Two choric odes in that play are,
doubtless, the special cause of this outburst, but the
criticism seems to include the employment of the chorus
in their whole function, whether Aristophanes himself intended this or not ;   and so (rightly or wrongly) Aristotle was perhaps content with a quite general criticism
of the Euripidean chorus as inadequately employed.[2]

Here his interest in the chorus appears to cease.
Although, both historically and practically, their functions had so intimate a connexion with tragic drama, he
nowhere expands his views on the precise link between
chorus and actors, nor (which is as important) between
chorus and audience.   The presence of fifteen maidens
or sailors or elderly citizens was so much a matter of
established convention that Aristotle could hardly have
the perspective to ask or answer the question whether
the tragic stage might not have followed the later comedy,

---

[1] *Schol.* on Aristoph. *Ach.* 442.   See also *schol.* on Eur. *Phoen.*
1018 f., where a charge of irrelevance is made.

[2] See generally G. Norwood, *Greek Tragedy*, p. 76 f. ;   R. C.
Flickinger, *Greek Theatre*, p. 144.   The chorus of Sophocles is
analysed by J. Errandonea (*Mnemosyne*, 51-54), that of Euripides,
by Phoutrides, *loc. cit.*

and have dispensed with them altogether. In modern criticism the existence of the Greek chorus has sometimes been defended by curious arguments : it has even been called " a deliberate sentry against realism, to exclude verisimilitude, to forbid the illusion that we are witnessing a scene from real life." [1] Such, no doubt, is often its effect, although, remembering the history of the chorus, we cannot call it a deliberate sentry. The practical problem lay in quite the opposite direction—how to *give* verisimilitude to a body of semi-actors whose presence is so often unconvincing. In any case, a Greek play was well protected against realism by a whole army of such " sentries "—masks and buskins, language, metre, conventional scenery. The same critic is more fortunate in pointing out that the chorus is a real bridge between the stage and the audience. This —as has already been noted—is its historical function. In theory, the whole city shared in the ritual act which was the core of tragedy, just as, in savage ceremonial, all the tribe or clan (or whatever the unit may be) are seated round chosen dancers, and " assist " by beating the tomtom or gong. Aristotle—in spite of his researches into barbarian customs—can hardly be expected to have realised that the fifteen members of the chorus represent the whole community, like the twelve good and true men on a modern jury ; but he at least knew that, both in outlook and station of life, the chorus was generally far nearer to the spectator than the other persons of the drama could be. No doubt it often moved on a higher plane. It has sometimes been called a body of ideal spectators, and in such a play as the *Prometheus* its (semi-divine) members certainly show a courage and self-devotion which lifts them from the ranks of

[1] W. M. Dixon, *Tragedy*, p. 53.

a merely sympathising " crowd." Often, too, they are
the vehicle of expressing the poet's own views, which
may by no means coincide with popular opinion. In
the main, however, their part is that of simple, average
humanity, a foil to the superhuman persons of the plot ;
and it is here that they can best mediate between stage
and audience. By their own sympathy with heroic
fortunes they transmit a sympathetic current to spectators, who are in this way drawn into closer contact
with the sphere of the action. In default of a chorus,
some modern producers, dissatisfied with the " pictur-
esque " theatre, have aimed at this communication by
the rather sophisticated device of " hobnobbing with the
audience," introducing an actor, such as a messenger,
by way of the auditorium ; and in revivals of the
Oedipus, the blinded hero has even outdone (and probably would have outraged) Athenian practice by an
agonised exit through the stalls.

This problem of communication does not come within
the scope of Aristotle's psychology. His interest lies
with the action in itself, and he mentions the chorus
only so far as it is concerned with action. Here he
starts with one of the famous pronouncements, whose
value has been said to consist in the fact that he asks
the right questions, if he sometimes gives the wrong
answers. And perhaps none of his answers has been so
much criticised as his preference for Action to Character.
In his own words : " tragedy is essentially an imitation
not of persons, but of action and life, of happiness and
misery. All human happiness or misery takes the form
of action ; the end for which we live is a certain kind
of activity, not a quality. Character gives us qualities,
but it is in our actions—what we do—that we are happy
or the reverse. In a play accordingly they do not act
in order to portray the character ; they include the

characters for the sake of the action. So that it is the action in it, i.e. its Fable or Plot, that is the end and purpose of the tragedy, and the end is everywhere the chief thing." [1]

Aristotle is here at grips with the very essence of drama, independent of time and circumstance; but it will help a discussion of his view to isolate, as far as possible, the character of Greek drama—his only material —and to examine whether his conclusion was justified by that material, before we approach the question in broader terms. Historically, at least, he could perhaps have made out a good case for this emphasis on action. As we have just seen, Greek tragedy was originally a piece of ritual in which the character of the participants —except perhaps in a collective sense—counted for little or nothing. At this stage of development, Mimesis (impersonation) is simply " to take the place of " someone else, whether god or hero, or even animal; it is the re-enactment of action. But Aristotle, however much interested in origins, was certainly not arguing from primitive ritual. To him it was not the germ but the flower of tragedy that mattered, and his preference for action is really due to his philosophy. He is riding his usual hobby-horse of teleology: the End is the chief concern of art as of life, and the plot, being the End of tragedy, is logically prior to character. As a mere abstract proposition this conclusion might be thought self-evident, since the essence of tragedy is certainly to exhibit " men in action." But a moment's reflection will reveal the fallacy of regarding these " men " as any sort of men. A railway accident is not a tragedy (whatever the newspapers may call it) in itself; it can only become tragic in relation to the characters of its

[1] 1450a, 16 (tr. Bywater).

victims.   Apart from this, a critic has not to deal with
abstract tragedy—if there is such a thing—but with
its concrete embodiment in the plays of Sophocles and
Shakespeare ; and the only pertinent question is whether
Aristotle was justified, if not by all manifestations of
the tragic spirit, at least by the only form on which he
could base his conclusions.

Here it should be noted that if the philosopher sins
in his depreciation of character, he sins against the light ;
for he admits that there are several types of tragedy,[1]
one of which is " ethical "—the drama of character.
Unfortunately we know nothing of his examples—the
Phthiotides and *Peleus ;* [2] but he clearly allows that, as
a fact, character may be at least as prominent as action.
He might well have instanced the *Prometheus Vinctus*,
where there is really no action (in the physical sense)
from the opening scene to the final catastrophe.   No
doubt we are rightly warned by Dryden against holding
" nothing to be action till the players come to blows,"
and Aristotle would agree on this general principle.
But still, whether we regard the Titan's character as
developing during the course of the play, or as fixed
and only apparently developed during its progress,[3] the
Prometheus is plainly classed in the category of
ethical or static drama, although Aristotle—if he refers
to this play—quotes it only as an example of the
" spectacular " or perhaps " marvellous." [4]   And, if he
discounted Aeschylus as old-fashioned, the *Philoctetes*
of his favourite Sophocles might have given him pause.
That play is at once the most static and—in the in-
terplay of characters—the most delightful of extant

---

[1] As, for example, the play with a happy ending, see p. 151.
[2] 1456*a*, 1.
[3] See Sikes and Wynne Willson, ed. *Prom. Vinct.*, p. xlvii.
[4] 1456*a*, 2, where the text is corrupt.

Sophoclean dramas. But, here as elsewhere, the philosopher is less anxious to discuss tragedy as it is than as it should be. His insistence on the plot may, in fact, be regarded as a protest against a common tendency to subordinate action to character.[1] He is in search of the highest type, and he finds it in the *Oedipus*, which, as a fact, precisely illustrates, if it did not originate, his theory : no other surviving work has so complicated a plot ; and the character of the hero—however we may regard it—is quite subservient to the action, even if we admit that the tragedy of *Oedipus* is heightened by his self-assurance. We could not imagine the play of *Hamlet* without the character of the protagonist exactly as Shakespeare has drawn it. Hamlet's personality *is* the play ; but we can surely conceive that the plot of the *Oedipus* would have been equally effective, if attached to a person of quite different psychology and morality.

While we need not go beyond Aristotle's philosophic bias to account for his own stress on action as the End of tragedy, the question still remains whether his statement may hold within at least the sphere of ancient drama. His depreciation of character has been defended on the ground that the persons in Greek tragedy are typical, not, like Shakespeare's, individual. This argument apparently presumes that, as the type is " general," it gives less opportunity to the dramatist than the variations of the individual. Aristotle himself would have disowned the argument, since he held that poetry deals only with the universal. None the less, we may consider its validity, because—if it can be proved that the persons of Greek tragedy are *merely* types—it may well follow that the development of the plot was of prime interest and importance, and Aristotle may after

---

[1] So M. Macgregor, *Leaves of Hellas*, p. 138.

all be justified, though not for his own reasons. In this connexion we may start with the incontestable fact that the Greek tragic personage is far more typical than the Shakespearian—the use of a mask itself demands conformity to the type. The difference can be summed up—much more of course could be said—in a brief quotation : [1] " We are interested in the personality of Orestes or Antigone, but chiefly as it shows itself in one aspect, as identifying itself with a certain ethical relation ; and our interest in the personality is inseparable and indistinguishable from the interest in the power it represents. This is not so with Hamlet, whose position so closely resembles that of Orestes. What engrosses our attention is the whole personality of Hamlet in his conflict, not with an opposing spiritual power, but with circumstances, and, still more, with difficulties in his own nature."

It is not necessary to labour the point that the Shakespearian character is more complex than even the Euripidean ; but we may remember that the Greek dramatists rarely drew such simple types as later Graeco-Roman critics demanded. To Horace, for example, Medea must always be fierce, and the writer of the Argument on the *Medea* remarks that people blamed Euripides for inconsistency : he should not have depicted the heroine in tears. Euripides was a better student of human nature—better, perhaps, than Aristotle, who misread the character of his Iphigenia.[2] So, in Sophocles, Antigone is no mere typical exponent of an idea—the force of natural affection—but, on the other hand, she does not display the individual marks of Desdemona or Lady Macbeth ; and so the ethical conflict—the disharmony of laws human and divine—

---

[1] A. C. Bradley, *Oxford Lectures on Poetry*, p. 77.
[2] See above, p. 116.

is less obscured by the persons who represent the struggle. Our attention, in fine, is more closely riveted on the action, because the issue is more clear-cut, less complicated by the intrusion of personality.

Are we then to accept Aristotle's neglect of character as borne out by Greek practice, if not justified by his own theory? The inference would surely be difficult to deny, if—as is often stated—the classical drama excluded Freewill. For if the action was entirely directed by an external cause (whether God, Fate or Chance) the persons of the play would be automata, so that the plot would become not only the main but the sole consideration. And it would seem, at first sight, that the Greek tragedy is almost wholly predestinarian. Sophocles appears to send the innocent to death simply because such is the will of higher powers. Antigone, Deianira, Oedipus himself, are, *to our mind*, innocent, whatever Aristotle may say.[1] But it is difficult to believe that the misfortune of the completely innocent was intended by a Greek dramatist.[2] The common motive of the hereditary curse no doubt implies that the sins of the fathers are visited upon the children, whose innocence may otherwise be assumed. Yet even the house of Atreus has some measure of Freewill. Such a curse produces a predisposition to crime—modern views on heredity would here agree—but it does not act by sheer compulsion. The Stoic inevitability of fate, foredooming before birth, and therefore independent of sin, has hardly a place in older Greek thought, which rarely, if ever, rules out a modicum, at least, of choice. Fate does not paralyse all action ; on the contrary, it often challenges opposition. As early as Homer, Zeus complains that mortals blame the gods, but are them-

[1] See Rohde, *Psyche* (E.T.), p. 427 f.
[2] See below, p. 142.

selves also to blame.[1] So in Aeschylean tragedy : the
chorus of the *Agamemnon* (who here certainly speak for
the poet and for his audience in general) condemn the
plea of Clytemnestra that the Alastor or avenging spirit
is solely responsible. They realise that the curse may
contribute,[2] but she herself is to blame. Aeschylus is
at pains to refute the belief that mere Prosperity is
enough to cause downfall. It is a " thrice-old tale,"
but it is not true. There is danger in riches—that view
is not only Greek—but the rich man *may* avoid the
impiety that leads to his destruction.

This limited freewill is not confined to Aeschylus.
All through later tragedy there runs the thoroughly
Greek idea that misfortune is the result of avoidable
sin, although Hubris must be followed by its inevitable
Ate, Pride by Punishment. The Pride has many manifestations, not all equally to be condemned. Perhaps
it is chiefly seen in that human presumption which
exceeds the due place of mortals in their attitude towards the divine. In the *Bacchae* of Euripides, Pentheus
is not a " bad " man ; he is a Greek ruler anxious to
preserve order in his state ; but he offends against one
of those primal forces of Nature, personified by Bacchus,
which are thwarted by man at his peril. So, again,
a modern may think Antigone to be in the right,
or at all events undeserving of her fate ; to a Greek,
however, she is not perfectly innocent. Both she and
Creon stand for two opposing principles, and the tragedy
lies precisely in the conflict.[3] She has freedom of will ;
only, as in Plato's tale of Er, she must take the consequences of her choice.

If this view of the relation between fate and freewill

[1] *Od.* i. 32.
[2] πατρόθεν δὲ συλλήπτωρ γένοιτ' ἂν ἀλάστωρ. See *Ag.* 1497 f., 717 f.
[3] See G. Norwood, *op. cit.*, p. 138.

is correct for Greek tragedy, it seems to follow that Aristotle undervalued the importance of character in the drama of his own country. For, if man, though he may be the sport of fate, has moral responsibility, character acquires a dignity and importance that raises it to the level of action, or even higher, in the scale of tragic values. Heracleitus had pronounced that character is man's deity or destiny ($\delta\alpha\iota\mu\omega\nu$), and the Greek tragic hero, if not master of his fate, is the captain of his soul. While we may admit that " we are happy, or the reverse, in our actions," these actions are, at least in part, the result of personality. The degree of individual responsibility of course varies in different plays. Hippolytus and Medea may not have equal freewill; but neither of the two seems, in the author's intention, to be entirely at the mercy of external power or caprice. Greek tragedy does not spring from the rigid and ruthless determinism which, in so many modern plays, can send a helpless victim—miscalled a hero—to his doom, without allowing him even the pretence of a choice.

But this is not all. Even if the action of a Greek drama were entirely predestined, this would not diminish —it might even increase—the importance of character. Phaedra and Hippolytus may be foredoomed to suffer through the anger of Aphrodite ; but it is just here, in their attitude towards this hidden fate, that the importance of the tragedy consists. This truth— so familiar to ourselves—seems to have been very imperfectly grasped by Aristotle, whose treatment of the subject implies a sharp distinction between character and action, whereas the two are intimately bound up together. Plot and Ethos cannot be so neatly dichotomised ; the two form a unity, and the end of the drama lies in this unity—the representation of character in action. This does not preclude the obvious fact that, in any given play, one of these partners may predominate. The course of European drama, since Athenian tragedy, has shown an almost unlimited range of oscillation between the two elements. In Shakespeare, as has already been noted, human personality is often so prominent that we are less interested in the story than in the reaction of character to circumstance. Hamlet is " a study in temperament," apart from his fortunes, although, in the play itself, we are only concerned with the effect of his temperament on the issue of the plot. In more modern drama, the growth of psychological insight has inclined the pendulum in favour of character —sometimes so excessively that in static dramas such as Maeterlinck's *L'Intérieur* action is entirely wanting, and the curtain is rung down in talk. Aristotle might have found a place for these plays among mimiambs— in which, to judge from Herodas, the action was often negligible—but he would certainly have refused them the name of tragedy. On the other hand, a modern cannot acquiesce in the Aristotelian definition which would logically give the palm to the cinema, where character seems to be very largely subordinate to action. Aristotle might find more support in plays (such as Galsworthy's *Loyalties*, or *Strife*, or the *Skin Game*) where the characters are rather symbolic embodiments of social groups, or (as in the *Dynasts*) of whole nations, than of individual personalities.

It would appear, then, that Aristotle's neglect of character is not only condemned by the general nature of later drama, but is doubtfully sound in the range of his own contemporary stage. Practically he allows for the effect of character on action only in his definition of the hero, whose downfall is due to an ἁμαρτία— whatever this " fault " or " error " may exactly mean. The hero must not be a perfect man—the later Stoic spectacle of a good man struggling with (and conquered by) adversity is not tragic but abominable;[1] it might excite pity and terror, but a moral indignation would ruin the pleasure of tragedy. Still less must the protagonist be thoroughly bad;[2] and, so far, critics may agree, provided that the badness is sufficiently thorough. A hero without redeeming faults (or virtues) is not likely to command sympathy; though, even here, the proved interest of a modern audience in a Passion play may suggest doubts as to this limitation. The real trouble lies in the hero's " fault," on whose exact nature Aristotle is, perhaps discreetly, vague. Is it a defect of character in an otherwise noble person, or an error in judgment— a flaw or a simple mistake? If a simple mistake, is it moral or intellectual, or—since Aristotle, like Socrates, puts a stress on right knowledge as a guide to conduct —is it due to ignorance in both spheres together? We should expect to find light thrown on the meaning by the *Oedipus Tyrannus;* in that play, if nowhere else, Aristotle must have found authority for his view. But the error of Oedipus is by no means clear. It has been explained as the simple ignorance of a man who justifiably killed an agressor, not knowing that his victim was his own father. But if this interpretation is correct, Aristotle may well be exposed to a charge of confusing morality with knowledge, beyond even the Socratic blend of the two; and, in the *Ethics,* the philosopher draws a sure distinction between culpable and innocent ignorance.[3] As Oedipus was ignorant both of his father and mother, his fault, on this hypothesis, was surely innocent. A more common line of thought is to

[1] 1385b, 13, 1386b, 34.

[2] 1452b, 34. For modern discussion of ἀμαρτία, see e.g. Butcher (2nd ed., p. 310 f.) and F. L. Lucas, *Tragedy,* p. 97 f.

[3] *Eth. N.* iii. 2.

assume that Aristotle saw a real defect of character in the hero. Oedipus has been accused of a hasty temper in avenging a blow with the sword. In answer it may be pointed out that he acted under strong provocation, quite sufficient for a Greek to excuse the act. Again, he has been thought "hybristic," although the exact nature of his Pride is by no means clear. Certainly no Greek would have condemned him for calling himself "Oedipus, famous in the eyes of all"—as in fact he was. Anyhow, his pride (if it existed) did not deserve so heavy a punishment on his land as well as himself.

The true explanation of the Oedipus-myth must be sought on quite other lines. Ultimately, of course, it shows the workings of Fate; but that power does not work at random. And here we come on the great distinction between ancient and modern theories of criminality. We regard the *intention* as supreme; to the Greek, the *fact* over-rides the motive. The prime law—enunciated by Aeschylus, and entirely upheld by Greek religion—is that the Doer must suffer—$\delta\rho\acute{a}\sigma a\nu\tau\iota\ \pi a\theta\epsilon\hat{\iota}\nu$. The sinner, however blameless in his intention, must take the consequences of his act. He may perhaps be allowed to pass the worst of the consequences on to a surrogate; as, in the Bouphonia, the guilt of slaughtering a sacred bull was transferred to the axe which was solemnly cast into the sea. But, in any case, sin left a contamination—a $\mu\acute{v}\sigma os$—that must be expiated.[1] It has often been noted that Justice is the key-note of ancient drama; but we have to remember, not only that the justice required by an old myth did not always satisfy Euripides, but that the code of Euripides, in his turn, cannot always be harmonised with modern ideas.

[1] See F. R. Earp, *The Way of the Greeks*, ch. 12.

The old myth of Oedipus was based on the primitive doctrine of Justice, that sin is a pollution to be cleansed by suffering ; and the duty of Sophocles himself, as an artist, was not to defend or explain the myth, but to give it a worthy representation. Of course the poet " sympathised " with his hero, as he must have sympathised with Antigone. But we need not therefore suppose that he did not think the penalty deserved, though he was less concerned with Fate in itself than with its bearing on the character of Oedipus. He was not Euripides, who would have thought (and said) that if the gods did such things, they are not gods. At all events, whether the penalty is deserved or not, the fall of Oedipus can be matched in real life, and we are ultimately thrown back on the mystery τοιόνδ᾽ ἀπέβη τόδε πρᾶγμα—" so has this matter happened."

But Aristotle himself lived at a time when the old ideas of crime and punishment were no longer as self-evident as they had seemed to the fifth century. He could scarcely have understood the semi-barbarous myth which laid so much emphasis on the fact and so little on the intention. Plainly, a tragic hero must have a fault, not merely because to err is human, but because the divine habit of *not* forgiving must somehow be justified. Aristotle would like the pleasure of tragedy to be supreme, and it is to his abiding honour that he insists on this pleasure. But, after all, there is nothing pleasant in the contemplation of rank injustice. The hero must therefore bring his punishment on himself by some fault, even if it does not merit the full amount of retribution. The degree of error may vary—there is a wide gulf between the sin of a Clytemnestra and the error (whatever it was) of an Oedipus. The gap could only be bridged by a term of the loosest connotation, for (as we have seen) ἁμαρτία can range from conscious

sin to innocent mistake. The exact amount of blame-
worthiness in the fault of Oedipus may well have been
obscure in Aristotle's own mind. It was perhaps sufficient for him to feel that Oedipus was not a perfect
man, but capable of making mistakes—one of which was
to end in disaster. So, too, if Aristotle had been asked
to explain the motive of the *Hippolytus*, he would
doubtless have answered that both hero and heroine
had erred—Hippolytus by defect, Phaedra by excess,
in the province of Aphrodite ; and that the " moral "
of the play was apparent : in love, as in other spheres
of human life, man is safe only by observing the Mean.
Aristotle was not the first—or the last—to require
ethical satisfaction from the drama ; the wonder is
that his æsthetic pleasure was so little contaminated
by the morality which all Greek tradition expected.

§ 2. Comedy

In an early chapter of the *Poetics* Aristotle had
promised to deal with comedy, and no doubt he kept
this promise in the lost part of the treatise.[1] There
are many incidental allusions to the Comic Form in the
extant part of the work, but these are insufficient for
a reconstruction of his theory in any completeness.
The philosopher remarks that although the spirit of
comedy is shown in Homer (the *Margites*), the origin
of the established Form is obscure, because it was not
at first " taken seriously." [2] But it is quite evident
that Aristotle himself took comedy with as much serious-
ness as tragedy. As a metrical " copy " of the universal,
it came equally within his definition of poetry, while

---

[1] 1449*b*, 21. See generally Lane Cooper, *An Aristotelian Theory
of Comedy*.

[2] Comedy was admitted to the City Dionysia by 486 B.C., and to
the Lenaea about 442 B.C.

it was exposed, in an even higher degree, to Platonic assault. Aristotle had not only to meet Plato's condemnation of Mimesis in general, but his special objection that if it is wrong to imitate at all, it is certainly worse to imitate the Ugly. His answer—as we have seen—is that while we do not take pleasure in the Ugly itself, we admire its likeness in art. Comedy, however, does not imitate all kinds of ugliness : it is " an imitation of men worse than the normal ; but worse, not in respect to any or every fault, but in respect to one particular kind, the Ridiculous, which is a species of the Ugly. The Ridiculous may be defined as an error or deformity not productive of pain or annoyance to others ; for example, the mask which excites laughter is ugly and distorted, but does not cause pain." [1] His chief object is not to deny the importance of comedy—" relaxation and fun are indispensable in life "—but to apply the doctrine of the Mean. Comedy must appeal to the witty man ($εὐτράπελος$), not to the buffoon ($βωμολόχος$) or to those who exceed the due limit of the laughable.[2]

So far, we can follow Aristotle from his own words ; but they do not take us very far. We are left in doubt as to his views on the philosophical relation of comedy to its sister-art. What is the precise connexion of Laughter with the comic spirit ? The question was certainly discussed by the Peripatetics, and a lost work On Laughter by Theophrastus was often quoted ; [3] but there is no ground for thinking that much of Aristotle's own views can be deduced from an extant treatise (the Tractatus Coislinianus) which is concerned with the effect of comedy.[4] The tract gives a definition in a

---

[1] 1449a, 32 f. ; cf. 1448a, 16.   [2] Eth. N. iv. 8 f.
[3] Cic. de orat. 2, 217 f.
[4] See A. W. Pickard-Cambridge, Dithyramb, Tragedy and Comedy (1927), p. 270.
10

semblance of the Aristotelian manner : " Comedy is an imitation of a laughable action . . . producing, by pleasure and laughter, the catharsis of such emotions." But this cannot be an accurate transcript of Aristotle, who does not regard pleasure as a passion, co-ordinate with laughter, but as a result.[1] It is possible that Aristotle regarded laughter as a thing to be purged by itself ; in which case, the spectator would be cured of any desire to laugh " immoderately," at the wrong time and at the wrong things.   But it is much more probable, on the tragic analogy of pity and fear, that Aristotle sought for a similar pair of impulses—perhaps anger and envy—to be purged by the comic spirit.   If so, laughter would not be a thing to be purged, but only the means of purgation.[2]

Another question—perhaps more interesting to a modern reader—must remain without a full or certain answer : Did Aristotle view the old or the later comedy as the acme of the Form ?   As the first play of Menander was produced in 324 B.C. (or 322, the year of Aristotle's death) his whole lifetime fell within the period of the Middle Comedy, which—with its stock characters and situations, and almost complete absence of politics— led directly and insensibly to the full art of Menander. On general grounds we should expect that Aristotle was mainly concerned with contemporary art, though even this supposition may be held doubtful, as he certainly preferred the great period of tragedy to that of Agathon and his successors of the fourth century.   But modern scholars—from Meineke and Egger to Butcher and Bywater—have in general agreed that if his theory of comedy had survived, we should probably have found

---

[1] See Svoboda, p. 147 f.
[2] See Cooper, p. 66 f. ; Svoboda, p. 148.

that his preference was for the comedy of his own age.[1]
The view rests partly on the *Comparison of Aristophanes
and Menander*, attributed to Plutarch, but believed
to represent a Peripatetic tradition. This tract, which
exists only as an Epitome, is violently hostile to the
Old Comedy, and has, at best, the negative value of
being of the most misguided pieces of criticism at
any time or in any language. Aristophanes is censured
for vulgarity—various terms of reproach (τὸ φορτικόν,
θυμελικόν, βάναυσον) hammer in this nail. But there
is even a more serious charge—a lack of " propriety ": the
poet fails to preserve the fitting character (τὸ πρέπον),
as dignity in a king, cleverness in an orator, simplicity
in a woman, but gives chance words to any person as
if taken from a ballot-box. This conclusion is as sweeping as Voltaire's epigram on Aristophanes—*ce poète
comique qui n'est ni comique ni poète*—and is about as
illuminating. It did not occur to a late Greek, who
knew Menander but not the *Mikado*, that the Old
Comedy had its own propriety, the precise antithesis of
the decorum required in ordinary life, although Aristophanes could very well observe the " proper character "
when it suited his purpose.

It is to be hoped that this Epitome does not represent
Plutarch's own opinion ; but it seems at least prompted
by the Plutarchan view of poetry as a channel of moral
teaching. That philosopher, as we shall see, was quite
unable to " take an airing beyond the diocese of the
strict conscience, and imagine a world with no meddling
restrictions," like Charles Lamb in relation to another
form of Comedy. Anyhow, whether Plutarchan or not,
the Epitome cannot represent the true tradition of
Aristotle himself, unless the great critic had sadly changed
from the sobriety and commonsense of the extant

---

[1] Butcher, p. 380 ; Bywater, p. ix.

Poetics. In that book, there is only one reference to Aristophanes, but he is then mentioned in the same breath with Homer and Sophocles, the two literary heroes of the author.[1] This would be an odd preparation for the disparagement of the Epitome. On the other hand, there are some hints in the *Poetics* that its author did not approve of the Old Comedy without reservation. Philosophically, he ought to have preferred the New Style, which he obviously had in mind in stating that "comic writers construct their plots out of probable incidents, and afterwards put in any chance names; they do not write about an individual, like the iambic satirists."[2] Aristophanes, of course, had no such scruples; and as the type counted for everything in poetry, the philosopher must surely have thought that comedy did not "find its true nature" until personal attacks were abolished. Moreover, his sole direct contrast between the old and later styles shows a definite preference in respect of decency. That passage (from the *Ethics*) remarks on the difference between the humour of a gentleman and that of an uncultivated person: "we may see this to be so at once by a comparison of the old and new comedy; in the former it was obscenity which raised a laugh, but in the latter it is rather innuendo, and this makes a great difference from the point of view of decorum."[3]

It may be added that—to judge from our fairly extensive knowledge of Menander—the use of even innuendo was very sparing, so that the two styles were on this ground in strong contrast; and Aristotle, with his ethical bias, may have reasonably preferred the "safer" style, apart from the fact that the later comedy was the true expression of his own times. He concurs with Plato

---

[1] 1448*a*, 27.   [2] 1451*b*, 11.
[3] *Eth. N.* IV. 8, 1128*a* (Welldon).

in forbidding a youth to attend comic performances until he has reached the age of sitting at public tables and drinking strong wine, by which time true education will have fortified him against evil influences.[1] The young should be taught to admire Polygnotus, who painted men as better, rather than Pauson, who painted men as worse ; and men of all ages are to be protected from an indecency that was only tolerable in Greek cults, as in certain Oriental temples at the present day.

So far, there is a clear indictment of the Old Comedy ; but it does not follow that this blemish counterbalanced the supreme excellence of Aristophanes as poet. Was the philosopher insensible to the charm of the *Birds*, the wit of the *Frogs*, the power of the *Knights*, the imagination that runs through every play until we reach the flatness of the *Plutus*, which—on this theory —Aristotle should have preferred to all the rest ? Perhaps we have no logical right to expect a better treatment of Aristophanes than of Aeschylus—the former, no less than the latter, was only a landmark in the history of drama, which, for all that Aristotle knew, had "stopped" in the Middle Comedy. Yet it is permissible to believe that Aristotle could at times separate the playwright from the poet, and that he could be the forerunner, not of Plutarch or the Pseudo-Plutarch, but of the Alexandrines, who were otherwise deeply indebted to the Peripatetic, and who transmitted their enthusiasm for the Old Comedy to Cicero and Quintilian, to the scholars of the Renascence, and to such modern poets as Goethe and Browning and Rostand.[2] It is hard to suppose that Quintilian, in particular,

---

[1] *Pol.* vii. 17, 1336*b*, 20.

[2] This view is taken by Lane Cooper, *op. cit.*, pp. 18-45. Among the Alexandrines, Lycophron, Callimachus, Eratosthenes, Aristophanes of Byzantium, and Aristarchus studied the Old Comedy. For Cicero's admiration of Aristophanes, cf. *de off.* 1 (29), 104 ; *ad Quint.* 3, 1 (6) 19 ; *Leg.* 2 (15) 37.

owed nothing to Aristotle in his admiration for the
Old Comedy, as " elevated, elegant and charming "—
adjectives comprehending all the styles of diction into
which the Greeks divided their literature.[1] But we
have always to remember that Aristotle, at least in the
Poetics, is almost exclusively concerned with the structure
of a play. The comedy of his own age had developed
a plot, which he certainly regarded as no less essential
in comedy than in tragedy. It is true that the Aristophanic play has a kind of plot ; but this is sometimes
very " thin," and is broken or delayed by episodes
which do not further the action. Even with the deepest
appreciation of Aristophanes in pure poetry, Aristotle
could hardly have failed to prefer the newer school. He
was, after all, the child of his age, and that age was in
course of evolving a drama destined to be the lineal
ancestor of our own, whereas the Old Comedy, although
one of the greatest achievements of Greece, belonged to
a single period, and could never again be imitated or
recaptured. Nor, indeed, is there any reason to think
that a contemporary of Diphilus or Menander would
have welcomed its recapture. In any case, the *Poetics*
is intended to be a practical treatise. Whatever views
Aristotle may have held on the merits of Aristophanes,
his business was primarily to deal with comedy as he
found it in his own day, ready for the final shaping of
Menander.

The immense vogue of Menander himself need not
here be discussed ; but it may be remarked that the
criticism of his comedy—as distinguished from mere
popular admiration—seems to have been largely Peripatetic. When Cicero voiced this general favour in his
well-known eulogy—*comoedia imitatio vitae, speculum*

---

[1] Quintilian, x. 1, 65.

consuetudinis, imago veritatis—he is probably repeating a criticism to which, in essence, Aristotle would himself have subscribed.[1] For the great Peripatetic started, or at least developed, the division of literary works into two classes, according to the characteristics of *pathos* and *ethos*, by his famous definition of the *Iliad* as pathetic, the *Odyssey* as ethical. These Greek terms are difficult to translate, and *ethos*, in particular, shifts in various authors and ages ; but, for Aristotle, *pathos* may be taken as representing the more sudden and passionate emotions, while *ethos* is " character " in its more regular states, or moral qualities observed in everyday life.[2] Hence—especially for the later critics —*pathos* became the distinctive quality of the *Iliad* and tragedy, *ethos*, that of the *Odyssey* and Comedy ; and it resulted that the judgment of poetry ($\kappa\rho\iota\sigma\iota\varsigma$ $\pi o\iota\eta\mu\acute{a}\tau\omega\nu$) was largely concerned with estimating the tone of a poem by reference to these two qualities. The Peripatetics certainly took this line of criticism, and it may be inferred, with some probability, that Aristotle himself gave them the lead. His own mistrust of " ethical " tragedy was no doubt in part due to its trenching on the ground reserved for comedy. The *Alcestis* and *Orestes*, in their different ways, seemed to overshoot the border-line between the two Forms. A play in which " nobody kills anybody " did not produce the proper stimulus for pity and fear, and the Arguments of both these plays show that the grammarians, following Aristophanes of Byzantium, were troubled by a catastrophe which was " too comic." To the latest times,

---

[1] *de rep.* 4, 11. Rostagni (p. 141) takes the original to be Peripatetic. The sentiment is familiar from the well-known lines of Aristophanes of Byzantium ὦ Μένανδρε καὶ βίε πότερος ἄρ' ὑμῶν πότερον ἀπεμιμήσατο; (Walz, iv. 101).

[2] Rutherford, *Hist. of Annotation*, p. 129 ; Rostagni, p. 111 f. ; cf. Quint. vi. 2, 8 *illud.* (ἦθος) *comoediae, hoc* (πάθος), *tragoediae simile.*

the tendency of the critics was to divide the drama into two separate compartments, and to complain that, in Euripides (and sometimes even in Sophocles) they were not always water-tight.[1]

§ 3. THE DICTION OF POETRY

Modern students of the *Poetics* are apt to concentrate on the famous definitions of poetry as a thing of the spirit. But, while Aristotle rightly regarded Nature as the mainspring of art, he would have been no Greek if he had neglected technique. The very title of his treatise (περὶ ποιητικῆς) implies an Art of Poetry, which, like that of Rhetoric, can be taught. Given nature or genius, he sets out to show how a poet can be not only born but made. In one important respect, indeed, he recognises the mark of nature: " By far the greatest thing is to be metaphorical. This faculty alone cannot be learnt from another; it is the sign of genius, for to make good metaphors is to see resemblances."[2] In other words, it is a perfect form of imitation. Even in prose, Aristotle was well aware of the value of metaphor (including the simile), but its restrictions in usage make it clear that prose-writers (and still more their critics) looked askance at metaphorical language to a degree which we can hardly appreciate. To call philosophy " a fort planted in the territory of laws," or the *Odyssey* " a fair mirror of life " does not appear too poetical for our own taste, in imaginative prose. But the Greeks were always mistrustful of the debatable ground between prose and poetry which Plato, alone of their great writers, was ready to occupy. In reasoned argument or analytical thought a strong

[1] See generally, A. P. McMahon, *Harvard Studies in Class. Phil.* 40 (1929), p. 106 f.

[2] *Poet.* 1459a, 5; cf. *Rhet.* iii. 2, 8 f.

metaphor seemed out of place; and the above instances, quoted from the sophist Alcidamas, are condemned by Aristotle as " too frigid," overshooting the mark. Even for poetry the use of metaphor (in the modern sense) was jealously guarded, if not confined. Epic tradition sanctioned the simile; but only Aeschylus and Pindar, perhaps, show the abundance of striking metaphors that readers of Shakespeare or Shelley have learnt to expect; and Pindar himself—with some reason—was not spared by the critics.[1]

We need not follow Aristotle's minute analysis of metaphorical language; but one point of special interest emerges in the *Rhetoric*: poetry, being occupied with human action, lays stress on such metaphors as vitalise the inanimate. Hence he quotes with approval the " shameless " stone of Homer, the arrow eager to fly, the quivering spear and the like—-in all these expressions, as he says, the thing is made alive and active.[2]

The section of the *Poetics* which deals with Grammar has no bearing on criticism, and the author himself confesses that the discussion of letters, syllables and parts of speech belong " not to poetry but to another art." But, intermingled with this jejune matter, there are hints and suggestions on subjects that really concern the poets and critics. The choice of words, the use of ornament, the perfection of style—these are all handled with a brevity suggestive of Coleridge's *Table Talk.* They are in fact lecture-notes, not intended to be exhaustive, but representing Aristotle's opinion on certain features of poetry which had been discussed since the days of Aristophanes. Among these questions, the old quarrel between the schools of Aeschylus and Euripides

---

[1] See below, p. 220 f.
[2] See Longinus, 33, 3, and Demetrius, 81 f.; [Plutarch], *de vit. Homeri*, ii. 19.

is brought up to date, although Aristotle does not
definitely contrast the pair.   But, unlike Aristophanes,
he holds no brief for the style of Aeschylus.   Starting
from the remark that the iambic verse of tragedy is,
in itself, the nearest of any verse-form to the spoken
language, he disapproves of an over-ornate style (ἡ
λίαν λαμπρὰ λέξις) as merely obscuring character and
thought, although it serves in the pauses of the action.[1]
It may have another use—to "sweeten the irrational":
parts of the *Odyssey* (the great stumbling-block of the
rational critic) would be absurd, if the improbability
were not glozed over by poetic charm.[2]   However, ornament must be used with discretion, "not piled upon a
commonplace object," in the manner of Cleophon, who
used phrases like the "lady fig-tree."[3]

On the other hand, Aristotle has no patience with a
certain Ariphrades[4] for protesting against tragic diction
altogether, as foreign to real life : the mere fact—he
replies—that the language is *not* ordinary, gives it
distinction ;   but, as he observes with terse finality,
"Ariphrades did not know this."[5]   In a word, the
speech of tragedy must be both "clear and not low,"
and this requirement leads to some rather surprising
estimates of the dramatists.   Aeschylus, of course, was
notoriously obscure, but we do not think of his language
as "low."   Yet Aristotle—perhaps not without a little
malice—deliberately reverses the common judgment.
He charges Aeschylus with a "mean" line, and com-
mends Euripides for his improvement in substituting
the rare word θοινᾶται, "banquets upon," for the

---

[1] *Poet.* 1460b, 2.
[2] On the "irrationality" of the *Odyssey*, see p. 231.
[3] *Rhet.* iii. 1408a, 10.   Cleophon was probably an epic poet.
[4] Possibly the garrulous man mentioned by Aristoph., *Eccl.*, 129,
and elsewhere.
[5] 1458b, 31.

common ἐσθίει, " eats." None the less, Euripides is himself criticised in the *Rhetoric* for excess of the ornate : his metaphor " a lord of the oar " seems to Aristotle to be above the dignity of the subject, and so destroys the illusion.[1] On the whole, however, Aristotle is in sympathy with the style of Euripides, for reasons which show the greatest insight. The aim of tragedy is to produce the semblance of common speech, varying in accordance with the characters. " Even in poetry, if fine language were spoken by a slave or very young man, or about trifles, it would be unsuitable. We must disguise art and seem to speak naturally. The illusion is successful when the poet selects and arranges words from common usage ; this is what Euripides does, and he first suggested the method." [2]

It need hardly be remarked that the last sentence summarises, in a brief but masterly way, the actual history of drama, which—both in Greek and modern eras—has constantly and consistently tended towards greater realism.[3] Aristotle may have had an imperfect conception of the high poetry which removed the *Agamemnon* from the category of realistic drama ; but he had a firm grasp on the basic principle of tragedy in his own day, in which Euripides had already approached the ideal of Menander as the " mirror of life." It is possible that Aristotle found arguments from his own philosophy in favour of a realistic style. Since poetry dealt with actions, it demanded expression in the language of fact, that is, of everyday life.[4] But, in any case, his system was not needed to sanction common-sense. Just

---

[1] *Rhet.* iii. 2, 11 κώπας ἀνάσσειν.

[2] *Rhet.* iii. 2, 5 κλέπτεται δ' εὖ, ἐάν τις ἐκ τῆς εἰωθυίας διαλέκτου ἐκλέγων συντιθῇ · ὅπερ Εὐριπίδης ποιεῖ καὶ ὑπέδειξε πρῶτος. See the epigram of Archimedes (p. 180).

[3] On this point see F. L. Lucas, *Tragedy*, vi.

[4] So Rostagni, *op. cit.*, p. 92 f.

as Socrates had brought down philosophy from heaven, Euripides had changed the superhuman into humanity, and a readjustment of language followed as a matter of course. As Aristotle notes in the *Rhetoric*, the writers of tragedy were still modifying their style, and it would be absurd to imitate a fashion which they had themselves discarded. Yet, for all this insistence on the apparent simplicity of poetic language, Aristotle always remembers that it is only an illusion. If Homer—however simple he may seem—is rewritten in " ordinary " words, his whole effect is ruined, as the philosopher proves by experimenting in such changes.[1] In general, he rightly sees that the epic is more tolerant of the rare word than tragedy, while the dithyramb is most tolerant of all. For—rather curiously—he seems to relegate, as proper to the dithyrambic style, many of the compound words which we think to be one of the special ornaments of Homer—epithets like the " white-armed " goddess or the " golden-bowed " Apollo, with a hundred others that give warmth and colour not only to the epic but to every kind of Greek poetry.[2] Here, perhaps, the doctrine of the mean may once more explain or excuse this apparent obtuseness. The dithyramb had certainly abused the privilege of compounding the adjective in verse, just as later prose was extravagant in compounding the verb. The astonishing forms in a poem of Pratinas (contemporary with Aeschylus) show the dithyrambic influence running wild,[3] and it may well be that, in Aristotle's ears, the old Homeric adjective suffered for the sins of Dionysiac excess.

[1] 1458*b*.

[2] On compounds see *Poet.* 1459*a*, 9 ; *Rhet.* iii. 3, 3 ; Philoxenus in *Athen.* xiv. 643*b* ; G. Meyer in *Philologus*, Suppl. 16 (1923).

[3] Smyth, *Melic Poetry*, p. 71. The poem seems to be a parody of the dithyramb, which, in its latest development, was characterised by the most corrupt musical style (see Dion. Hal. *de comp.* 19).

Later critics divided Style under the heads of Selection and Arrangement of Words ; and, although Aristotle does not explicitly treat of the latter division, he is fully aware of its importance in poetry, as appears from the reference to Euripides already quoted. Like all the Greeks, he would no doubt have agreed with Coleridge that poetry consists of the best words in the best order. As a fact "right" arrangement played a greater part in Greek (and Latin) than it can claim to play in English or the Romance languages, where the order, even in poetry, admits of very little variation. No one indeed would deny that, in a modern language, the whole beauty of a verse may depend on the exact place of a single word. In a line such as

> The vision and the faculty divine

we may hold, with Vernon Lee, that the poetry would be spoiled by any transposition of the adjective.[1] Shakespeare could supply hundreds of examples—

> *Sweet* are the uses of adversity

or Milton—

> With wandering steps *and slow*

in which we may feel that (apart from familiarity) the order is inevitably right. But inversions, though affected by a certain class of modern poets, cannot be very conspicuous in English, or—if we remember M. Jourdain's lesson—in French, whereas the Greek order is infinitely flexible, and each variation has its peculiar force. Moreover, both in prose and verse, the Greeks found a satisfaction from quantity far exceeding our own rhythmical needs ; and though quantity in verse was largely determined by the metre, the hexameter and most other

---

[1] *The Poet's Eye,* p. 18.

forms admitted a certain variety in structure.[1] But, when all allowances are made, it is still hard to appreciate this classical stress on order in poetic expression, except as a legacy from rhetoric, where it is more in place, since the art of persuasion so largely depends on a strictly logical order of words and clauses.   If this is so, it is but one instance out of many in which the Greek critics were handicapped by their usual failure to distinguish the ends of poetry and prose.

[1] See below, on Dionysius, p. 187.

CHAPTER VI.

ALEXANDRINE CRITICISM

§ I. Philosophers and Scholars

THE two centuries which followed from the death of Aristotle to the Roman conquest have been called the age of criticism; but it is no small paradox that the age failed to preserve a real critic until, at the very end, we reach the respectable, if not great name of Dionysius. It is probable that if the literary studies of Theophrastus had survived, the foremost pupil of Aristotle would be ranked as a good second to his master. Among the Peripatetics there was a considerable output of books on " style," " poetry " and the like—including " Lives " of poets, such as that of Euripides by Satyrus—which prove that the present gap between Aristotle and the Graeco-Roman Dionysius was certainly well filled—with what results, we shall best see from Dionysius himself.[1]

Of these works, the most important—to judge from frequent quotations—was that of Theophrastus *On Style*.[2] The well-known division of rhetoric into three

---

[1] For Peripatetic Lives of Poets see *Greek and Roman Biography*, by D. R. Stuart (1928).

[2] λέξις is used both for choice of words (ἐκλογὴ ὀνομάτων) and for " style " in general, including ἁρμονία. For Theophrastus see A. Mayer, *Theophr. περὶ λέξεως* (Teubner, 1910), and generally Rostagni in *Studi Ital. di Fil. Class.* (N.S.), 2, p. 105 f.

classes seems due to Theophrastus himself, although
the sophist Thrasymachus has been credited with the
trichotomy. Strictly, these styles apply only to the
" choice of words," and are not to be confused with the
three (or four) " harmonies " or modes of composition
which Dionysius and Demetrius describe. In both
methods, there is no clear distinction between poets
and prose-writers, who are classed together in one or
other category, often with unhappy results. It was
assumed that prose and poetry, though their means
might differ, pursued the same end—to please, enthral
and persuade the hearer. The two were not opposed
to one another, but rather shared in a joint opposition
to philosophical teaching, whose sole aim was truth.[1]

The alliance was not altogether unholy. It is a good
thing to recognise—as Longinus was to point out—
that " greatness " of style depends on qualities, both
formal and spiritual, that are common to verse and
prose composition. And there was, in fact, some
justification to be found in the peculiar nature and
circumstance of the poet, who was always thought to
be " akin to the orator." [2] Greek poetry was never
regarded as the musing of a solitary spirit, communing
with self, and rather to be overheard than heard;[3] it
was not primarily to be read, but sung or recited, as
a contribution of an individual to the delight and wel-
fare of society. The theatre and odeum were as public
as the agora and law-court, and the recitation of the
historians or the declamation of the rhetoricians and

---

[1] See Theophr. fr. 65 (Wimmer), quoted by Mayer, p. 14.

[2] Cic. de orat. 1, 70 ; est enim finitimus oratori poeta, numeris
astrictior paullo, verborum autem licentia liberior. Cf. orator, 20, 66.

[3] Even in sixth-century lyric, self-communing is surprisingly rare.
Archilochus, in well-known lines, addresses his soul (Bergk [4], 66), as
does Sappho in a new fragment, with the authority of the Homeric
hero, and the imitation—after many centuries—of Hadrian.

orators differed in degree, rather than in kind, from the drama. Even the " pleasure " of poetry was compared to the delight in rhetorical display, and metre was only a particular development of the rhythm which all orators affected ; and finally, if the art of poetic transport differed from that of oratorical persuasion, the orator himself was acknowledged to play on the emotions in order to convince.

But, by the fourth century, the law-court had ousted the theatre as the centre of public life, and the art of Lysias and Demosthenes had become the great preoccupation of the critic. The tendency was more and more to treat poetry as a sub-species of rhetoric, so that even Homer (like Virgil) was admired as a master of all the oratorical styles. If poetry was still distinguished by the doctrine of universality (which was never displaced), its form could be analysed as if it were simply a grammatical exercise. The vital difference between the two arts was blurred by the identity of their medium —the spoken word ; and comparisons between orators and poets were freely drawn, as if their chief distinction lay more in language and form than in their object and attitude of mind. Indeed, it was too often assumed that the distinction was *only* linguistic : there is a characteristic passage in Isocrates, in which that " old man eloquent " rather peevishly complains that eloquence is easier for poets, who have many graces ($\kappa\delta\sigma\mu o\iota$) denied the rhetorician—they are not confined to usual language, but can employ strange and new words ; they can be metaphorical, and they compose in metres and rhythms which have such charm that, even if there is a failing in language and ideas, they transport their hearers by their eurhythmy or symmetry of form alone.[1]

---

[1] Isocr. *Evag.* 9 f.

Isocrates, in fact, seems a little jealous of " poetic licence," which a late writer quaintly describes as the power of adding or omitting at will.[1] But the great rhetorician may be partly excused, since he was here referring to *encomia* such as he had then written in eulogy of Evagoras, and no doubt the Hellenistic encomiasts could do their work as competently as the poets of the period. But the age of Simonides and Pindar would have resented the suggestion that the arts of rhetoric and poetry could serve indifferently in praise of great men.

To Theophrastus is largely due the idea that the Word is not only interesting as the logical and grammatical, but as the æsthetic unit of expression. The study of " beautiful words " was at least as old as the Sophistic age, when Licymnius, a pupil of Gorgias, defined the beauty or ugliness of a word as lying either in sound or sense. Aristotle had examined the subtle changes of emotional effect in the use of " rosy-fingered " or " crimson-fingered " or " red-fingered " Dawn ; and had told the story of Simonides, who declined to celebrate the victory of mules on the ground that half-asses were undignified ; but, when the pay was increased, he wrote of the " daughters of wind-swift steeds," although, as Aristotle (with lecture-room humour) remarked, " they were the daughters of donkeys as well." [2] Theophrastus, therefore, was not breaking new ground in his definition of verbal beauty as " what gives pleasure to the ears or sight, or has value to the mind " ; i.e. a word may be beautiful either in itself or for its associations.[3] As

---

[1] ἄδεια ποιητική. See Apollon. Dysc. (Schneider and Uhlig, ii. 2, p. 52). Cf. Hor. *ars poet.* 10, *quidlibet audendi potestas.*

[2] Arist. *Rhet.* iii. 2, 1405b.

[3] Theophr. quoted by Demetrius, *de eloc.* 173 ; cf. Dionys. *de comp.* 16 ; Hermogenes, περὶ ἰδ. ii. 4, 15. See generally Mayer, p. 51 f.

Demetrius (in quoting him) explains, the term for a thing seen with pleasure is itself pleasant ; while certain words are euphonious in themselves. But his influence in developing the formal side of style—with its incidental repercussions on the art of poetry—is obvious in the history of Rhetoric.

With this meticulous study of the Word—both in itself and in composition—it was inevitable that the Peripatetic interest should decline from the philosophic side of literary criticism to the more pedantic side of verbal scholarship. We need not belittle the immense service of Alexandrine scholars to the cause of humanism in preserving and editing the texts of Homer and other classics. But it must be confessed that, although at least two of these scholars—Callimachus and Eratosthenes—were also poets, their comments on Homer, as a poet, are nearly always worthless, or, rather, non-existent. Homeric *scholia* (like *scholia* in general), which reflect the spirit, and often quote the actual words of the great Alexandrines, have the highest value in exegesis ; but their importance in æsthetic judgment is negligible.

The Alexandrine scholar was still hampered by some of the prejudices which had long obscured the study of Homer. It is true that, after Aristotle, the old bugbear of immorality had lost its chief terrors, largely owing to a convenient recourse to allegory. And, when the allegorical method was unsuitable, Aristotle's reminder, that Homeric customs did not coincide with those of his own times, at least opened the way to an historical method. But the Alexandrines never succeeded in developing this sense of history. Grammarians were interested in what they called ἱστορία, but this went no further than the subject matter of mythology or geography, as shown by the stock subjects of discussion

at Roman dinner-parties—Where did Ulysses wander?
Was Penelope chaste? [1] A Baconian interest in "what
song the sirens sang" may be harmless, but it hardly
forwarded the study of Homer. The real defect of
Alexandrine scholarship was that Homer, although
theoretically acknowledged to speak for his own age,
was required, in practice, to conform to Alexandrine
standards. If the poet failed to do this, he was explained
or censured according to the bias of the commentator ;
but the difficulty or " problem " was very rarely seen
in the light of historical evolution. The scholars—
even the greatest—assumed that Homer's idea of
" decorum " must be their own, and rejected as either
unworthy or spurious any passage which did not satisfy
this canon.[2] In general, the poets were of course judged
in terms of the Figures, from which there was no appeal.
Thus, the excision of five lines in the *Iliad* is demanded
because " they are too prosaic and frigid in their con-
ception " : i.e. they offend by the fault of $\psi\upsilon\chi\rho\acute{o}\tau\eta\varsigma$.[3]
It was not until the very end of criticism that the charge
recoiled on the critics themselves, when Lucian made
Homer acknowledge the paternity of his " spurious
lines," protesting against the " frigidity " of Zenodotus
and Aristarchus.[4] But this true word, spoken in jest,
came too late to influence classical criticism, and even
modern editors, in their Aristarchean zeal, have often
neglected the warning of Lucian. The underlying
principle is, of course, the assumption that Homer

[1] Seneca, *Ep.* 88 ; Quint. i. 8, 20 ; Juv. 6, 450 ; and often.

[2] Decorum or propriety ($\tau\grave{o}$ $\pi\rho\acute{\epsilon}\pi o\nu$) was a wide term for any
statement in keeping with the character (not necessarily moral) of
the person concerned ; cf. schol. on *Il.* 24, 130 ; Dion. Hal. *ars
rhet.* ix. 4. See also N. Wecklein, *Ueber Zenodot u. Aristarch ;*
W. Bachmann, *die aesthetischen Anschaungen Aristarchs.* For the
Latin equivalent *decorum* see Cic. *de off.* i. 27, 93 f.

[3] 3, 432.   [4] *vera hist.* 2, 20 (117).

should never sleep, although the fact that he *does* sleep was noticed long before Horace. But the Alexandrines could not easily escape from the ingrained habit of regarding the Homeric poems as written for their example, and if the example proved to be bad, so much the worse for Homer.

If Alexandrine scholars could so misinterpret the epic, Alexander himself, setting out to conquer Asia in the spirit of Homer,[1] may be forgiven for taking Achilles as an example, when he sacrificed at the tomb of his reputed ancestor, and matched Hephaestion with Patroclus. In his affection for the *Iliad* as a perfect vade-mecum of warfare, he could do no less.[2] But "the poet of kings" was a dangerous model, when Alexander thought fit to imitate the shame as well as the glory of his prototype. Achilles had wreaked vengeance only on the dead body of Hector; but the Macedonian outdid this savagery by ordering that a living man should be dragged to death.[3] As Homer had mitigated the punishment—in the old saga Hector seems to have been dragged alive [4]—the poet may here claim to have given the king a better lesson than he could learn.

Perhaps the inadequacy of "decorum" to explain Homer is most painfully illustrated by Alexandrine comment on certain characters whom the scholars and philosophers were quite unable to understand. A single instance—the character of Nausicaa—may suffice. The most delightful figure in Homer's gallery of women, she might be expected to pass even the stringent test of Alexandrine propriety. An ideal no less than Helen

---

[1] See J. A. Symonds, *Greek Poets*, i. p. 104.
[2] Plut. *Alex.* 8.   [3] Dion. Hal. *de comp.* 18.
[4] See Soph. *Aj.* 1031 ; Eur. *Androm.* 399 ; G. Murray, *Rise of the Greek Epic*², p. 145.

or Penelope, she can yet be easily translated into a " not impossible She," simple, unaffected, untouched by false modesty ; a princess, not of featherbeds or fairyland, but a girl who can wash clothes, and, if she throws a ball, is womanly enough to miss—the forerunner, not indeed of the modern athletic girl, but of the Greek woman who could only be disguised as a male defender of a besieged city, provided that she refrained from throwing missiles.[1]   Nausicaa, in fine, is " in character " from her first meeting with Odysseus, to her parting words, " Farewell, stranger, and remember me when you are in your own land again ; for it is to me first that you owe the price of life."

Her character was not misread in the great ages of Greek poetry.   Homer had inspired Alcman, the earliest of the lyric poets, to repeat her prayer " Father Zeus, would that he might be my husband " ; and though only one or two fragments of his poem on Nausicaa survive, Alcman's *galanterie poétique*—in Croiset's happy phrase—must have found the heroine a congenial subject.[2]   In the next century Sophocles not only wrote a play on the Phaeacians, but himself took the part of the princess in her ball-playing scene.[3]   But the romantic charm of this story was lost on the Alexandrines.   The lack of historical perspective, the actual change in feminine status, the growing demand for a moral—all combined to blur the picture of Nausicaa and Phaeacian manners.   An age which appreciated the *Lock of Berenice* could not understand the simplicity of Homeric womanhood.   In the sphere of " propriety " the court-poets swallowed the camel of Ptolemaic *amours*, while straining at the gnat of a Phaeacian girl who wished

---

[1] Aen. Tact. 40 πόρρωθεν γὰρ κατάδηλος βάλλουσα γυνή.
[2] Edmonds, *Lyra Gr*. i. 28-35 ; Smyth, *Melic poets*, 8 and 9.
[3] Athen. i. p. 20.

for a husband like Odysseus. Aristarchus rejected or doubted this incriminating passage ; and, later on, he struck out the lines in which (as Odysseus had not mentioned Penelope) Alcinous innocently offered his daughter to the hero,[1] on the ground that fathers do not make such proposals to a perfect stranger. It is only fair to add that the Phaeacians had already earned a rather unenviable fame for luxurious living, which seemed to reflect on Nausicaa's own character. Plato had reproved Homer for describing their love of feasting—it was an offence to Sophrosyne ; and even Eratosthenes, who should have known better, thought fit to emend the passage.[2] Nausicaa had indeed her defenders—no doubt her conduct was one of the fashionable Questions —and the historian Ephorus praised her for simple virtue ; but a scholiast quotes him with the pontifical remark, " *I* attribute it to the luxury of the Phaeacians." [3]

Nausicaa's own character was bound up with that of Homer himself ; for we have already seen the Greek inability to distinguish between the poet and his creations. There were two views about Homeric morality in general, and Nausicaa must needs be drawn into one side or the other. The Alexandrines left this lamentable confusion unsettled to the end. Plutarch, true to his principles, gives her the benefit of the doubt : she may, after all, pass muster as an example to the young. If she felt the love of a Calypso for the stranger, her boldness and incontinence were of course blameworthy ; but if she recognised his character and admired his intelligence, she was to be commended for preferring Odysseus to

---

[1] Schol. on *Od.* 6, 244-245 ; *Od.* 7, 311-316. See Lehrs, *de Arist. stud.*[3], p. 334. Ludwich, *Arist. textk.* p. 568.

[2] Plat. *Rep.* 390*a* ; cf. Luc. *Paras.* 10. For Eratosthenes' " bowdlerlising," cp. Athen. 1, p. 16*d* ; and see Plut. *de aud. poet.* 33*c* ; Lehrs *de Arist. stud.*[3], p. 335.

[3] Schol. Q.T.

some sailor or man who goes to dances (ὀρχηστικῷ)
among her own people.[1] Even later than Plutarch,
a Christian bishop takes a hand in the controversy.
St. Basil, influenced no doubt by his teacher Libanius,
believed that all Homer's poetry—except for certain
details—was in praise of virtue. He therefore supplements the Plutarchan apology: Odysseus, naked and
shipwrecked, is clothed in his virtue (Basil does not
discuss this virtue in regard to Calypso), and thus he
won the reverence of the princess and all the other
Phaeacians.[2] Nausicaa, if not canonised, or even be-
atified, is at least safely within the fold; and Basil
—if he ever read the *Constitutions* of Aristotle—must
have been pleased to find that she became, much more
suitably, the wife of Telemachus.[3]

This warped judgment of the poets is ultimately due
to the philosophers, from whom the scholars took their
cue. The general relation of post-Aristotelian philosophy
to poetry (especially the Homeric) cannot here be fully
discussed, since opinions varied between the extremes
of regarding Homer as an inspired teacher of wisdom
to a complete neglect of his bearing on philosophy.
Connected with this, there was an equal discrepancy of
views as to acceptance of allegory in explaining—or
explaining away—the theological and moral " difficulties." It is usually assumed that Plato's contemporary—Antisthenes, the founder of the Cynic School
—was a thorough-going allegorist, whose methods were
adopted by the Stoics. But there is more than a doubt
whether Antisthenes was an allegorist in any real sense
of the word. Although he was a keen student of Homer,

[1] *de aud. poet.* 8.
[2] Basil, *On the Use of Greek Lit.* 5 (ed. E. P. Maloney) ; see generally F. M. Padelford, in *Yale Stud. in Engl.*, 15, 1902.
[3] Arist. fr. 506, Rose.

his main object was to draw moral lessons from the epic characters—e.g. to show that Odysseus is the type of the wise man ; and, as has been pertinently remarked, the moral of the tale is not to be confused with allegory.[1] There seems no doubt, however, that he followed a common distinction in believing that Homer sometimes wrote according to popular opinion ($\delta\delta\xi a$), sometimes according to truth—an explanation which we have seen adopted by Aristotle to avoid inconsistencies. Antisthenes was at least anxious to save Homer's credit ; but later Cynics were not so careful. Among the new, or revived forms of Alexandrine poetry, the satiric poems (Silloi) were well suited to express the disillusion-ment of Cynic moralists, notably Crates and Cercidas, while others—like Phoenix and Timon—belonged to the same group. A marked feature of their general style was the parody of Homer, with satiric application to the morals of the day. In Cynic hands, this sort of parody did not spring from admiration, and easily passed into direct attack. It is probable that Zoilus, who earned notoriety as the " Scourge of Homer," was influenced by the school, even if he may not have been a professed Cynic. Part of his castigation is traditional, based on Plato, whom he followed in condemning the grief of Achilles as excessive. In another vein, he objected to the irrational element which Aristotle had tried to meet ; and he found fault with the exact symmetry of the six men whom Odysseus lost from each ship—an appalling piece of " common-sense " which sufficiently discounts his value as a critic.[2]

---

[1] See J. Tate in *Class. Quart.*, Jan. 1930, p. 4 f.

[2] For references see Sandys, *Hist. of Class. Schol.* i. p. 108 f. Zoilus must belong to the latter half of the fourth century. More than one of the objections " solved " by Aristotle are attributed to him. They were presumably contained in two works mentioned by Suidas, ψόγος Ὁμήρου and κατὰ τῆς Ὁμήρου ποιήσεως λόγοι ἐννέα.

Turning to the Stoics, we find a gradual development in the use of allegory, but not always out of respect for the poet. Dio says that Zeno " censures nothing in Homer " ; [1] but it was no part of Stoic dogma to hold that the poet was infallible—he might express merely " opinion," or he might misunderstand the myth which he transmitted. On the whole, however, the Stoic tendency was to regard the early poets as philosophers, and this attitude of course implies a free use of allegory. Chrysippus certainly held this view, which became a commonplace, although later Stoics could disagree without loss of orthodoxy. Seneca, for instance, denied that any philosophy could be extracted from Homer, and Cornutus held that, while philosophy existed in the most primitive times, it was corrupted by the poets, who confused it by their mythology.[2] This violation of the historic sense was too much to be stomached by some outside the Stoic fold. The Epicureans, at least, protested against making Stoic philosophers of the most ancient poets " who never even suspected such a thing." [3]

Only one leader of the school seems to have stood somewhat apart. Cleanthes, being himself a poet, treated poetry with more than mere toleration. He held that " metre and song and rhythm come nearest to the truth in contemplation of the divine " ; [4] and his great hymn to Zeus is a proof of his sincerity. But the Zeus of that poem is not the god of Greek mythology ; indeed, the hymn is a protest against Homer rather than in the epic tradition. Cleanthes would not have been disowned by Plato himself.

[1] *Or.* 53.
[2] *ep.* 88.   For Cornutus see J. Tate in *Class. Quart.* Jan. 1929, Jan. 1930, where Stoic allegory is discussed.
[3] Cic. *N.D.* 1, 41.
[4] Philod. *Vol. Herc.* i. 28.   I have discussed the later connexion of Stoicism with poetry in *Roman Poetry*, ch. 5.

In the later history of the Porch, the prevailing fashion was to make the best of the two worlds of poetry and philosophy by turning Homer into a teacher of the young, among whom the illiterate adult was to be classed. Strabo, who may be taken as an average example of " laymen " in the Stoic creed, remarks that the marvellous and portentous give an increase of pleasure, which acts as a philtre, whether to deter or to incite.[1] By making poetry the handmaid of philosophy, the Stoics not only rid themselves of a troublesome rival near the throne, but used the rival for a useful end. Philosophy, as Strabo adds, is for the few, while poetry is more useful to the people and can fill the theatre. Homer, in particular, uses his myths for education, but mingles the false with the true, to win favour for his truth. The wanderings of Odysseus are fabulous ; but here and elsewhere, these are only the trappings to decorate the facts of history. So far, even a poet and Epicurean might agree, since Lucretius himself acknowledged that his sweetness was but to coat the pill. But, as time went on, the Stoics became more stiff-necked, and poetry was either patronised or shelved. The later Romans were sufficiently contemptuous : Seneca's real or assumed disregard for criticism — and indeed for poetry itself—is handed on, as a magnificent gesture, to Marcus Aurelius, who thanks heaven that he has learned to eschew " rhetoric, poetry and fine language " —their importance in his mind being shown by the next words, that he had also learned not to wear full dress at home.[2] All he can say for tragedy is that it may be useful : it may teach us to bear, " on the larger stage," such troubles as are shown on the tragic boards. Comedy fails to win even this modified approval, although Marcus

---

[1] Strabo, i. 2, 8 f.   [2] M. Aur. i. 7 ; xi. 6.

has a word of praise for the utility of the old style in
" rebuking pride."

There remains Epicureanism, which ought to have
done better. A hedonistic doctrine could easily have
included the appreciation of poetry, whose object was
itself Pleasure ; and, since the poets were still regarded
as teachers, they might seem to have a double claim for
respect, or at least for toleration. The fact that poetry
provides *intellectual* pleasure—to which Epicurus gave
priority—might have been a further bond of sympathy.
But the attitude of the school directly falsifies these
anticipations. Its founder, for a Greek, was singularly
devoid of a feeling for poetry or, indeed, for any form
of literature. Claiming to be self-taught, he warned
his followers to avoid all education, by " taking to the
boats," as if culture were a sinking ship.[1] Epicurus
would have strongly disowned parentage of *Marius the
Epicurean* or of its author's æsthetic view of life. No
doubt he was not entirely consistent, as he is said to
have frequented the theatre ; but he certainly despised
any literary criticism—including the " problems " of
the dinner-table.[2] His rejection of poetry was clearly
due to various causes, quite unconnected with Plato's
grand refusal. It might give a certain pleasure, but
not the pleasure demanded by philosophy.[3] As an art,
he regarded it as a species of rhetoric—a κακοτεχνία
or device unworthy of a philosopher. If he and his
followers wrote on rhetoric it was (in Plutarch's words)
to abolish the rhetorician.[4] There were other objections.
Homer and his followers were largely concerned with

---

[1] Diog. L. x. 6.
[2] Plut. *non posse suav.* 13.   [3] κύριαι δόξαι 10.
[4] Amm. Marcell. 30, 4, 3 ; Plut. *adv. Colot.* 33. See other references in Usener, *Epicurea*, p. 109 f., and p. 170 f. ; C. Bailey, *Greek
Atomists*, p. 234 f.

the praise of gods and heroes, and these needed no eulogy.[1] Still worse, poetry was bound up with the myth which, as the foe of scientific truth, must be swept away. To the Epicurean, it does not matter how the thunderbolt is to be explained " provided that myth is eliminated." Darwin confessed that science had killed his taste for poetry ; and though Epicurus was by no means scientific in the modern sense, he was equally immersed in the study of phenomena. Anyhow he seems to have been one of the few Greeks (even of his own period) for whom poetry had no appeal. His style, at least, betrays no spark of imagination ; it is simply dull. He showed his own wisdom in remarking that " only a wise man could speak rightly on music and poetry, but in practice he would not compose poems." His greatest pupil—Metrodorus—wrote a treatise on poetry, but this must have been very negative, since he stated that it was unimportant to know the side on which Hector fought, or the first lines of Homer, or any other part.[2] In the Roman period, some followers of Epicurus may have conveniently forgotten their master's advice ; but the age of Cicero still thought an Epicurean poet to be an exception.[3] One of the chief ironies—and gains—of literature is that a school of these antecedents should have produced a Lucretius.

§ 2. The Poets as Critics

It is a relief to turn from the philosophers to the poets of the age. They, at least, had a fellow-feeling for Homer, even if imitation of the old Epic was outworn. The " artificial " epic of Panyasis, Antimachus of

---

[1] Philodemus, *Rhet.* iv (Sudhaus, i. p. 215).
[2] Plut. *ib.* 12 ; cf. Cic. *fin.* 1, 7, 25.
[3] See Cic. *in Pison.* 29.

Colophon and Choerilus—the last unfavourably criticised by Aristotle—had exhausted the cycle of Homeric
myths, and an attempt of Choerilus to borrow from
history (in the *Persica*) seems to have fallen flat. A
distaste for the long epic is shown in the famous line
of Callimachus—" I hate the cyclic poem [1]—and in his
still more celebrated remark " a big book is a big
nuisance." [2] Theocritus, too, protested against those
birds of the Muses who vainly chatter against the Chian
singer. As is well known, both these poets, in different
ways, favoured the short hymn or epic idyll which
carried on the Homeric style at a more manageable
length. Aristotle had himself hinted that a modern
epic might well be shortened, so as " to embrace the
beginning and the end in one view," like a tragedy, [3]
much as Poe and Baudelaire required a poem to be
limited by " capacity of attention." On the other side
Apollonius adhered more closely to tradition, although
even the *Argonautica*, in four books, is a sort of com-
promise between the old epic and the idyll. For his
quarrel with Callimachus, which began with a difference
of poetic aims and ended in violent personal animosity,
new evidence appears in the recently discovered fragments of his rival's chief poem, the *Aetia*. In one
fragment, Apollonius (then an exile at Rhodes) and his
friends are disguised under the name of the Telchines—
the mythical wonder-workers of the island—who are
represented by Callimachus as attacking him for not
having written a continuous poem. The other fragment claims that Apollo had given Callimachus the

---

[1] So *Anth. Pal.* II, 130 τοὺς κυκλίους μισῶ.

[2] Athen. iii. 73a, τὸ μέγα βιβλίον ἴσον ἔλεγεν εἶναι τῷ μεγάλῳ κακῷ.
M. M. Gillies, *Argonautica*, iii. p. xliii, suggests that this may be
a petulant comment of a librarian on a heavy papyrus roll ; but
it is surely a literary criticism.

[3] *Poet.* 1459b, 19, on which see Bywater.

advice to "keep his Muse thin," and to choose an un-
trodden path, even if narrower. He sings like a cicala
for those who do not love the bray of asses.[1] We need
not pursue in detail this Battle of the Books; it is
more profitable to turn from these rival poets to one
who, like them, was both scholar and poet, but who
seems to have far surpassed either of the two as a literary
critic.

Eratosthenes of Cyrene, who succeeded Apollonius as
head of the Alexandrian Library, was one of the most
remarkable scholars of the third century.[2] Astronomer
and geographer, mathematician and poet, he deserves to
rank, after Aristotle, as a man of encyclopædic knowledge although his nickname (Beta) implied that he
was not thought first-rate in any one capacity; but
we are here concerned with him only as poet and critic,
even if the loss of his chief critical work *On the Old
Comedy*—a few fragments survive—is probably less
deplorable than that of Aristotle's own discussion of
Comedy. It may well have been his interest in Aristophanes that helped to form a judgment of the poetic
end, which places him not merely above his coevals but
among the soundest critics of any age. For Eratosthenes threw over the whole incubus of Teaching, boldly
stating that every poet aims at transport, not instruction.[3]
Strabo, who quotes this pronouncement, makes the
orthodox comment of a Stoic: it may be absurd to

---

[1] *Oxyrh. Pap.* xvii. (1927), 2079. See E. A. Barber, in *New
Chapters in the Hist. of Gk. Lit.* (2nd series), p. 4 f.; R. Pfeiffer, in
Hermes, 63 (1928), p. 302 f.

[2] Circ. 276-176 B.C. See Hiller, *Eratosthenis Carm. rell.*; Sandys,
Hist. Class. Schol. i. p. 123; Pauly-Wissowa, *Real. Encl. s.v.*

[3] Strabo, i. 2, 3, ποιητὴν πάντα στοχάζεσθαι ψυχαγωγίας οὐ διδασκαλίας.
cf. i. 2, 30 f. Strabo's own view was surpassed by Rymer, who held
that "a poet is obliged to know all arts and sciences" (*Pref.* to
translation of *Rapin's Reflections on Aristotle*, 1674).

credit Homer with all knowledge and every art ; but
it is equally absurd to deny him vast learning, and to
call his poetry the invention of an old wife's tale for
the sake of entertainment. That geographer would obviously prefer to regard Homer as an " epitome of art
and science "—a view, as we may remember, which
lingered until finally exploded by Bentley.[1]

No less honour is due to Eratosthenes because the
trend of criticism had been pointing to his conclusion
since the beginning of the fourth century, although
that time was not ripe for its full acceptance. Even
Aristotle had been too much under the influence of
moral instruction to reduce that element of poetry to
its due proportion. His contemporary Isocrates seems
also to have halted between the two opinions. Unable
to throw his weight without reservation into either
scale, he divided the poets into two categories : the
gnomic poets (Hesiod, Theognis and others) were instructive, while Homer and—curiously enough—the
dramatists were classified as ministers of pleasure.[2]
This view of tragedy would have shocked Aristophanes ;
and otherwise the position of Isocrates was not satis-
factory—a formula was needed to cover all poetry, and
Eratosthenes was left to find it. He approached Homer,
not from the standpoint of a rhetorician, like Isocrates,
but as a poet and scholar, who, in his way, could justly
be called a Higher Critic. His denial of Homeric teaching involved a new attitude towards the epic. As a
geographer, he might have been expected to show interest in the identification of places which Odysseus had
visited. There were (and still are) many who have tried
to give a local habitation to Circe or the Cyclops, and to

---

[1] See R. C. Jebb, *Bentley*, p. 146.
[2] Isocr. *contra Nicocl.* 43-49.

track the wind-god to his lair. Eratosthenes strongly
disagreed, and perhaps carried his dissent too far, since
no one would now hold that *all* this geography was
purely imaginative. But he was sound in his main
contention that Homer was not to be treated as a
historian : " the wanderings of Odysseus will be charted
when you find the cobbler who sewed up the bag of the
winds." [1] It might have been thought that this single
illustration would have cleared the critical air of all the
mists of allegory, and have finally established Homer as
an imaginative poet whose only aim was to please.
But the philosophers were not to be convinced ; and
even the approval of Longinus is not unqualified. For
at no time was the Greek world anxious to divorce
poetry from instruction, when even Horace could do
no better than to propose morality *or* pleasure as alternative Ends. In the empire, Eratosthenes had his
followers, as when Galen thought that the Muse of
poetry meant to astonish and charm, but not to teach ; [2]
but, as a rule, the absence of poetic teaching was regarded rather as a reproach than a merit. We need
only remember that Dryden felt qualms in claiming
poetry for pleasure alone, and that Dr. Johnson reverted
to the classical theory of " uniting pleasure with truth."

No doubt Eratosthenes preached his theory better
than he practised it. His own poems are certainly
not free from the didacticism of an age that produced
Aratus and Nicander, besides a whole school of moralists
whose poems, coloured by Cynicism, were gnomic and
instructive—remote ancestors of the Roman satire with
its Horatian text *ridentem dicere verum.*[3] Learning was

[1] Eratosth. *ap.* Strab. 1, 2, 15. In ancient times Polybius and
Strabo, in modern, Victor Bérard, have held the view that the
wanderings of Odysseus can be mapped in the Mediterranean.

[2] Galen, *de usu partium* iii. 1 (with reference to Pindar).

[3] On these σπουδαιογέλοιοι see Powell, 202 f.

12

the keynote of Alexandria, and its effects are seen even
in the epic idylls which should have been free from
its baneful influence. The *Hermes* of Eratosthenes, as
an idyll, is technically in the tradition of the *Homeric
Hymns* rather than that of Aratus ; its subject is the
early exploits of the boy-god who, on ascending to
heaven, discovered that the music of the spheres harmonised with his new invention, the lyre. But the
longest surviving fragment—an account of the five
zones which Virgil honoured by imitation [1]—seems
frankly didactic : here, at least, the astronomer outran
the poet.[2] On the other hand, the tendency of
Eratosthenes was no doubt mainly Callimachean, and
Callimachus, for all his learning, never sank to the
depths of Nicander. Too much stress may be laid on
the didacticism of an age which counted Theocritus
among its shining lights ; for the bucolic poet might
have fairly agreed with the definition of Eratosthenes,
and have pointed to his own idylls in confirmation.
And, apart from the greater names of Theocritus and
Apollonius, the mimes of Herodas, the elegies of Philetas
and the erotic epigrams of Meleager are only some
instances of the new poetry which redeemed the
Alexandrine period from the taint of instruction.

The greatest achievement of the Hellenistic age—
the New Comedy—was equally free from didacticism
in the strict sense of the word. If Menander was the
Mirror of Life, his instruction in the art of living was at
least oblique ; and the comic poets, as far as we can
infer, were satisfied with this indirectness. Few of their
fragments have any close relation to criticism, although
we find some interesting passages which show that
literary questions were still—as they had been in the

[1] *Georg.* i. 233 f.
[2] Hiller, *Erat. carm. rell.* ;   Powell, p. 58 f.

days of Aristophanes—a proper subject for comic discussion. Antiphanes, for example, in the period of the Middle Comedy, is concerned to point out the difficulties of a comic poet as compared with his tragic rival.[1] He remarks that the latter has only to breathe the name of Oedipus, and the audience know what to expect (Aristotle, by the way, did not credit them with so much knowledge of mythology),[2] whereas the comic poet had to " invent " from beginning to end, with new names, new situations and an original plot. Equally interesting, on other grounds, is a fragment of Simylus,[3] which has been quite needlessly suspected. It is true that we know practically nothing about this poet, but the fragment itself contains no thought too advanced for a writer between the time of Aristotle and the Graeco-Roman age. Simylus enumerates the needs of a successful poet as follows : nature (genius) by itself is not enough, nor art without nature—a pronouncement which was certainly trite since the age of the sophists, if it remained unsettled till Horace and Longinus. Then—Simylus proceeds—the poet must find a producer, and needs " love, skill, a happy occasion, time (? to spend on his work) and a judge able to understand his words." The order is a little curious, as the poet's work seems to be chronologically confused with the circumstances of its production. But few will deny that a comic writer of the period could have realised all these difficulties in his own experience. Commentators have boggled at the word " passion " ($\xi\rho\omega\tau\alpha$), on the ground that " the principle that we should all love our work, if known, was not commonly expressed in antiquity."[4]

---

[1] *Circ.* 408-332 ; cf. fr. 191 Kock.
[2] Arist. *poet.* 1451*b*, 25.   [3] Stob. *flor.* ii. 352.
[4] I quote from Mr. D. W. Lucas, who, however, rightly defends the fragment as of the fourth century.

May we not rather say that the principle was so well known that it was hardly necessary to express it? Even the arch-enemy of the poets had acknowledged that their works are a labour of love—the " children " created by their Desire, the *dulcis labor* of a Lucretius.[1]

No account of Greek criticism would be complete without some reference to the Epigrammatists, who may be conveniently mentioned among Alexandrine writers, although the history of the Form is of course far longer—at both ends—than the three hundred years of this period. We need not look for professional critics among the writers like Leonidas and Meleager, whose proper business was to write poetry themselves; but many of the sepulchral and declamatory epigrams, belonging to this age, show a love of the great poets which the scholars and philosophers might well have envied. It is interesting, for example, to find that Aristotle's preference for Sophocles was fully recognised, as by Simias, whose two epigrams on the " star of the tragic muse " are among the most exquisite of their class.[2]   There is also fine appreciation of his two rivals, in epigrams of a much later date : of Aeschylus, who is praised by Antipater, the Thessalonican, for raising the language and sublime song of tragedy in a tower of massive eloquence—a reminiscence, no doubt, of the *Frogs ;*[3] of Euripides, by a certain Archimedes (whose date is unknown), where the ancient editors of that poet are soundly trounced—his path is smooth, to look at, and well-trodden, but if one treads upon it, it is rougher than the point of a sharp stake ; beware of scratching even the surface of the *Medea.*[4]   And—as

---

[1] See above, p. 84.
[2] Paton (Loeb. ed.), ii. 21, 22 ; cf. Erycias, 36 and Dioscorides, 37.
[3] *Ib.* 29.   Antipater is of the Augustan age.
[4] *Ib.* 50 (*Anth. Pal.* vii. 50).

a corrective to Plutarchan spleen—it would be hard to match the eulogy of the same Antipater on Aristophanes, whose pages are " steeped with Dionysus," and full of that " terrible grace which hates and mocks what deserves hatred and mockery." [1]

Perhaps, however, the Epigrammatists (of whatever date) are at their best in praise of the lyric poets, to whose charm—in spite of Aristotle's real or apparent silence—the Greeks of all periods never failed to respond. Here, again, it is impossible to date many of the poems in honour of Anacreon and other members of the lyric canon ; but several Alexandrines—notably Asclepiades, Dioscorides and Antipater of Sidon—turned their very considerable powers to the commemoration of the great lyrists.[2] The odes of Sappho, naturally, have perhaps the greatest appeal, summed up in the imperishable words of Meleager himself — βαιὰ μὲν ἀλλὰ ῥόδα, " few but roses." Finally, although the " nightingales " of Heracleitus, the Halicarnassian, no longer sing, we may remember that even that obscure poet could inspire Callimachus to write the most beautiful of all Alexandrine elegics. If the *Garland* of Meleager had lost its proem, the six lines on Heracleitus might still be sufficient proof that the Hellenistic age had not yet " sunk its sun " in the judgment as well as the practice of Greek poetry.[3]

When we review the general tendencies of the Alexandrine period, we are forced to the conclusion that the " age of criticism " must be interpreted with much

[1] Paton, iii. 186.

[2] See e.g. Paton, ii. 11 (Erinna), 29, 30, 31 (Anacreon), 34 (Pindar, " the Pierian trumpet ").

[3] ii. 80, famous through Johnson Cory's translation.

reserve. It was the time of the scholar and biblio-
grapher, of the philosopher and the scientist, but it
seems to count for little in the history of æsthetic values.
From the scholars, at least, nothing could be expected
after the treatment of Homer by Aristarchus, the
greatest of the so-called "critics." Horace, in his
claim to be a Roman Aristarchus, well sums up the
duties required of his kind; he is to mark the harsh
and inartistic lines, to prune excessive ornament, to
reprove obscurity.[1] There is too much of Zoilus in this
attitude—though Horace himself means to help a young
author—and too little of Longinus.

With these limitations, it may be agreed that the
Alexandrines were critics; and the period has often
been mentioned in support of the foolish belief that an
age of criticism cannot be an age of poetry. The
centuries of Ronsard and Pope and Coleridge—themselves both poets and critics—might sufficiently dispel
this notion; and, at all events, it derives no support
from Alexandria, where the achievement of the poets is
certainly equal to that of the critics, with their one-
sided concentration on Form and their misguided trust
in Decorum. On the spiritual side, they seem to have
added little or nothing to Aristotle, who—like Homer
in another sphere—was " enough for all," except for
the philosophers, for whom he was too much.

[1] *ars. poet.* 445 f.

CHAPTER VII

GRAECO–ROMAN CRITICISM

§ 1. DIONYSIUS OF HALICARNASSUS

IF the scope of this book included the criticism of prose, we should have to discuss the Graeco-Roman writers on rhetoric with much greater fulness than is here necessary. But teachers of rhetoric were of course primarily concerned with the orators themselves, or with the prose writers, such as Thucydides and Plato, from whose style a student could naturally learn far more than from the poets. Quintilian's summary comparisons of Greek and Latin poetry are strictly limited by this condition; and although Dionysius goes much deeper than Quintilian into the characteristics of certain Greek poets, his main task is the formation of a prose style. Like all rhetoricians he starts with Homer; but his attitude towards the epic is not that of one who studies the greatest manifestation of the poetic spirit in and for itself; Homer is the fountain-head from which the orator is to draw his own stream of eloquence. The notion that poetry is a species of oratory, which we have seen in Theophrastus and even in Gorgias, was too deeply planted in all Greek criticism to be uprooted, least of all by a teacher of rhetoric.

The most voluminous of these was Dionysius, who was

teaching in Rome during the Augustan age, from 30 B.C. to 8 B.C. or later.[1] He had thus lived through the greatest period of Roman oratory, and was a contemporary of Virgil and Horace ; but he nowhere mentions Cicero or any Latin writer by way of literary comparison. This is the more remarkable, since his friend Caecilius had " compared " Demosthenes and Cicero, although it is true that Plutarch rebuked him for his rashness.[2] The fact that Longinus apologised for drawing a parallel— and a very good one—between Demosthenes and Cicero (" if we, as Greeks, may be allowed to express an opinion ") is instructive.[3] It was obviously a point of honour, or at least of etiquette, for Greeks not to invade the province of Latin literature, just as the Romans, in their turn, were very chary of art-criticism, which was better left to the Greeks. The reason for the reticence, in either case, may well have been different : a typical Roman, with all his admiration for Greek art, was apt to be proud of his ignorance on æsthetic questions ; the Greek teacher of eloquence was anxious to deprecate any authority in the language of his patrons —on such matters, as Longinus politely tells his young Roman pupil, " your countrymen (ὑμεῖς) will decide."

This lack of the comparative method has been, perhaps excessively, deplored. In the absence of a true historical sense, it may be doubted whether Greek criticism was ripe for the use of other literatures. Longinus has been complimented for a fine (though loose) citation from *Genesis ;* and, if this is not an interpolation, it is in the highest degree interesting to us, that a Greek critic should have looked to a lawgiver of the Jews for an example of the sublime and a worthy

---

[1] See generally W. Rhys Roberts' ed. of Dionysius *On Literary Composition*, 1910, and his earlier ed. *Three Literary Letters*, 1901.
[2] Plut. *Dem.* 3.   [3] Long, *de subl.* ch. 12.

conception of the divine.[1] It would have been no less
interesting if Longinus had (for example) " compared "
Aeschylus and Job or Isaiah ; but it is probable that
Greek criticism would not have been greatly helped.
When the Romans set up Virgil to match Homer, the
study of literature was rather hindered than served.
The true poet must be judged by his own poetry, not
by comparison with another's. A knowledge and appreciation of foreign literatures is of immense value
in understanding the history of poetry, but it is of no
importance in any attempt to fathom the mind of a
particular poet. In the hands of Roman critics, the
method was only harmful, because it was almost wholly
concerned with estimating the amount of " imitation "
which could be detected between one poet and another.

Of the various treatises written by Dionysius on
rhetoric, the most important is that on Composition
of Words ($\pi\epsilon\rho\grave{\iota}$ $\sigma\upsilon\nu\theta\acute{\epsilon}\sigma\epsilon\omega\varsigma$ $\grave{o}\nu o\mu\acute{a}\tau\omega\nu$). The term
primarily means the order or arrangement of words ;
but it is extended to the whole framework of clauses
and periodic sentences.[2] Logically, as he explains, the
Choice of words precedes their arrangement ; but, as
many philosophers and political writers had already
discussed this branch of rhetoric, he begins with Order,
promising however to complete the whole subject in
the following year.[3] Taken together, the two treatises
covered the whole ground of formal style, both in verse
and prose ; and Dionysius is clear that Order or Arrangement is the more important of the two, since this gives

---

[1] *de subl.* 9, 9. Many scholars consider the passage as a late
interpolation arising from a desire to match Homer with Moses ;
see K. Ziegler in *Hermes*, 50 (1915), p. 572. Rhys Roberts (p. 231 f.)
thinks it probably genuine.

[2] *de comp.* 2, 9.

[3] *Ib.* 1, 6. The latter treatise, if ever written, has been lost ;
see Radermacher, *Dion. opusc.* ii. p. 251.

" greater pleasure and persuasion and force than the vocabulary." Although the selection of words is in theory outside the main scope of his Arrangement, it is by no means excluded in practice, so that we may regard this treatise as the first extant discussion on Style (λέξις) in the purely linguistic sense. At the very outset, Dionysius makes it perfectly clear that the laws of style apply equally to poets and prose-writers. He takes a passage from Homer and another from Herodotus, to show that the order is more important than the choice of words.[1] After quoting the lines which describe the meeting of Odysseus and Telemachus,[2] he remarks that " the language is woven of the most ordinary and humble words, such as might have been employed by any farmer or seaman or workman or anyone who takes no care about fine language."

On the subject of Homeric diction, no student of English criticism will fail to recognise Arnold's debt to Dionysius, in drawing attention to the " plainness " of the Epic style.   If it is objected that common Epic words were not necessarily common in the first century B.C., we may reply, with Arnold, that all Greeks knew Homer from boyhood and that his diction was perpetuated to the latest imitations.[3] The meaning of certain words was (and is still) disputed ; but the dialect, as a whole, was as familiar to an Alexandrine Greek as that of the Authorised Version is to ourselves.   Indeed, except perhaps for a single compound (ὑλακόμωροι) — itself derived from a common root in use—there is no word which a later Greek would have felt as unfamiliar. So far, Dionysius is Wordsworthian in a general preference for this common language ; and he also anticipates Coleridge in emphasising the importance of

---

[1] de comp. 3.   [2] Od. 16, 1-16.
[3] Arnold, Last Words, p. 125.

arrangement. But he would not have agreed with Coleridge's distinction between prose as " words in the best order " and poetry as " the best words in the best order," since he made no such invidious comparison between the two. He recognised of course that poets *did*, as a fact, use language different from that of prose —the dithyramb in particular was always allowed full latitude ; [1] but his main object is to prove that the best poetry does not depend on the " poetic " word. The Homeric passage, he adds, has no metaphors or other figures or rare and poetical language : what then remains but Order, to account for its nobility ?

The weak point in this argument is obvious. Dionysius has chosen one out of the countless passages in Homer which are pure narrative, not striking or exciting, but—as Dryden noted in Milton—" flats among the elevations." On such lines Arnold said conclusively that " they are very good poetry *in their place*." They are poetical just because they are not pompous. Their effect depends at least as much on the simplicity of the words as on their order. Again, this order is largely, though not entirely, settled by the metre ; and Dionysius really means to show that the hexameter is the perfect metre for a long poem, as Aristotle had already held.[2] He actually claims as much by transposing epic lines into other metres, and so proves—perhaps unnecessarily —that Homeric thought cannot be worthily enshrined except in hexameters. But he does not deal with the difficulty that the order of words in a poem must largely be determined by the metre. Homer, no doubt, chooses the best possible order—the most lucid and euphonious collocation of words ; but Dionysius hardly seems to recognise the limitations under which the poet has to

[1] See above, p. 156. [2] *Poet.* 1459*b*, f.

act. Greek prose, of course, was not hampered in this
way ; but even prose had its own rhythms, and a considerable part of the treatise is occupied in a minute
analysis of its structure. With this we are not directly
concerned ; but it leads to the discussion of a literary
problem relating to the border-line between prose and
poetry, which even a modern writer can call " that
No-man's land of literature, claimed now by one side,
now by another, and securely held by neither." [1]

The problem itself was not new ; as we have seen,
Aristotle had felt the need of a " class " between prose
and poetry, for spiritual rather than for metrical reasons
—the Socratic dialogues were too dramatic to be easily
fitted into the class of historical or rhetorical prose.
Dionysius, in approaching the question, seems to have
taken into account both spirit and form. In one of his
letters, he boldly speaks of " the poems " of Herodotus
and Thucydides, with the half-apologetic explanation
" I should not shrink from so calling them." [2] This
may be a gesture of admiration, but it is at least a
considerable advance on Aristotle, who had denied the
name of poetry to historical works even if versified. In
other passages Dionysius is more guarded—Herodotus
by choice of words, composition and variety of figures,
made his prose *like* the finest poetry, in respect of
persuasion, charm and the highest pleasure. [3] Sometimes, indeed, he thinks that the prose-writer becomes
" too poetic "—it is a shame that Plato should have
deliberately confessed to writing in the style of dithyrambs. [4] Here Dionysius lapses ; he might have re-

---

[1] J. L. Lowes, *Convention and Revolt in Poetry*, ch. 8. See *de
comp.* 20 f.

[2] *Ep. ad Pomp.* 3. So Demetrius, *de eloc.* 215 (of Ctesias) ποιητὴν
γὰρ αὐτὸν ⟨ἂν⟩ καλοίη τις εἰκότως.

[3] *de Thuc.* 23.

[4] *ad Pomp.* 2 ; *de Demosth.* 7 ; cf. Plat. *Phaedr.* 227a-238d.

membered Aristotle's defence of a poetic style—justifiable not only when the audience is in an emotional mood, but also when the speaker is ironical, as in the *Phaedrus*.[1]   To Dionysius, as to other critics, the dithyrambic style was always a scandal ; but Plato was more sympathetically treated by those who realised his poetic genius.   Cicero (who here brackets him with Democritus) remarks that although he does not write in verse, his " imitation," added to his brilliance of style, makes him more poetic than the comic poets—a high praise in view of Menander's reputation.[2]   Cicero no doubt drew from a Peripatetic source, and it is interesting to note that this claim for the poetry of Plato rests on the spiritual basis of Mimesis, as much as on formal beauty of style, which seemed only an " exaggeration (ὄγκος) to Dionysius." [3]   But, after making allowance for his prejudice against Plato, we may admire with little reservation his chapter on the near approach of prose to verse,[4] even if we should not now take Demosthenes as the highest example of the prose writer's kinship to the poet.   The relation, however, is purely formal—depending on Choice and Order—and we have to wait for Longinus to develop the spiritual side. Briefly, Dionysius comes to the conclusion that metre is the significant test : prose must not be metrical, " that it may not transgress its own character," but it may resemble poetry by virtue of its rhythm ; and " in this way it would be poetical, although not a poem ; lyrical, but not a lyric." [5]   The same conclusion is reached by the converse process of taking lyrics, which if read by

---

[1] *Rhet.* iii. 7, 11.

[2] *orator*, 20, 67 : (locutionem) *etsi absit a versu, tamen quod imitatione feratur et clarissimis verborum nominibus utatur, potius poema putandum quam comicorum poetarum.*

[3] See e.g. *ad Pomp.* 764, *de comp.* 25.

[4] *de comp.* 15.   [5] *de Demosth.* 50.

" divisions " (κατὰ διαστολάς) i.e. the natural pauses
required by the sense, can easily be mistaken for prose.
Dionysius in fact forestalls the method, fashionable
among critics of Free Verse a few years ago, of showing
that such poems, if printed continuously, could easily be
read as prose. The parallel is not quite accurate, since
Free Verse has no strophic correspondence; but Dionysius
happens to choose a lyric—the famous *Danae* of Simonides
—in which his contention is only too successful, for no
modern scholar has been able to distinguish the strophe,
antistrophe or epode.[1]

So, after rehandling the old Aristotelian problem,
Dionysius comes to the conclusion, foreshadowed if not
definitely stated by Aristotle himself, that poetry and
prose converge, according as metre tends to become
merely rhythmical, or rhythm metrical. The " No-
man's land " had therefore an existence in fact, but only
in so far as the two Forms stepped beyond their proper
bounds. In theory there was no prose-poem, because it
would be a confusion of the Forms ; but, in practice,
the border line was sometimes crossed. From Aristotle
to the end, Metre remains the rigid test of poetry,
though metre alone does not make a poem.[2] Dionysius
is mainly concerned with the metrical and linguistic
tests ; but it may be here convenient to summarise the
other hall-marks of a poem, as recognised by the later
Peripatetics. The definition is fourfold : metre, myth,
" history " and a certain quality of diction. Metre, it
will be noticed, comes first ; but, true to Aristotle, it

---

[1] *de comp.* 26. Simonides, fr. 27 (Edmonds). Dionysius' argument has most force in relation to the Nome (νόμος) which was not
written antistrophically (Aristot. *probl.* 19, 15). Such verses were
ἀπολελυμένα, but Hephaestion notes that they were metrical, although
the metre was not fixed (περὶ ποιημ. 3).

[2] On Aristotle see above, p. 97. Cf. Cic. *Orator*, 56 f. ; Quintil.
ix. 4, 60.

is added that every composition which lacks the other requisites is not a poem, even if metrical. The Pythian oracle and the astrologers, as well as Empedocles, are excluded. The insistence on "myth" and "history" may be easily misunderstood, but is to be explained by the Aristotelian emphasis on action. Aristotle himself would have been content with μῦθος alone, which is a "synthesis of action," but later critics distinguished between "myth," as old stories (whether credible or incredible) and "history," as informative facts which have happened or might happen—the latter category being often called πλάσμα, "fiction." In each division the subject-matter is equally concerned with πρᾶξις, an active human state.[1]

Whatever allowance he may elsewhere make for the spiritual distinction between prose and poetry, in the *Composition* Dionysius deals almost wholly with formal characteristics of Style. Like other critics after Theophrastus, he classifies all literature into modes or styles, adopting the usual division of the "severe" the "smooth" (or florid) and the "mixed";[2] and, in discussing the last, he quotes the Aristotelian Mean with the approval to be expected from a follower of Theophrastus—"it deserves to win the first prize."[3]

There would have been no great harm, perhaps, in this system of compartments, if the method had been strictly subordinated to a sounder form of criticism. It may not be very helpful to be told that Aeschylus and Thucydides are leaders in the "severe" style;

---

[1] See Schol. on Dionys. Thrax, p. 166, 13, and p. 168, 8 (Hilgard) = Diels, *Vorsokr.*[4] *Empedocles*, A25. Other references in Hilgard, p. 300, 35, and 449, 14.

[2] (a) λέξις αὐστηρά ; (b) γλαφυρά, ἀνθηρά ; (c) εὔκρατος are the usual terms for the three styles or "characters," which often intermingle in the same writer.

[3] *de comp.* 24 ; see generally 21-24, and *de Dem.* 37 f.

that, in the smooth, Sappho and Isocrates make a pair (ill-assorted, one might think, on other grounds) with Euripides in the same galley; and finally, that the mixed or highest class contains (among others) the name of Sophocles — again the Aristotelian influence — with Herodotus, Plato and Demosthenes to balance him in prose. Homer, of course, belongs to this category, with a special mark of distinction as the Ocean " from whose source all rivers, every sea and fountain arise." Still, as far as it goes, the method has a certain value. Since language is the common medium for both prose and poetry, there may often be a gain in illustrations of its use by examples drawn from the two divisions of literature. Pope's comparison of the *Iliad* and the Bible for " pure and noble simplicity " was approved by Arnold, and—within its own limits—the criticism is useful. But, at most, it is only a point of departure, a preliminary survey of the common ground from which two great artists (or groups of artists) start on widely-diverging paths towards quite distant goals. Even when Dionysius and his followers compare poets with poets, the defect of their method far outweighs its occasional helpfulness. The radical flaw in the doctrine of styles is plain : a poet or prose-writer is fitted into a style, to the subordination or exclusion of all the other qualities which make up the character of the individual artist. The method tended to sink the person in a collection of writers, often oddly associated. It is true that the influence of rhetoric was strong enough to except the great orators and historians from this summary treatment : a prose-writer was always thought to deserve the dignity of a monograph. But the poets—except Homer—were not privileged to the same extent. There is no extant work of the Graeco-Roman period, corresponding to the full studies of Dionysius on Thucydides or Demosthenes.

In theory, of course, individuality of style was recognised, and not least by Dionysius himself. At the very outset of his discussion on the three modes, he asserts without ambiguity that each person has his own way of writing as much as each man has his own individual appearance: words are like the artist's colours; all use the same pigments, but in different ways.[1] There was nothing new in this, since Socrates, apparently, and Plato, certainly, had observed that "style is the man," which had become a proverb in the days of Cicero and Seneca, and Menander had anticipated Buffon in the epigrammatic line ἀνδρὸς χαρακτὴρ ἐκ λόγου γνωρίζεται;[2] but in practice the writers on rhetoric reversed the relative importance of the style and the man.

Dionysius represents, for both good and evil, the Greek apotheosis of Form. His discussion on Order starts with the vowels and consonants and investigates every possible combination of words, in rhythmical or metrical arrangement, which produce style. His analysis of poetic effect is far too subtle for modern taste. He lingers, for example, on the devices of onomatopoeia, as if Homer's art were best revealed by noting that when the stone of Sisyphus rolls down, its rush is described in the dactylic line—

αὖτις ἔπειτα πέδονδε κυλίνδετο λᾶας ἀναιδής.

This sort of verbal analysis no doubt pleased Pope, and explains his well-known eulogy :

> See Dionysius Homer's thoughts refine,
> And call new beauties forth from every line.

---

[1] de comp. 21.
[2] Walz, Rhet. Graec. vi. 395 οἷος ὁ βίος τοιοῦτος καὶ ὁ λόγος (ascribed to Socrates) ; Cic. Tusc. 5, 47 ; Sen. Ep. 114.

13

But we are surfeited by too much of this refinement. A modern reader may well mark and admire, in passing, some onomatopoeic beauty in Homer, as in Virgil or Tennyson, but Dionysius has no mercy. His dissection of a few verses from Sappho or Pindar is so exhaustive that we are not only unable to see the Sacred Wood for the trees, but even to see the trees for the leaves. No doubt it is better to err with Dionysius than with Epicurus in literary criticism ; yet, after reading whole chapters on letters and syllables, we are inclined to sympathise, in the mood of a Gallio, with " the Epicurean Choir " who, as the rhetorician disdainfully remarks, " cared for none of these things." [1]

But the Greek artists themselves did care for these things ; only they cared for much else beside—for the matter as well as the manner, for the spirit as much as the form. Being a Greek, Dionysius was well aware of the writer's double sphere, of saying well what is worth saying at all ; and he is not to be blamed for assuming the worth and concentrating on the expression. A more pertinent criticism would be to remark that, in his chosen sphere, he is more classical than the classics. For, too often, he parades the art which they concealed ; and, too often again, he finds painful skill where we should rather see the instinct of genius. Homer, in particular, is judged by a method which turns an early poet not merely into an elaborate artist but into a sedulous rhetorician. As usual, the historical sense is lacking, and Homer is credited with the preciosity of a Callimachus, while (which is infinitely more serious) there is a corresponding neglect of Homer's " native genius." Even so, however, Dionysius shows the qualities of his defects : it is a good thing to recognise that

[1] *de comp.* 24.

Homer, after all, *is* a great artist, and no mere singer of unpremeditated lays. The Greek rhetorician was a safer guide than the Renascence critics, who denied conscious art in the Epic, or than Pope himself, who— for all his love of Homer—called Virgil a better artist. And, when we come to the finest Attic period, we feel that Dionysius has at least a strong case. As he reminds us, Isocrates spent ten years on the *Panegyric*, and Plato, even when eighty years old, " combed and curled his dialogues." [1]   Here, again, we may be inclined to agree with those whom Dionysius calls " lacking in general education," [2] and to ask, with them, whether Demosthenes was so unfortunate that, whenever he wrote a speech, he inserted metres and rhythms " like clay modellers " ?   Perhaps the answer of Dionysius is sufficient—when a Demosthenes had once mastered the rules, the application came easily, from force of habit. [3]

If this were the whole story, a modern reader might be excused for asking where the great merit of Dionysius can be found.   The purely formal and verbal method of criticism is no longer in fashion—although R. L. Stevenson used it with good effect—and Dionysius pushed it even beyond the warrant of Greek literature. His real title to our respect lies not in his method but in the man himself.   The verbal analysis is not sheer pedantry, but a clue by which the Greek critic tries to discover the " mystery " [4] (the metaphor is striking) of a beautiful style.   Within the limits of his own choice, he has, in a marked degree, the chief virtue of a critic. Less interested than Aristotle in the theories and definitions of literature, he has far more interest in the actual

---

[1] *de comp.* 25.
[2] *Ib.* τῆς ἐγκυκλίου παιδείας.
[3] See also *de Demosth.* 52.
[4] *de comp.* 25.

texts.   Whether he quotes Homer or Sappho, Pindar or
Euripides, he follows the practice of those poets in " keeping his eye on the object " of criticism.[1]   His great exem-
plar, of course, is Homer, and here he is quite free from
the incubus of moral teaching.   Homer writes, σεμνῶς
καὶ ὑψηλῶς, with distinction and elevation, and that
is enough for Dionysius.   A modern critic would hardly
contrast passages from Homer and a third-rate historian
(Hegesias) to point the difference ; but the main thing
is that Homer's " nobility " *does* appear from the comparison.[2]   And besides Homer, his survey extends over
the whole field of Classical poetry, not least in the region
of lyric, which Aristotle had apparently neglected.   It
is not without significance that he chooses Sappho's
hymn to Aphrodite to illustrate a Style—not indeed the
highest in his scale, but showing the " grace and euphony "
of the Lesbian poetess.   Pindar, also, though analysed
too minutely, is not merely praised in generalities but
quoted in a whole dithyramb—an ode which entirely
justifies his eulogy of it as a fine specimen of the earlier
dithyrambs, before they lapsed into floridity : Pindar's
own poem is still severe, rugged in the beauty and
magnificence of the past.[3]   These quotations, with his
comments, give us confidence in his taste even when—
as in the treatise on *Imitation*—his account of poetry
from Homer to Menander is not documented by actual
citation.[4]   Indeed, his estimate of Pindar, in particular,
shows a masterly knowledge of the great poet's eminence
—not only stylistic but ethical.   In the *Judgment of
Ancient Authors*, Pindar is praised, among other points,
for dignity and force—various terms emphasise this
character—for a gentle irony or mordancy (πικρίας

---

[1] *de comp.* 16, πρὸς χρῆμα ὁρῶντες ;   cf. Aristotle, *poet.* 1455a, 22.
[2] *de comp.* 18.   [3] *de comp.* 22 (Pind. fr. 75).
[4] *de imit.* B. vi. 2 f.

μετὰ ἡδονῆς), for general largeness and opulence, as well as for mastery of the Figures. Moreover—and here Dionysius makes amends for his verbal treatment in the *Composition*—Pindar exhibits, to the fullest degree, the ethical qualities of continence, religious feeling and grandeur of character.[1] The list of qualities —here abbreviated—is a little alarming, but we are by this time prepared for its mixture of art and morality, and are not surprised to find that Dionysius supplements the verbal commentary of the *de Compositione* with a tribute to the whole significance of a poet who was not only a supreme artist, but a great personality.

Still, in the end, Dionysius, the teacher and historian of rhetoric, finds his chief satisfaction in the technique rather than the morality of Pindar. Always, and every-where, he is in quest of " sweet and fair speech," [2] and his judgment is remarkable. He is no *castigator*; in his own words, he avoids the impiety of a Zoilus, though he claims full liberty to mingle blame with praise ; his enthusiasm saves him from petty fault-finding. Some-times this enthusiasm overpowers his judgment, as when a zeal for Homer leads him to disparage Plato, whom he absurdly accuses of expelling the poets from jealousy.[3] But, apart from such rare lapses, Dionysius is a true critic, if not four-square and blameless (in the definition of his beloved Simonides), at least one who, in the phrase of Simylus, " can grasp the word."

§ 2. Plutarch

By the time of Dionysius, the main tendencies of Greek criticism were fixed. On the formal side, the

---

[1] *de vet. scr. cens.* p. 224 (2, 5), quoted in full by Gildersleeve, *Pindar*, p. xxxiv. n. Quintilian (x. 1, 61) follows.
[2] *de comp.* 11.   [3] *ad Pomp.* 1.

de Compositione left little or nothing to be said. Verbal analysis had been pushed to its extremity ; and if (as Dionysius is apt to think) the secret of style were purely linguistic, the lock of poetry had been found—or forced. The poet turned out to be a near kinsman of the orator : both moved their audience by the pleasure and persuasiveness of the spoken word, differing mainly in their spheres of action. But the End of poetry was still in dispute. Aristotle, with all his emphasis on the pleasure of art, had not been quite able to cut adrift from morality ; and just as the followers of his own master developed and exaggerated one branch or another of the Socratic teaching, the post-Aristotelians were one-sided in following up the rather scattered hints of the *Poetics*. If Eratosthenes concentrated on Pleasure, the Stoics saw poetry as philosophy without tears ; and, with the predominance of Stoicism in the Empire, it is no wonder that even eclectic philosophers felt the influence of the Porch.

The foremost scholar of the first century was undoubtedly Plutarch ; [1] and, although his greatest achievement was outside the province of criticism, his views on poetry are characteristic not only of his own personality but of his time and race. An eclectic philosopher, he combines the æsthetics of Aristotle with the Stoic emphasis on morality. He is Aristotelian in refusing to accept purely instructive verse as poetic— the works of Empedocles and Parmenides, Nicander and Theognis, have only borrowed their dignity and metre from poetry, as men take a carriage to avoid walking.[2] Again, he is sound on the basic distinction that prose is intellectual, while poetry, though not entirely emotional, is an appeal to the mind through the emotion.[3] His

[1] *Circ.* A.D. 45-125.   [2] *de aud. poet.* 2.   [3] *Symp.* 5, 1.

treatment of Ugliness in art is equally Peripatetic. Here the doctrine of Imitation was useful enough. Plutarch accepts the fact that poets *do* describe base actions or characters, and defends their practice by the analogy of painting. Poetry is vocal painting, just as painting is silent poetry—he attributes this remark to Simonides—and, in both arts, we praise the imitation of the Ugly if it is successful, i.e. true to the original.[1] So far, Plutarch is Peripatetic ; and, in dismissing allegory, he is no less a follower of Aristotle, although here he is perhaps not quite logical, as he has no objection to an allegory on the banks of the Nile—in Egyptian myths.[2] Nevertheless he is a Stoic in moralising Homer, as a conscious teacher, even though his lessons are not all of equal value. In his tract *How to study the Poets*, he starts with the axiom that all the poets are didactic, and he condemns, directly or by implication, any action or sentiment of their characters which is reprehensible. It follows that he is often hard-pressed to find the moral ; and his methods are more ingenious than convincing. For example, if the sentiment in a certain passage is of doubtful instruction, the same poet may prove a better teacher elsewhere. He reminds us that Euripides, when reproached for the impiety of his Ixion, replied " I did not let him leave the stage before binding him to the wheel." Again, if the poet cannot save himself, he may be saved by another, called in to redress the balance—the metaphor, too suggestive perhaps of the " swings and roundabouts," is Plutarch's own—so that no harm is done.[3] Boys, when properly trained to appreciate poetry, will learn to extract

[1] *de aud. poet.* 3, *utrum Athen.* 3. On the theory of *ut pictura poesis* see I, Babbitt, *The New Laocoon*, ch. I.
[2] See H. P. R. Finberg in *Class. Quart.* 20, p. 148.
[3] *de aud. poet.* 4.

advantage, somehow or other (ἀμωσγέπως) from the most dubious passages.[1] So, if the advice of Thetis to her son seems improper, we should remember what continence Achilles displayed, in spite of it.[2] Finally, should this method fail, Plutarch does not hesitate to re-write an offending passage, quoting with approval the precedents of Cleanthes and Antisthenes. The latter, hearing in the theatre the line

What is the shame, the doers think not shame?

at once exclaimed

Whether they think or think it not, 'tis shame.

There is much more to the same effect, but we need not follow Plutarch further in his profit-and-loss account, which is naturally drawn up to show a handsome balance of advantage for the student. Even then, however, the youth is not to rest content with his poet, who is after all only an elementary schoolmaster. The real teacher is of course the philosopher, to whom the poet offers a friendly means of introduction. Yet Plutarch is not impervious to æsthetic pleasure—indeed his wide knowledge of the poets could scarcely have been won without a real appreciation of poetry. Her charms are Siren-voices, and some say that the ears of the youth should be stopped, so that he may voyage past these Sirens "under Epicurean sail."[3] Plutarch is less drastic: for him poetry is "the Muses' vine," and, rather than hew it down, like a Lycurgus, he would make it harmless by mixture with the pure waters of philosophy.[4] He

---

[1] de aud. poet. 12.

[2] See Il. 24, 130, where Aristonicus had noted ἀθετοῦνται στίχοι γ', ὅτι ἀπρεπὲς μητέρα υἱῷ λέγειν ἀγαθόν ἐστι γυναικὶ μίσγεσθαι, i.e. the advice did not suit the person.

[3] See above, p. 194.   [4] de aud. poet. 1.

prefers the Moderation of an Aristotle to the Prohibition of a Plato. Otherwise, it must be acknowledged, Plutarch has learned too much from the Stoics and too little from the Peripatetics. A confused idea—so prominent in his essay *On the Glory of the Athenians*—that it is " deeds, not words " which matter ; a lurking suspicion that poetry may after all, be merely a pastime or a toy ; a more-than-Stoic desire to point the moral —all these attitudes may serve for the generation of a philosopher, but they are surely the corruption of a critic.

§ 3. DEMETRIUS

The author of the *de Elocutione* (to give the work its Latin name), who was certainly a contemporary and possibly a friend of Plutarch,[1] belongs to the Peripatetic school. Demetrius not only admires and quotes Aristotle, but follows the principles laid down by Theophrastus and his successors in their definitions of the styles. But a fourth style is added to the original three—the " strong " ($\delta\epsilon\iota\nu\grave{o}s \chi\alpha\rho\alpha\kappa\tau\acute{\eta}\rho$) which seemed to mark out Demosthenes from all other models. With this addition (which does not concern us) his analysis agrees with the usual classification into (*a*) the plain, (*b*) the elevated, and (*c*) the elegant.[2] Without going into details, it may be sufficient to note that the first three of these types correspond with Cicero's classification into (1) *subtilis* or *tenuis*, (2) *gravis* or *grandis*, etc.,

---

[1] $\pi\epsilon\rho\grave{\iota}$ $\dot{\epsilon}\rho\mu\eta\nu\epsilon\acute{\iota}as$, which may be translated " *On Style.*" See W. Rhys Roberts' larger ed. of Demetrius, 1902 ; Loeb ed. *On Style*, 1927.

[2] (*a*) $\dot{\iota}\sigma\chi\nu\acute{o}s$; (*b*) $\mu\epsilon\gamma\alpha\lambda o\pi\rho\epsilon\pi\acute{\eta}s$; (*c*) $\gamma\lambda\alpha\phi\upsilon\rho\acute{o}s$. See generally, W. Rhys Roberts, Introduction in Loeb ed., p. 265 f. For the debt of Demetrius to Aristotle and Theophrastus, see also A. Mayer, *op. cit.* ; and G. L. Hendrickson, in *American Journal of Phil.* 1904, 1905.

(3) *medius*. Demetrius himself does not use the term
" middle," but his description of the third type shows
that it is identical with the Peripatetic mean.   For
" elegance "—as he says—can be found in combination
with both the plain and the elevated, whereas the
elevated is essentially contrasted with the plain.[1]   In
fact, he adds, except for the irreconcilable contrast of
this pair, the types may be freely combined by the
greatest writers in verse or prose.   Homer, of course,
has the excellencies of all the types.

The most valuable part of the work is the section
dealing with the elegant style, since it is here that
Demetrius shows his keenest appreciation of Greek
poetry as a thing of beauty.[2]   It is characteristic of
his attitude that he quotes the famous comparison of
Nausicaa to Artemis as an example of " noble grace "
in Homer, while he is quite free from moralising the
story in the Stoic or Plutarchan manner.[3]   Throughout
his work, indeed, the author seems perfectly unconscious
of any message or moral to be derived from literature—
the beauty of Style, in all its varieties, is an end in
itself.   His term " elegance " has a wide connotation,
ranging from the dignified charm of Homer to the grace
of Sappho and the humour (if in season) of Aristophanes ;
and nowhere is the catholic taste of Demetrius more
apparent than in his homage to the lyric poetess and
the comic dramatist alike.   He may not do full justice
to the latter—perhaps Plato alone had discovered, with
the Graces themselves, the soul of Aristophanes—but he
has the great merit of standing with Quintilian against
Plutarch or the pseudo-Plutarch, while his allusions to
Menander and Philemon [4] do not suggest any preference

---

[1] 36.   [2] 128-189.
[3] 129.   See p. 167.   [4] 153, 194.

for the New Comedy. Aristophanes, on the other hand, is fully recognised in some, at least, of his myriad aspects —for the charms of quotation, for his burlesque, and for the use of the " unexpected " ($\pi\alpha\rho\grave{\alpha}\ \pi\rho\sigma\sigma\delta\sigma\kappa\acute{\iota}\alpha\nu$) and of humorous hyperbole.[1] If—to use the phrase of Meredith—Demetrius cannot quite see Aristophanic wit as " the laughter of Hercules," his appreciation is at least not that of the men whom Rabelais would call agelasts.

But it is Sappho who rouses his enthusiasm. As we have seen in Dionysius, and shall see even more clearly in Longinus, the fame of the " divine " poetess never stood higher than in the first century of the empire.[2] The three critics unite in shelving the moral question —poets like Ovid had no such scruples—and concentrate on her charm. Part of this *charis*, according to Demetrius, is due to the subject-matter of her verse— the gardens of the nymphs, weddings and loves : " no one," he naïvely adds, " can sing a marriage-song in anger." [2] If this insistence on the subject runs counter to the modern doctrine that " the subject is nothing, the treatment everything," we may be relieved to find, in the next paragraphs, a recognition that not only does language add charm to a graceful subject, but can rescue even an unpleasant theme by its own gracefulness.[3] The common belief that the Greeks paid too much attention to the choice of a subject, has, in fact, little countenance either in their theories or their practice. It is true that the poets had no use for trivial themes, at least until the Alexandrines, who were satisfied with the rape of a lock. Demetrius correctly interprets the great

---

[1] 150 (*Clouds*, 401), 152 ; (*ib.* 149), 161 ; (*Ach.* 86).

[2] 132. Even the Stoic Strabo speaks of her as a marvel, unique among her sex (xiii. 617).

[3] 133-135.

period of Greek poetry by an analogy from another art :
he quotes the painter Nicias, who advised the artist to
choose a theme of magnitude (e.g. a battle) just as the
poet chose the ancient myths.[1] The Greek attitude
towards the unpleasant in art was precisely the same.
The subject of a tragedy must have dignity ; but, from
the nature of the case, it cannot be pleasant; the
pleasure of the *Oedipus* comes from treatment alone.

Demetrius, therefore, simply argues that, by choosing
a pleasant subject, Sappho starts with a certain initial
advantage, which is indisputably true. He is not so
foolish as to confuse the poem with the subject. Here
his remarks, if a little obvious, are quite sensible : even
a great theme may be ruined by forcible-feeble treatment ; and if Sappho was helped by her themes, she,
too, was exposed to her own dangers in dealing with
matter which is itself " difficult." [2]

On the whole, then, the Greek view of the relation
between subject and treatment need not offend the
most modern critic : whatever the material, it is only
the handling that counts. And in this Demetrius sees
the supreme mastery of Sappho. Like all the Greeks,
he finds a poet's lapse from Reason a fault hard to forgive ; but Sappho is excused—or rather, even praised
for her hyperbole, " more golden than gold "—the
impossible, in her hands, has become a charm. Here,
as elsewhere, Demetrius cannot forget the Figures,
which he finds " most evident and abundant " in
Sappho ; but Repetition, Metaphor, and the like, lose
much of their pedantry in view of his real admiration
of the poetry. He sees, and explains in a single sentence,
the true power of the poetess, in whom the greatest
passion is expressed with grace.[3] If he does not go

---

[1] 75 f.   [2] 127.
[3] 140 ἡ δὲ καὶ τοῖς δεινοτάτοις καταχρῆται ἐπιχαρίτως.

as deeply into Sappho's psychology as Longinus, his quotations—including fragments as exquisite, though not as famous as that on the Evening Star—show how fully he understood her lyric, in the various themes which range from "love and spring and the halcyon" to a boorish bridegroom and a door-keeper at the wedding. To each mood its own expression ; and Demetrius applies to lyric the Peripatetic distinction of the beautiful word for the beautiful theme, and the ordinary, prosaic word for poems more attuned to conversation than to the lyre.[1]

A width of criticism which embraces Homer, Sappho and Aristophanes leaves certain gaps. We find that Demetrius cares little for the tragedy. It may not be surprising that he omits Aeschylus altogether ; but a single reference to Sophocles [2]—and that uncomplimentary—is a curious tribute from one who owes so much to Aristotle ; and two citations of Euripides do not make amends for the neglect. Still more curiously, both of these passages are quoted in connexion with acting, as though the poetry of Euripides was unimportant ; [3] and although Demetrius expressly disclaims any intention of writing about the author's or actor's technique, it is clearly the constructive rather than the poetic side of the drama that appeals to his taste.[4] In this respect, he has the precedent of Aristotle himself, whose outlook on tragedy is so often limited to the formal construction of a play.

To weigh Demetrius by his own method of classification, it must be confessed that, as a critic, he is more "pleasant" than forcible. His view of literature does not seem to be markedly original ; and his chief value is perhaps in preserving some part of the Peripatetic

---

[1] 166 f.

[2] fr. 515 Nauck, *Ion*, 161 f.

[3] 114 ; see p. 222.

[4] 58, 193-195.

tradition, which has been so badly mutilated.   And here Demetrius reflects the later followers of the School rather than the founder himself.   Much as he certainly reveres the authority of Aristotle, he rarely, if ever, follows the master in his wider and more spiritual point of view.   He has no great definitions of the poetic aim, no discussion of poetic thought ; his whole interest lies in the expression which applies to poetry and prose alike.   If Demetrius had alone survived to speak for the last phase of Greek appreciation, we should have been obliged to infer that the main stimulus of the *Poetics* had been lost with the death of its creator. The fortunate survival of a single work, which we have still to consider, proves that neither Dionysius nor Demetrius represents the final development of ancient criticism.

CHAPTER VIII

LONGINUS

§ I. GENERAL PRINCIPLES

THERE remains what is perhaps the last, and is undoubtedly the greatest contribution of the Greeks, after the *Poetics*, to the study of their own literature. This is not the place to discuss the various problems concerning the date and authorship of the treatise *On the Sublime*.[1] The author was certainly not the learned minister of Zenobia ; it is equally certain that he was not Dionysius of Halicarnassus ; and strictly we can go no further than the inscription of one manuscript (ἀνωνύμου περὶ ὕψους) and call him Anonymous. But the writer who, since the first edition of 1554, has been known to the world as Longinus, may be allowed to retain the name under which he was honoured by Dryden and Addison, by Pope and Gibbon.

The chief argument against the claim of the historic Longinus is to be found in the treatise itself, for the whole outlook belongs to the first century rather than to the third. Its tone is in keeping with the age of Tacitus and Quintilian, when Greek criticism was taking a final shape, soon to be distorted and blurred by the sophistry of the Antonines. In his final extant chapter, the author laments the loss of Freedom, and its conse-

---

[1] See W. Rhys Roberts' edition of *Longinus*, 1899.

quent effects on literature, in language which, as Roberts has noted, implies that this Freedom has not long been dead : " we seem to catch the accents of a Tacitus." None the less, in his actual criticism, Longinus is rather to be contrasted than compared with Tacitus and Quintilian. The writer of the *Dialogus* is an early precursor of Taine—too busy with the " causes " (the environment and concomitants of literature) to find much time for the literature in itself. Quintilian, again, views poetry in relation to rhetoric alone. His opinions on the poets, though sound in general, are entirely subservient to his thesis—the education of an orator ; and, while he mentions every considerable name from Homer to his own day, he never comes to grips with their works. He is content to label each of them with a striking phrase or even a brilliant epigram. Longinus has a very different object. He approaches literature from the standpoint of Value—the cardinal problem of modern criticism. What quality (he asks in effect) makes one work more valuable than another ? This quality must be common to prose and poetry, since, like Aristotle and the rest, Longinus draws no ultimate and absolute distinction between the two divisions of literature. The Peripatetics had found special virtues in all the three (or four) " characters " ; but Longinus concentrates on a single quality shared equally by Homer and Sophocles with Plato and Demosthenes—that " height and excellence," which is not merely a matter of logic or persuasion, but produces transport and ecstasy.

How, precisely, are we to translate this ὕψος ? The traditional rendering " sublime," like the author's name, has at least the merit of antiquity, since Quintilian often uses *sublimis* or *sublimitas* for an elevated style.[1]

---

[1] See Roberts, p. 209.

But, in English, the word is doubly unfortunate. In the first place, "the sublime," in popular language, suggests ideas rather than form. We should primarily apply the word to the conception of the *Divine Comedy* or *Paradise Lost*, even if we allow that the execution of both poems is worthy of the imagination. The term, in fact, has often been associated with the sense of mystery and infinity which Burke noted as characteristic of Hebrew rather than of Greek poetry, although the *Agamemnon* or the *Prometheus* may well be thought sublime in this Hebraic sense. Secondly, the term is not wide enough. If, in its upper range, it includes the highest flights of Greek imagination and expression, it also covers a style which need not rise to such heights. Applied to Pindar, the term might best be translated as the "grand" style; but this would be less suitable to describe Herodotus or Thucydides, who are not grand in the Pindaric or Miltonic sense. But the various words used by Longinus, as more or less equivalent to ὕψος and its adjective ὑψηλός all connote distinction or elevation;[1] and if the name of the book were not fixed by tradition, we might best convey its character by the title *On great writing*.

Such a title would be at least more comprehensive than *On greatness of style*, for—in spite of Buffon—we are apt to regard style as artistic rather than moral, whereas Longinus, as a Greek, insists that character, not less than art, is necessary for a good writer. He himself defines ὕψος as the echo of a lofty mind.[2] So, even when it seems most purely artistic, style is the expression of a noble character: "beautiful words"—which the rhetoricians had discussed in terms of sound

---

[1] τὰ μεγέθη, τὸ μεγαλοφυές, etc.
[2] 9, 2, ὕψος μεγαλοφροσύνης ἀπήχημα.

or sight—become, for Longinus, " the peculiar light of
the thought." [1] The keynote of his criticism is to be
found in this union of fine thought with perfect expression.

As they stand, the two last quotations might suggest
that Longinus regarded literature, or at least poetry,
with the vision of a Stoic. Nothing could be further
from his real attitude. At a time when there was every
temptation to be a Plutarchan moralist, he never even
hints that it is a poet's business to teach. The poet
must have a great mind, but this greatness is never
interpreted in terms of any conventional code—least of
all, the code of the Stoics, who demanded that a good
poet should be a good man.[2] But Longinus was no
Stoic, although certain views of the school—by this
time common property among the educated—may be
traced in his treatise. Philosophically, indeed, he is
not easy to class. Greek criticism, in general, was so
largely Peripatetic that his natural tradition would be
Aristotelian ; but he mentions Aristotle (with Theophrastus) only once, apparently with reference to the
lost part of the *Poetics*, and even so the allusion—on
softening metaphors—is quite unimportant.[3] His admiration for the *Oedipus* is no doubt due to Aristotle,
although many who have never read the *Poetics* have
admired that play.[4] Spiritually, at least, he is the very
antithesis of Aristotle. In place of the cold, formal and
intensely logical analysis of the Peripatetic founder,
he shows a passion for the best literature, that is his
principal claim to be reckoned a master of criticism.
Aristotle has given good reasons for our admiration of
Sophocles, but it may be doubted whether his method

---

[1] 30, I, φῶς γὰρ τῷ ὄντι ἴδιον τοῦ νοῦ τὰ καλὰ ὀνόματα.

[2] Strabo, I, 2, 5, οὐχ οἷόν τε ἀγαθὸν γενέσθαι ποιητὴν μὴ πρότερον
γενηθέντα ἄνδρα ἀγαθόν.

[3] 32, 3.   [4] 23, 3 ; 33, 5.

would convert an unbeliever. Longinus, on the other
hand, has the supreme gift of being able to make the
reader share in his own fervour and delight. Gibbon is
not conspicuous for enthusiasm ; but, after reading the
ninth chapter of Longinus, he felt the infection, and
acknowledged that Longinus had thrown a new light
on the enjoyment of literature : " he tells me his own
feelings upon reading it, and tells them with such energy
that he communicates them.[1] The praise is deserved ;
for Longinus really fulfils the ideal, assigned to criticism
by Matthew Arnold, as " a disinterested endeavour to
learn and propagate the best that is known and thought
in the world."   In this infectious zeal, Longinus finds
a forerunner in Plato—the object (after Homer) of
his warmest admiration.   For the strength of Platonism
lies in the fact that it is not a creed but an inspiration,
flowing in diverse channels, æsthetic as well as philosophical ; and one of these channels led directly to
Longinus.   Of the many ironies in history, not the least
pleasing is the silent refutation of Plato's poetic heresy
by a follower not, like Aristotle, alien to the Platonic
spirit, but deeply imbued with the imagination of the
Phaedrus and *Symposium*.   Longinus is no blind admirer.   He acknowledges that Plato sometimes trips, as
much as Homer or Demosthenes ; [2] but no great genius,
he insists, is free from flaws.   He is not directly concerned with Plato's opinions on the poets ; but he fully
recognises the poetic side of Plato himself, who " would
not have so often attained the matter and expression of
a poet, if he had not challenged Homer for supremacy,
as a young competitor with a tried champion." [3]

---

[1] *Misc. Works*, v. p. 263.   The passage is well known, and need
not be quoted in full.

[2] 36, 1.

[3] 13, 3.   Maximus Tyrius (36, 3) goes so far as to say that Plato,
in mind, though not in style, is nearer to Homer than to Socrates.

The treatise opens with a discussion on the requisites for great writing; and in the second chapter the rival claims of Nature and Art are examined. As we have seen, this age-long question had been practically settled in Alexandrine times, and there was little left to be said, beyond the summary of Horace that the two partners must needs be allied. But Longinus was not one of those who, as he acknowledges, thought the question superfluous. There is a gap in the manuscript at the place where he discusses the subject;[1] but the fragmentary chapter is decisive as it stands: of course "Nature" must come first; but Nature—and here Longinus is Aristotelian—does not act at random and without method. She herself suggests the system which it is the business of Art to develop. "Great writing needs the curb as well as the spur"; and it is clear that Longinus regards the Rules as, in a large part, a safeguard against the possible extravagance of undirected nature.[2] But Art has not merely this negative value as a "good counsellor" to direct the "good fortune" of genius. Her positive function is to reveal the secrets of natural expression—to act as an interpreter as much as a monitor.

What, then, is this art of literature? We have seen that, since the fifth century, what moderns feel to be the elusive mystery of style was, to the Greeks, a much simpler thing to explain. Style depended on the successful employment of the Figures, regarded as touch-stones of literary excellence. Here, at least, the Greeks were "always children," holding the ingenuous belief that the art of writing could be taught by attention to apos-

---

[1] 2, 3.
[2] Cf. ch. 2 generally, and 36, 4, τὸ ἀδιάπτωτον ὡς ἐπὶ τὸ πολὺ τέχνης ἐστὶ κατόρθωμα.

trophe, asyndeton, periphrasis and the rest.[1] Of course
the Figures had—and may still have—a certain value
as convenient labels of virtues (or vices) in style. The
danger of analysing literature in figurative terms is due,
not so much to the recognition that language *is* largely
figurative, as to the misuse of the method by the rhetorical teachers, who seem always to suggest that Homer
or Demosthenes may be successfully imitated by borrowing or plundering their tropes. Longinus is not entirely
free from this perverted method. He cannot disabuse
himself of the reverence which every Greek paid to the
Figures : " if treated in the fitting manner, they contribute not a little to elevation." [2] But, after giving
examples of the effect produced by such devices as
Demosthenic apostrophe, he warns us that art must be
concealed—a figure is most successful when the very
fact that it is a figure escapes notice. Otherwise, as
he sensibly observes, the audience will resent, as a personal affront, the patent trick of the rhetorician. The
antidote to this suspicion can only be found in real
elevation and passion.

In the eighth chapter Longinus, after his preliminary
discussion of Nature and Art, proceeds to define more
precisely their respective shares in creating " elevation."
Under the head of Nature, fine writing demands two
qualities : firstly, the power of forming large conceptions,[3]
and secondly, strong passion.[4] In modern language,
a poet is great by his imagination and the gift of feeling
and communicating emotion. It is true that Longinus
has no word for the imagination. The term φαντασία,

---

[1] Besides these, Longinus discusses interrogation, anaphora, repetition, hyperbaton, metaphor, hyperbole. See esp. 16-32 and 37, 38.
[2] See generally, 16-29.
[3] τὸ περὶ τὰς νοήσεις ἁδρεπήβολον.
[4] τὸ καὶ σφοδρὸν ἐνθουσιαστικὸν πάθος.

which the neo-Platonists were to extend, was still commonly restricted to the sense of " visual representation "—the power of seeing what you describe and placing it before the eyes of your audience, as when the poet himself sees the Furies and " almost compels his hearers to see them." [1] But Longinus admits a more general sense of the word as covering every mental concept that gives birth to speech; [2] and, as a matter of fact, the poetic examples which he gives are all highly imaginative. He cannot, of course, cut adrift from Imitation, which—as Philostratus recognised—hampers or even strangles imagination ; but he widens and deepens the powers of Imitation so that, in practice, that term already embraces the image-making faculty of the poet. And here he drops one of the remarks which show how thoroughly he distinguished the poet from the orator, even if the same qualities go to the making of both.   To the orator, the purpose of an image is clarity or vividness (ἐνάργεια) ; to the poet, enthralment (ἔκπληξις).   The orator shares with the poet the aim of stirring the emotions ; both, by means of elevated speech, should not only " persuade " their hearers but should rouse them to the greater height of transport.[3] But what is incidental to the orator is essential to the poet, as the supreme maker of images.

The second gift of Nature—here aided by Art—is summed up in the word πάθος, emotion or passion. Indeed, elevation is so largely emotional, that Longinus can even use the words ὕψος and πάθος as if convertible,[4] though not completely identical, since some passions

---

[1] 15, 2.

[2] 15, 1, πᾶν τὸ ὁπωσοῦν ἐννόημα γεννητικὸν λόγου.

[3] I, 4, οὐ γὰρ εἰς πειθὼ τοὺς ἀκροωμένους ἀλλ᾽ εἰς ἔκστασιν ἄγει τὰ ὑπερφυᾶ.

[4] 17, 3 ; 23, 1.

are mean and low, such as lamentation, self-pity, fear.[1]
There may be a touch of Stoicism in this limitation of
the passions ; but nothing distinguishes Longinus from
the true Stoic so much as his insistence not on their
suppression but their proper expression.   Here, again,
the poets are mainly concerned.   From Homer he draws
an instance—" one out of many "—to show the elevation, not of base or cowardly fear, but of awe, in a
passage describing a storm, when " the sailors shudder
in dread, for they are but a little removed from the
clutch of death." [2]   With this sheer simplicity Longinus
contrasts the triviality of Aratus, who thought to make
the flesh creep by the line " And a little plank averts
destruction," on which the critic briefly remarks, " well,
it *does* avert "—οὐκοῦν ἀπείργει.   In this couple of
words, he lays bare the Alexandrine weakness—the sub-
stitution of a neat phrase, an epigrammatic point, an
artificial finish, for the plain dignity of Homer.

Even more striking is his appreciation of love-poetry.
As an example of sublimity in handling this emotion,
he chooses—and we owe the preservation of the poem
to his choice—the great ode of Sappho to Anactoria.[3]
In few ancient poems—the *Song of Solomon* is of
their number—have the purely physical aspects of
passion been revealed with so much frankness.   Times
had changed since Aristophanes had protested against
the dramatic portrait of a woman in love ; and Sappho's
motif, circumscribed or proscribed for serious poetry
before Euripides, had been fully restored in Alexandria,
where Apollonius led the way in treating the psychology
of Love.   Here, indeed, Longinus might have fitly
chosen the third book of the *Argonautica*, with its
wonderful analysis of Medea's passion.   But the critic

---

[1] 8, 2.   [2] 10, 5 from *Il.* 15, 624 f.   [3] 10, 2.

—as we shall see—had little good to say of Alexandrine art ; and, in any case, he shows an unerring instinct in going back to the fountain-head of Greek love-poetry. The song to Anactoria illustrates his definition of the elevated, as the utterance of a great mind expressed by a supreme artist.   We owe an equal debt to Dionysius for his rescue of another of Sappho's finest poems ; but, as critics, the difference between that writer and Longinus is nowhere better shown than in their respective comments.   Dionysius had been content to indicate the formal beauty of a poem in the " smooth " style ; Longinus goes far deeper, penetrating the spiritual qualities of the poetess as reflected in her work.   He is not concerned with her moral character ; it is enough that Sappho has loved greatly ; and her poem is supreme in elevation, because it " selects and combines the most conspicuous and striking effects of love."   The effect —he sums up—is that not one emotion only is described, but a concourse of all the passions.[1]   It is not remarkable, of course, that Longinus admired a poem to which Theocritus and Apollonius, Catullus and Lucretius were debtors.[2]   But he not only admires—he gives sound reasons for his appreciation.   While rightly refusing to " explain " genius, he shows how art can be used in its service.   Selection, as a technical term, had hitherto been confined to verbal choice ; it has now been widened, so that (with its corollary, Combination) it passes into the sense of Simplification—the first principle that guides every artist in the choice and management of his significant material.

In the main, however, though Longinus draws instances of elevation from the three great tragic poets, as well as from Sappho and Pindar, it is to Homer that

[1] 10, 3, ἡ λῆψις τῶν ἄκρων καὶ ἡ εἰς ταὐτὸ συναίρεσις.
[2] Theocr. 2, 106 ; Apoll. Rhod. 3, 962 ; Catull. 51 ; Lucr. 3, 154.

he most often recurs. If he often quotes from the epic to show the effect of some Figure, he is illuminating not only on Homer's art, but on his psychology. Nothing can better show how deeply he pondered over the heroic character than his comment on the famous prayer of Ajax:

Father Zeus, save the sons of the Achaeans from the darkness; make day, and let us see with our eyes. Destroy us, but in the light.[1]

" This is the true emotion of Ajax. He does not pray for life, for such a prayer would be unworthy of the hero. But since in the darkness, where deeds cannot be done, he can use bravery for no noble purpose, he chafes at his impotence for battle, and begs for light without delay, resolved at least to find an end worthy of his valour, even if Zeus should meet him in the fight."

Such a comment, by itself, is worthy of a scholar who was also a great humanist. But Longinus also takes the occasion of insisting on the same passage as illustrating the essence of poetry—" in this battle Homer is swept away by the action, and he, too, raves like the war-god or a forest fire." [2] A poet, in modern phrase, must " live his subject." Of course the idea that an artist must immerse himself in his subject is obvious enough, and could not escape the most elementary critic; but it is an idea capable of infinite degrees, ranging from the power of simply " keeping one's eye on the object," which we have found in Aristotle and Dionysius, to the entire absorption of the poet's personality in his creation. There is a difference between *seeing*, externally, the passions of others (which satisfied neo-classical critics), and the " living " of emotions, without the intrusion of the intellect—a poetic process on which some modern

---

[1] 9, 10 : *Il.* 17, 645, ἐν δὲ φάει καὶ ὄλεσσον.
[2] 9, 11, quoting *Il.* 15, 605 for the simile.

critics lay so much emphasis.[1] Even this latter theory, in a crude form, must have been familiar to fifth-century Athenians, since it was ridiculed by Aristophanes— when Agathon is writing a feminine play he must needs dress as a woman.[2] Longinus, no doubt, was too Greek to reject the part played by the intellect. He would hardly have followed Plato in dethroning Reason from her place as the poet's supreme director. But Reason may willingly abrogate her own function, and yield to Emotion. His quotations from the lost *Phaethon* of Euripides are introduced to prove that this poet so completely merged himself in his subject that the author's soul had " mounted the car of Phaethon, and shared the danger of his winged horses."[3] If a poet must relive his subject, it is no less the critic's duty to absorb his poet ; and perhaps the finest praise that Longinus could earn would be a claim that he not only loves the epic, but can project himself into the spirit of Homer. It is inevitable that Homer should have many avatars, of whom Longinus was only one. The classical critic was unable to recapture the first flush of Greek poetry, as yet uncontaminated by later self-consciousness. But it is to the lasting credit of Longinus that, far more than any other Greek, he divested his criticism from the accretions of moralists and philosophers, and relived the essential Homer *sub specie aeternitatis*.

§ 2. CRITICISM OF POETS

The foregoing account may throw some light on the general principles which guided Longinus in his approach to the poets. It remains to consider the appli-

---

[1] See e.g. J. Benda, *Belphégor*, p. 76 f.
[2] Aristoph. *Thesm.* 148, quoted by Benda.
[3] See 15, 3 f.

cation of these principles in more detail. His catholicity
is best shown by the fact that no considerable poet
from Homer and Hesiod to Theocritus and Apollonius
is omitted. Naturally, after the lyric age, the great
Athenians have the fullest share of his attention ; and
his estimate of the three masters of tragedy is the more
instructive because it may be taken as the established
judgment of antiquity.

Aeschylus does not escape from the time-honoured
charge of bombast ; but, on the other hand, he is praised
for the most heroic images, which Longinus illustrates
by a passage from the *Septem*, describing the oath taken
by the seven leaders over a slain bull. Even so, he
admits, these images are often " woolly " ($\pi o \kappa o \epsilon \iota \delta \epsilon \hat{\iota} s$) as
in the line

> The house is frenzied ; bacchanal, the roof

—where the metaphor is too " strong " for any Greek,
and Euripides is praised for toning it down.[1] It is
perhaps in his estimate of the latter poet that Longinus
is seen at his best. He quotes from at least seven
Euripidean plays with a remarkable appreciation of
their merits and defects : Euripides is unsurpassed in
his tragic description of love and madness—the *Bacchae*
and *Orestes* are quoted for the latter—and " though his
nature is not elevated," he often compels it to be tragic.[2]

There remains Sophocles, whose primacy, in the
opinion of Longinus, is perhaps sufficiently marked by
his estimate of the *Oedipus Tyrannus*, and by his quotations from two other plays.[3] But here again, the
critic is no blind partisan—the greater the poet's person-

[1] 15, 5, 6. Chapter 32 is devoted to metaphors, but mainly those
of Plato.

[2] Ch. 15 ; see also 40, where his power of composition and use of
common words (as already noted by Aristotle) are commended.

[3] 15, 7.

ality, the greater the need of caution in criticism. No
saner principle has ever been laid down than the famous
appreciation of the thirty-third chapter, where the
argument is that no high genius is flawless, whereas a
mediocrity often produces work of impeccable finish.
Homer himself trips—the admission, as we know from
Horace, had become a proverb—and Longinus had himself noted " slips that gave him no pleasure."   " But,"
he asks, " should we therefore choose to be Apollonius
or Theocritus rather than Homer, or the blameless
Eratosthenes rather than Archilochus ?   Bacchylides
and Ion, too, are free from blemish—both polished writers
in the elegant style, while Pindar and Sophocles, though
they sometimes burn everything in their fiery career,
are often strangely extinguished and fall lamentably flat.
Yet, would anyone in his senses prefer to be Bacchylides
instead of Pindar, or Ion instead of Sophocles himself,
whose single *Oedipus* outweighs all the dramas of Ion ?"

Posterity—the final court to which Longinus appealed—
has remarkably confirmed this judgment.   If there are
points of reservation, they arise out of the inevitable
differences between the ancient and the modern outlook.
Apollonius is no longer " compared " to Homer ;   and
if—as will appear—Longinus is perhaps a little blind to
the merits of the *Argonautica*, he is rightly conscious
of its defects.   In tragedy, we must take his opinion
of Ion very largely on trust ;   at any rate he is supported
by classical verdict, since only a few fragments have
survived.   It is possible that Ion might more strongly
appeal to later taste ;   but, on classical principles, he
was certainly no rival of Sophocles.   As regards Bacchylides, we are on safer ground, for the modern discovery
of his Epinikian odes has proved—if proof were needed
—that Longinus correctly gauged the difference between
" faultless art " and genius.

On the whole, therefore, his censure of those who fail
to reach the standard of his poetic " heroes " seems
justified. But what of the heroes themselves ? So far
from over-estimating their excellence, it may even
be that he is too ready to admit their flaws. Where,
for example, does Pindar fail lamentably ? If cross-
questioned, Longinus would possibly have objected to
some of his metaphors. According to Galen, " Even a
Pindar is not praised for calling fountains the ' leaves of
Ocean,' still less, when he speaks of ' sharpening the
tongue on an anvil of truth.' " [1]   It is of course a
commonplace to remark on the wealth of Pindar's
imagination, which here and elsewhere runs to riot ;
but we must remember that the classical mistrust of
excessive metaphor may have prejudiced Longinus more
than a lover of poetry would now think to be warranted.

But what, precisely, are the faults of Sophocles ?
Mr. Saintsbury asks whether all these were in the lost
plays. Others, however, besides Longinus, complained
of his " inequality " ; [2]   and certainly we need not
search beyond the extant plays to discover their reasons.
In the *Ajax* (an early play) the prolonged quarrel over
the arms was condemned by a scholiast, who thought
the scene sophistic : " in his wish to lengthen the play
he showed frigidity and spoiled the tragic pathos." [3]
Many moderns have agreed with the scholiast ; notably
Goethe, who hoped that Sophocles did not write the
last scene.[4] As to the " lengthening " itself, the charge
is simply due to misunderstanding. The subject of the
play is not merely the death of Ajax, but the removal

---

[1] Galen, *de puls. diff.* 3, 6.

[2] Dion. Hal. *de vet. script. cens.* 2, 11 ; Plut. *de aud. poet.* 13.

[3] Schol. on *Aj.* 1123. So on 1127, a passage " more comic than
tragic."

[4] *Eckermann's Convers.* i. 371.

of the stigma attached to his death, and the recognition, by burial, of his rights as a hero with an Athenian cult.[1] We might as reasonably object to all that comes after Caesar's death in Shakespeare. There may be more in the scholiast's complaint of sophistry. To our minds, the wrangle over the arms is tedious and lacking in either poetic or dramatic interest. A much greater play—the *Antigone*—has been censured, at least by many modern critics, in respect of its final scene.[2] We may conclude that, after due allowance for ignorance, ancient and modern, there is good ground for the charge of " inequality "—which, after all, might be brought against Shakespeare or any other genius, as Longinus was the first to show. Here Sophocles himself gives the clue, by his own acknowledgment—if Plutarch is correct—of a development from the early influence of Aeschylus to a stage of " character " drama—such as we find in the characterisation of the later *Philoctetes*.[3] A line from one of his first plays certainly gives a good instance of the frigidity which Demetrius, who quotes it, calls a " neighbour " of the elevated :

$$\dot{a}\pi\upsilon\nu\delta\acute{a}\kappa\omega\tau o\varsigma \; o\dot{\upsilon} \; \tau\rho\alpha\pi\epsilon\zeta o\hat{\upsilon}\tau\alpha\iota \; \kappa\acute{\upsilon}\lambda\iota\xi \text{[4]}$$

—" a cup unbased hath no entablement " for " a bottomless cup is not placed on the table." No better example of the thin division between the sublime and the ridiculous

---

[1] See Norwood, p. 136. According to A. C. Pearson, *Class. Quart.* 16, 3, p. 124 f., the last part of the play is meant to show that Ajax was not a traitor.

[2] *Ant.* 904-912.   [3] Plut. *de prof. in virt.* 7.

[4] From the *Triptolemus* (about 468 B.C.). See Pearson, *Fragm. Soph.* ii. p. 251 ; Demetr. 2, 114. In *Cl. Rev.* 40, 4 (1926), p. 115, Roberts held that Demetrius' words τὸν Αἰσχύλου διαπεπαιχὼς ὄγκον must mean more than " imitation," and (in *Greek Rhetoric*, p. 66), he suggests that the line may have been spoken by some drunken slave, a homely character like the watchman of the *Agamemnon*.

could easily be found than this pomposity. Demetrius seems to have thought that the line was a conscious travesty of Aeschylean style ; but, though ancient dramatists—as we have seen—could freely criticise one another, it is difficult to believe that deliberate burlesque was a tragic weapon ; as Demetrius himself says elsewhere, " laughter is a foe of tragedy." The verse is surely nothing but a proof that Sophocles, like Homer, could nod ; and the chief point in recalling such failures lies in the fact that Sophocles outgrew them. They are experiments tried and discarded in his progress towards the perfect style of the *Oedipus at Colonus*. That development—from the " swelling " of Aeschylus to the lucidity and simplicity of the severest diction compatible with the highest poetry—is perhaps the most remarkable achievement of Greek literature. The severity, indeed, is such that the beauty has often been missed by those who have no grasp of the true Attic ideals—who find coldness in the sculptures of the Parthenon and even in the Hermes of Praxiteles. In literature, as in sculpture, the Greeks did not attain this perfection of restraint without making mistakes on the way, though the goal was gained within the lifetime of Sophocles as well as Pheidias. One fault of Longinus himself—shared by other Greek critics, who viewed their classical authors too statically—was to neglect the development possible within the limits of a single life. It is a trite observation to note the rapid florescence of Greek literature and art ; but it is often forgotten that individual poets and artists had their own " periods." In other words, the wonderful progress of the fifth century was quite as much due to the development of the individual as to the improvements of his contemporaries or successors. Sophocles, in particular, did not stand still during his long life ; and the marvel of the *Oedipus at Colonus* proves that he developed to the very end. But Classical critics, while fully aware that a poet might change his style or his outlook on life, seem to have undervalued the importance of " comparing," not one writer with another, but one writer with himself.

With Sophocles and Euripides, Longinus really closes his canon of great poets. The fourth century was, as a fact, almost negligible in poetry ; and the critic passes to the Alexandrines, for whom, as we have already seen, he has only faint praise, just as he finds little to admire in the prose after Demosthenes. He recognises the art and polish of the school, but for this a high price is paid in the face of glaring faults pervading both prose and poetry. The Romans of the Ciceronian and Augustan periods had learned too much (for good or evil) from Alexandria to belittle her influence, and Virgil, in particular, had turned Apollonius to magnificent use for Rome. But the Greek critics were not concerned with Latin poetry, nor were they historians of comparative literature. Possibly the Alexandrines were too near for a truer perspective ; but, in any case, they were thought to challenge Homer, and could not stand the test. Hence both Demetrius (who ignores the great Alexandrine poets) and Longinus failed to appreciate the *Argonautica*, whether for its own merits or for its influence on Rome. Nevertheless, if Apollonius seemed " outclassed " by Homer, it is remarkable that Theocritus made no favourable impression. For the Idyll started a new movement in Greek literature, and deserved to be appraised without prejudice. No doubt Longinus thought Bucolic poetry to be merely " graceful," and he was only occupied with the " elevated " style. But, even with this limitation, he might have singled out the Simaetha of the second idyll, since her passion was not unworthy of the Sappho whom he loved. Or,

again, he might have felt, with Virgil, the charm of the
seventh idyll, which breathes the spirit of the country-
side. The Roman Gellius—a critic immeasurably below
Longinus—had at least the taste to admire the " native
sweetness " of Theocritus, which even Virgil, as he
says, could not reproduce.[1] Longinus had good reason
for his dislike of Alexandrine literature as a whole, but
he was unable to separate the scanty wheat from the
abundant chaff. His eyes were fixed on the great ages,
and their brilliance obscured an author, like Theocritus,
whose aim and achievement were foreign to fifth-century
ideals. Addison (oblivious of *Lycidas*) warned the poet
not to rest content with " pastoral and the lower kinds
of poetry " ; and, although Theocritus had anticipated his advice to " acquaint himself with the pomp
and magnificence of Courts," even this stage of poetic
development would not have weighed with a critic
fresh from the study of Homer and Sophocles.[2] Judged
by the true Hellenic standard, the Bucolic poet was not
ungenerously described as a " most fortunate " artist,
but still not to be reckoned among the glories of Greece.
In his own day, Theocritus had complained that Homer
was held to be " enough for all " ; and a Greek critic
of the Roman age could at best regard the idyll as
he—or we—might approve of a Tanagra figure or a
Syracusan coin, perfect in its own way, but not grand
and sublime with the Pheidian majesty of the *Iliad*.

§ 3. Longinus on Homer

It is perhaps not too much to say that a Greek critic's
reputation must stand or fall by his estimate of Homer.
We have already seen how, in the course of the centuries,
from Xenophanes to Plutarch, the pride and delight in

---

[1] Gell, N.A. 8, 9, 8.   [2] *Spectator*, 417.

15

the supreme manifestation of Greek poetry were sometimes tempered, sometimes completely ruined, by the
intrusion of moral and religious qualms, never entirely
laid to rest.   To the uncritical, no doubt, these difficulties
did not matter.   In every age there were many for whom
the wrath of Achilles or the " surge and thunder " of
the *Odyssey*, needed no excuse ; but the critics were
compelled to face the trouble, unless (like Dionysius
or Demetrius) they shelved it by concentration on the
pure poetry of the epic.   Here, as elsewhere, Longinus
represents the considered judgment of those who, while
regarding Homer as first and foremost a poet, refused to
shirk the moral difficulty.   He confronts the old problems, and without dismay.   Plato, with his thorough
purge, might now be neglected, even by a whole-
hearted admirer of Plato's genius.   But that philosopher was at least an open enemy ; Longinus had
still to save Homer from his very dubious friends
—the Stoics.   It is not surprising that, in this final
bout, he yields a little ground.   The ninth chapter—
the essence of his poetic creed—makes some concession
to the pressure of philosophy.   He admits that there
are certain features in Homer—the feuds of the gods,
their vengeance and all their passions—that cannot be
reconciled with religion or even with common humanity.
In all this side of the epic—as he finely clinches the
matter—Homer has done his utmost to make gods of
the men in the *Iliad* and men of the gods.   Here a
modern could reasonably explain the paradox : as has
been well written, the heroic age " has so high a sense
of the dignity of man that it can afford to make fun of
the gods." [1]   Stoicism, however, preferred to think the
gods away rather than to think them undignified ; and
so Longinus has no choice but to say in comment that

[1] C. M. Bowra, *Tradition and Design in the Iliad*, p. 239.

" these stories are wholly impious if they are not understood as allegory." [1]

No Greek, if he were not impious himself, could have said less. Perhaps it would have been better if no Greek, who loved Homer, had said more. Longinus, at least, is content with this brief recognition of the difficulty, and then turns to his real interest—to the epic as literature. He appeals, as it were, from the poet drunk (but the drunkenness is only apparent) to the poet sober, when Homer represents the gods as worthy of their godhead, and—still better—when he describes the nobility of men.

The same chapter contains what is perhaps the most striking proof of his intuitive wisdom—the handling of a problem which, if it had not yet grown the hydra-heads of the modern Homeric Question, was at all events a snake already hatched in Hellenistic grass. Down to the beginning of the Alexandrine age the unity of Homer —that is, of the *Iliad* and *Odyssey*—was unquestioned even by those scholars who, with Zenodotus, suspected or rejected the Cyclic poems as un-Homeric. But higher criticism, once started, is not easily restrained ; and Zenodotus had his natural successors in Xenon and Hellanicus, who took the ultimate step of Separatism. Unfortunately, we know little of the arguments on which these " Chorizontes " relied, beyond the fact that they pointed out minor discrepancies, such as a difference between the number of Cretan cities mentioned in the two poems, and objected that the heroes ate fish in the *Odyssey*, but not in the *Iliad*. The snake was not only scotched but killed by the great Aristarchus, and only its skin survived in the days of Seneca, who

---

[1] Hermogenes ($\pi\epsilon\rho\grave{\iota}$ $\imath\delta$. 1, 6) evades the trouble by explaining that the poet, aiming at pleasure, may speak of the gods in a human way ($\dot{\alpha}\nu\theta\rho\omega\pi\sigma\pi\alpha\theta\hat{\omega}s$).

thought that life was too short to discuss so unprofitable a subject.[1]   Besides the recorded objections of the
Separatists (which are trivial enough), it is possible
that there were other difficulties, of more value, which
Aristarchus dismissed in his refutation of Xenon's
" paradox." [2]   Aristotle had already commented upon
the broad differences between the two poems : the
Iliad was simple in plot and " passionate," the *Odyssey*,
complex and " ethical," full of character, and, since it
ends happily, producing a pleasure akin to that of
comedy.[3]   The former was the prototype of tragedy, the
latter, of comedy ; and those who thought, with Plato
(in one of his moods), that the same man could not
write both tragedy and comedy, might readily apply
the argument to their prototypes.

Longinus was not of their number. Even if the
heresy had not been crushed, his reverence for a " personal " Homer would no doubt have prevented any
tampering with tradition. The niceties of Wolfian
scholarship were of course beyond the scope of ancient
grammarians ; while, on the other hand, the essential
likeness of the two great poems was thought sufficient
evidence of identity in authorship. At the present
time, when many students of Homer have rejected
Separatism, and have practically returned to the
Aristarchan Unity, it is not surprising that Longinus
does not seem to betray the slightest consciousness of
any Homeric Question. None the less, the palpable

---

[1] Sen. *de brev. vit.* 13.   On the Separatists, see Susemihl. *Gesch.
der griech. Litt. in der Alexandrinerzeit*, ii. p. 149.   Long before this
final step, the way had been prepared by denying the authenticity
of the *Cypria* (Herod. 2, 17).

[2] Schol. Ven. on *Il.* 12, 45.   The Separatists are mentioned on
Il. 2, 356, 649 ; 10, 476 ; 11, 430, 692 ; 12, 96 ; 13, 365 ; 16, 747 ;
21, 416, 550.

[3] *poet.* 1453*a*, 30 f. ; 1459*b*, 15.

differences of tone and treatment, already noted by Aristotle, and probably stressed by Xenon, could not be entirely neglected. Longinus found or adopted a solution which—granted his premises—is both simple and inevitable: Homer had composed the *Iliad* in his prime, the *Odyssey*, in his old age. The *Iliad* "was written at the height of his inspiration, full of action and struggle, while the Odyssey is for the most part narrative, as is characteristic of old age."[1] Action, it will be observed, still stands as the end of poetry; whereas narrative implies garrulity or prolixity. "So" —Longinus proceeds—"in the *Odyssey* Homer may be compared to a setting sun, whose grandeur remains without its intensity. . . . I have not forgotten the storms in the *Odyssey* and the tale of the Cyclops and the like. If I speak of old age, it is still the old age of Homer. . . . The genius of great poets, as their passion declines, finds its final expression in the drawing of character."

The Odyssey, then, is like a comedy of manners (οἱονεὶ κωμῳδία τις ἠθολογουμένη); and such a character ranks second to the tragic pathos of the *Iliad*. So far, the discrimination is perfectly just, since the *Odyssey*—quite apart from much imitation and even parody of the earlier epic—is certainly akin, both in subject and treatment, to Comedy in the ancient connotation. Moreover, bearing in mind the New Comedy,[2] where character-drawing is seen to be a late-comer in literature, Longinus could not avoid the conclusion that the *Odyssey* belongs to the old age of Homer.

[1] Cf. οἱ γέροντες μακρολόγοι διὰ τὴν ἀσθένειαν. The notion occurs in *Hom. h. Aphr.* 5, 237, of Tithonus, whose voice, from weakness, ῥέει ἄσπετος.

[2] Longinus does not mention the great writers of the New Comedy (apparently because they are not "elevated"), although he allows that Aristophanes is sometimes dignified (40, 2).

Scholars who follow the present fashion of clinging to the one and indivisible author of both epics are presumably content with this theory of old age in its literal sense. On the other hand, those who stress the undoubted fact that the epic age in Greece exceeded the limits of a single life, can easily re-state the argument in more modern terms. We may hold that the *Odyssey* exhibits many traces of advancing years, not indeed of an individual, but of a period, whose age—still, however, like Charon's, *cruda viridisque*—has declined from the fresh vigour, the passionate intensity, of the Wrath of Achilles.

With regard to the "garrulity," it is clear that Longinus does not object so much to the narrative in itself (although he is Aristotelian enough to prefer Action) as to its matter and content. The *Odyssey* dealt with the marvellous, and marvels were not lightly stomached by any critic after Aristotle. Not that the Greeks, at least before the Enlightenment, were insensible to the charm of the fairy-tale, as distinguished from the true myth, although these two forms tend often to merge into one another. Aeschylus had adorned the wanderings of Io with wonders no less incredible than those described in the voyage of Odysseus. Herodotus had filled the fringes of the known world with strange tales of Arimaspi and Hyperboreans, on the principle (which even Aristotle approved) that, whether truly or not, "people say so." Even the sophistic Reason could not eliminate the marvellous, as the later "historian" Megasthenes and other purveyors of *mirabilia* are sufficient to prove. In the twentieth century, there is no need to excuse this delight in the fairy-tale; but Greek philosophers and critics thought otherwise. They were forced, indeed, to make some concession to the Tale—children are not drawn from their play, nor old men from their chimney corner, for nothing. Aristotle himself, the champion of Reason, had to make room for the irrational. He felt the pleasure of the Tale, although he was well aware that marvels are more suited to epic than to dramatic poetry. It was Homer who " chiefly taught the proper use of the falsehood," and even then, he adds, the irrational parts of the *Odyssey* would be intolerable in the hands of an inferior poet, without Homer's brilliant treatment.[1] A line must somewhere be drawn ; and Longinus seems to draw it in much the same place as Aristotle. He passes, and indeed admires " the tempests in the *Odyssey*, and the story of the Cyclops and the like "—incidents, by the way, which seem fabulous enough—but he protests against glaring absurdities, such as the story of Circe and the swine, or of the infant Zeus nurtured by doves, or the slaying of the suitors.

The *Odyssey* has been called a great romantic poem, which is true, if we remember that it is no less a perfect example of classicism. In the highest poetry the modern distinctions of the classic and romantic have no more ultimate value than the ancient divisions of style, which the Greeks themselves recognised as inadequate to account for Homer. Still, the elements in the *Odyssey* that appeal only or mainly to the " Romantic mind " are so considerable that the poem, as a whole, could not win the unqualified approval of purely classical critics, even if they seem to quote passages from both poems with equal admiration. But the folk-tales, at least, were a strain on Longinus, as on all others who were concerned with the proper use of the lie.

The growth of Romanticism needs no discussion here ; but it may not be impertinent to recall how hardly and

---

[1] *poet.* ch. 24.

recently the fairy-tale has won acceptance in high poetry. In no other sphere, perhaps, was neo-Classic prejudice so rampant. Half a century after the *Midsummer Night's Dream*, Mr. Pepys—a constant and, on the whole, a judicious playgoer—described that romantic drama as the " most insipid ridiculous play that I ever saw in my life " ; so that we are prepared to find that, a few years later, Dryden was compelled to apologise for " the fairy way of writing." [1]   With the full triumph of Reason in the next century, Addison had occasion to protest against " the men of cold fancies and philosophical dispositions " who despised the fairy way, as too improbable to affect the imagination.[2]   Still later, Dr. Johnson's faint praise of Shakespeare in his " wild and fantastical " mood is as damning as Pepys' more robust disapproval, and surely deserved more than the mild expostulation (*Fie !*) with which Keats erased the Johnsonian comment in his own copy of Shakespeare.[3] Even the author of the *Ancient Mariner*—the most Homeric and the most Romantic of voyagers—thought it not superfluous to ask for that suspension of disbelief which constitutes poetic faith.   The wheel moved slowly before it was spun full-circle by Novalis, who defended fairy-tales as the highest form of poetic art precisely because they are illogical.[4]

Compared with the deadly logic of the neo-Classicists, the Reason of the Classics seems almost mild.   Longinus, at least, is temperate in his strictures on the old age of Homer.   His fables are incredible—but they are the dreams of Zeus.   The phrase, like so many in Longinus,

---

[1] Pepys, *Diary* (29th Sept. 1662) ; Dryden, *The Author's Apology for Heroic Poetry* (1677), mentioning (with others) the *Midsummer Night's Dream*.

[2] *Spectator*, 419 (1712).

[3] *Keats' Shakespeare*, by Dr. C. Spurgeon (1928).

[4] See I. Babbitt, *New Laocoon*, p. 80.

is arresting. It would of course be an anachronism to
credit him with a modern theory of poetic intuition, as
a dreamlike working of the imagination, to be rehandled
in the later stage of consciousness. To the Classic mind
the poet is inspired, but no dreamer. If the Muses
appeared to Hesiod in a dream, they only warned him
of his mission to write poetry in waking hours. Yet
Longinus, the Platonist, may well have seen that the
ecstasy of the poet is nearly akin to the dream. The
grand impossibilities of Homer were, indeed, such stuff
as dreams are made on—they had never been subjected
to the supreme test of Reason ; but, none the less, as
Virgil might have said, the mind of the divine poet
could serve for the Ivory door, through which these
dreams, however false, should pass into the world of
poetry.

In the foregoing account, no attempt has been made
to gloze over the limitations of Longinus. Himself a
modest man—after expressing his own opinion on a
point of literary interest,[1] he adds " let everyone sub-
scribe to the view which pleases him best "—he would
have asked for no better treatment than he metes
out to the great poets, whose virtues and faults he so
impartially records. In certain aspects, he naturally
shows the drawbacks of his age and race. He was
hampered by the doctrine of Imitation, still in un-
disputed possession of the æsthetic field. Theoretically,
Mimesis was not seriously misleading. Aristotle had
nowhere understood it as mere " copying "—on the
contrary, an artist should improve Nature. The mischief came when the representation of Nature was
logically extended to the imitation of the Book. This

[1] 36, 4.

extension was at least implicit in the mind of Aristotle : for, as he held that Homer and Sophocles could not be surpassed in their imitation of Nature, it followed that these masters were models themselves to be imitated.

In strict reasoning, such a theory would imply the extinction of all later literature. Homer would indeed be " enough for all," since the only excuse for imitating the masters lay in " emulation." But, *ex hypothesi*, Homer—being (practically) perfect—could not be excelled or even equalled. The Romans evaded the difficulty by claiming that a new environment and a new language entitled them to imitate ; and the greater Latin poets proved their own justification. It was not till the Silver Age that both poets and critics realised the impossibility of surpassing or even of equalling the models—the effort, as Velleius knew, could but end in despair.[1] Later Greek poets had not the Roman excuse of a fresh start. They were working on the old lines, and their credit could only be saved by the most liberal interpretation of Mimesis. So the word turns out to be, not *metathesis*, or servile copying (which of course no one defended), but a proper deference to tradition, which does not preclude originality. As Demetrius explains,[2] Thucydides may borrow from Homer, but he makes the borrowing his own—a line of argument that satisfied many defenders of Virgil from Macrobius to Dryden. Viewed in this light, Imitation may lose its force, but it certainly loses its terrors. For no Greek could have accused Thucydides or Plato of " copying " Homer. Unfortunately, Longinus is sometimes moved to use Mimesis in its narrower sense. To say that Plato's debt to Homer is not plagiarism but taking a mould from beautiful forms or works of art, is a most unhappy

---

[1] See *Roman Poetry*, p. 96.   [2] *de eloc.* 112 f.

metaphor.[1] But we need not condemn Longinus for a single loose expression. His reverence for the models is really nothing more—though nothing less—than a respect for the continuity of tradition. If Herodotus and Plato are inspired by Homer, they, in their turn, should inspire their successors in the unbroken line of great literature.

In recent years, tradition has been ably defended,[2] but it has also been attacked for good reasons as well as bad. Its rigid observance is often regarded as a cramping of originality, as (for example) the history of later Roman epic appears to show. But one instance does not prove a rule. Both Silius Italicus and Milton followed the epic tradition. The difference between a poetaster and a great poet cannot be explained by reference to a Form whose possibilities, when they seem most exhausted, may be suddenly revived by a fresh inspiration. In poetry, at least, new wine can be poured into old bottles. Longinus has been condemned for advising the young author to ask himself : How would Plato or Demosthenes have expressed this ? If, indeed, the critic had meant to recommend " respectful plagiarism "—as traditional art has been called or miscalled— he would have been a poor champion of the principle ; but Longinus is merely insisting that every author must have a standard—a demand which a poet may surely accept, unless he claims to be his own standard. We are not misled by Keats for acknowledging his debt to Chaucer :—

> That I may dare, in wayfaring,
> To stammer where old Chaucer used to sing ;

---

[1] 13, 4.

[2] A notable defence can be found in T. S. Eliot's *The Sacred Wood*.

nor do we think Morris a plagiarist because he confesses that his *Jason* was derived from the same fountain-head of English poetry.

Again, Longinus (like all Greek critics) has been accused of laying too much emphasis on the imitation, and too little on the creation. His native poetry is itself the finest example of these two qualities perfectly combined ; for, as has been well said, Greek literature, at its best, is to a remarkable degree a creative imitation of Homer.[1] The Greek critics would have accepted this sentence, although they seem to lay no stress on the importance of creation. This, however, is only a verbal discrepancy : the word " creative " is included in Mimesis ; Sophocles, if not a creator in virtue of the term ποιητής, none the less creates in the process of imitation. But, for Longinus, the true Mimesis closed with Plato and Demosthenes and still earlier in poetry, with Sophocles and Euripides. Alexandria, with its perfect art, had lost the union of spirit and form that alone could make for permanence. In his own day, something had gone even more seriously wrong with literature, whether the cause was the loss of political freedom or (as he preferred to believe) the indolence and luxury of the times. Greek literature was a closed book —which is certainly true of Greek poetry, as far as the authentic spirit of Hellenism is concerned. Only that spirit could give the permanence which he thought was the final proof of validity. Even this criterion, which may seem self-evident, has not been allowed to pass unchallenged. It has been said that " far more of the great art of the past is actually obsolete than certain critics pretend, who forget what a special apparatus of erudition they themselves bring to their criticism.

[1] I. Babbitt, *Literature and the American College*, p. 233.

The *Divina Commedia* is a representative example." [1]
No one doubts, of course, that mere survival does not
count. Silius Italicus has outlived much that we know
to have been of more permanent value. But Longinus
was not thinking of haphazard survival. His point is
that certain works deserve to survive, and that they
prove their value by the *consensus* of generations,
represented by the " serious " or " intellectual " men
on whose judgment Aristotle had relied. The precise
amount of " erudition " required for such judges is of
minor importance, provided that we do not hold that
literature should appeal only to the uneducated. With
this proviso, we may agree with Longinus in his anti-
cipation of St. Vincent's test of great literature—*quod
semper, quod ubique, quod ab omnibus*—in his own words,
" every living age, which cannot be convicted of in-
sanity, has given Homer, Demosthenes and other noble
writers prizes that have been preserved to this day, and
are likely to be preserved ' as long as water flows and
the tall trees flourish.' "

The treatise *On the Sublime* completes the critical
achievement of Greece, by uniting and reconciling the
divergencies of Plato and Aristotle. Longinus understands, with Plato, that poetry is inspired ; but, unlike
Plato, he neither fears nor distrusts inspiration. He
understands, with Aristotle, that poetry works through
the emotions ; but, if its process is cathartic (and he
nowhere mentions the Aristotelian theory), the purgation is higher, more stimulative, than the *Poetics* appears
to suggest. The attempt to class him as the " First
Romantic critic " [2] is as misplaced as the view that he
is to be identified with the minister of Zenobia—his

---

[1] I. A. Richards, *Principles*, p. 222 (see ch. 29).

[2] R. A. Scott-James, in his interesting book, *The Making of
Literature*, ch. 8.

attitude towards the *Odyssey*, his reverence for tradition, his contempt of Alexandria, his disregard of nature-poetry, are all alien to the spirit of romance. But he not only stands on the apex of criticism for his own Greek literature ; he is the last of the ancients, but also the first of the moderns, in holding the principles common to all good writing, irrespective of changing fashions or peculiarities ; and in recognising—without the Stoic extravagance of statement—the prime truth of literary creation, that " it is impossible for these, whose lifelong thoughts and habits are petty and servile, to produce noble work, deserving immortality."

After Longinus, there continued to be criticism, of a sort ; but there were no new principles, except one which, although of supreme value in the history of æsthetics, came too late to be of any service to the classical critic. The neo-Platonic abandonment of Imitation, in favour of Imagination, gave no impulse to a fresh study of literature. At most, the theory disposed of Plato's heresy, and this had long been shelved or refuted by common-sense. Proclus turned the tables on Plato by the apposite remark that he was as good a poet as Homer, and would have been expelled from his own Republic. The way had been prepared for the triumph of Imagination by the neo-Pythagoreans, among whom Numenius had held that sensible things are symbols of divine ideas ; the whole world is a symbolic poem, a revelation of some spiritual truth. It followed that the poet, being inspired, was no mere copyist of nature, but the revealer of the non-sensible. A little later, the sophist Philostratus [1] gave a new

---

[1] *vit. Apoll.* 6, 19. Philostratus is dated *circa* 170-245. Sandys, i. p. 237. On the whole subject see H. P. R. Finberg, in *Class. Quart.* 20, p. 148 f.

content to the term φαντασία : Pheidias and Praxiteles
are not imitative, but imaginative ; imitation can only
produce what it sees, imagination creates what it has
not seen, on the analogy of the visible. Plotinus settled
the matter by his pronouncement that the arts " go
back to the reasons from which nature comes ; and
further they create much out of themselves and add to
that which is defective, as being themselves in possession
of beauty." [1] Plato's æsthetic was finally convicted by
his own idealism. We are within sight of the modern
view that the function of art is not to imitate our ex-
periences but to transcend experience. But the practical
failure of the new æsthetics is sufficiently shown in the
lamentable incursion of a neo-Platonist into criticism.
Porphyry's Homeric *Questions* may not be worse than
Aristotle's in the same vein ; but his *Cave of the Nymphs*
is a startling proof of critical bankruptcy. The simple
and beautiful description of natural scenery, in the
cave of Ithaca, becomes a solemn allegory—the most
perverted example of a method which for so many
centuries had misled Greek critics the more seriously
because, like most serious errors, it contained a measure
of truth.

In actual criticism of documents, the end is reached
with Dio of Prusa (Chrysostom), the friend of Plutarch,
and perhaps more or less the contemporary of Longinus
himself.[2] His æsthetic is that of his period, symbolic
—art seeks to reveal the unseen and imageless in the
visible. The ancient poets were like attendants outside the temples of the Muses : and, though not them-

---

[1] Bosanquet, *Hist. of Æsth.*, p. 113. On the æsthetic of Plotinus
(205-270) see W. R. Inge, *The Philosophy of Plotinus*, 3, 11, 211 f.
(*Enneads*, i. 6 ; v. 8, 1 ; vi. 7 ; IX. 2, 11) ; and P. E. More,
Hellenistic Philosophies, p. 184 f. Maximus Tyrius (XVII) refutes
Plato on other grounds.

[2] *circa* 40-114 (Sandys, i. p. 290).

selves initiate, they could hear mystic sounds proceeding
from the inner shrine, and were thus inspired with brief
flashes of the truth ; but the successors of Homer and
Hesiod lacked even this partial inspiration, so that, in
a vain attempt to initiate the multitude, they could
only set up an open booth in the market-places of
tragedy.[1] But Dio's æsthetic is really no improvement
on Plato : he still misunderstands the nature of the
imagination, and is still worried about the " lies " of
Homer. He can do no better in explaining the fables
of the *Odyssey* than by offering the naïve suggestion
that Homer started well ; but as the poem went on,
he found his audience easily persuaded, and so supplied
them with marvels to their heart's desire.[2] Homer,
presumably, had sunk to the level of the hack-writer
who gives the public what it wants.

Still, in a single speech, Dio forgot all this crudity,
and—if not himself inspired—became a sensible critic
in his well-known valuation of the three great dramatists,
who suggested an obvious comparison by their treatment of the same subject—the myth of Philoctetes.[3]
His criticism, while largely conventional, is at least
sound in so far as it reflects the agreed opinion of antiquity. Aeschylus is described as lofty and dignified ;
Euripides, as " political " (i.e. rhetorical), and not only
excellent in technique, but showing wonderful power
in dialogue and lyric. Sophocles is midway—Dio, of
course, speaks of his style without reference to the
actual date of his play, which was much later than the
Philoctetes of Euripides.[4] Without the simplicity and

---

[1] *Or.* 36 (Dindorf, ii. p. 58 f.).
[2] *Or.* 11 (Dindorf. i. p. 17a). On the other hand, he is a warm
admirer of poets, especially, of course, of Homer ; see *Or.* 12, etc.
[3] *Or.* 52.
[4] Euripides produced his play in 431, Sophocles in 409.

originality of Aeschylus, or the realism of Euripides,
Sophocles is first of the three for nobility, elevation
and splendour of language; and he manages the plot
of his *Philoctetes* more convincingly.

Where only the Sophoclean play survives, it is difficult
to estimate, with any certainty, the justice of Dio's
comparison. This very fact of survival is itself, perhaps, an argument in favour of Sophocles, whose play
gained a first prize. We know at least the general
treatment of the myth in the two other plays, and we
may assent to Jebb's interpretation of Dio, that by the
presence of Neoptolemus, Sophocles invested the story
with a dramatic value of deep significance.[1]

The whole piece of criticism has an interest, if only
rather negative; for Dio adds little to Aristotle, beyond
pushing the comparative method to a degree unknown
in the *Poetics*. Yet, however dependent on Aristotle,
we feel that Dio has seen the three plays with his own
eyes. And more: he has escaped from the absolute
dominion of Euripides—no small achievement, since
that poet is more akin than his rivals to Dio's own age.
Though eminently fair to both of these, he sums up the
glory of the Attic stage in the person of the poet whom
Aristotle and Longinus had marked out as its truest
representative. Like these two critics, he has the
double criterion of morals and technique, and is thus
in the genuine line of Greek criticism. His preference
for " noble " characters—" in Sophocles, Odysseus is
far gentler and franker than in Euripides "—harks
back to the old ethical prejudice; and Euripides is
himself praised for the moral influence of his lyrics.
But morality never protrudes; if Dio does not insist
on the pleasure of tragedy, his final criterion is the com-

---

[1] R. C. Jebb, ed. *Philoct.* p. xxvi. f.

16

bination of beauty and elevation, and his final praise
of his favourite is not for the moralist but for the artist,
in quoting Aristophanes on an admirer who

> Licked sweetness from the mouth of Sophocles
> As from a jar whose lips are honey-smeared.[1]

Of Dio's successors, little need be said. The age of
Marcus Aurelius shows that the ancient classics were
studied with avidity, including the Old Comedy, whose
appeal—despite Plutarch—is evident in the wit of
Lucian. Among the rhetoricians or sophists of the
Antonine age, we find no name to put in the same
category as Longinus. Aristides has a value of his own,
as showing the repute (or disrepute) of dramatic performances in the second century, and his attacks on the
comedy of his time may be compared with Tertullian ;
but his more or less incidental remarks on poetry are
either not original or worthless. In his views, for example, that poetry did not precede prose, that metre is
the sole distinction between the two forms, and (following Isocrates) that eulogies are easier in verse than prose,
Aristides only proves how early the lessons of Aristotle
had been forgotten.[2] Hermogenes of Tarsus is important
for the later history of rhetoric, if only as an exponent
of its decadence. With him and his contemporaries
or successors, the stream of Attic eloquence has been
lost in the marshes of technical analysis. The formal
side of oratory—tolerable in the hands of Longinus,
who can appreciate the spirit that inspires the form—
henceforward completely swamps the once-living art of
Demosthenes in the stagnant waters of the figures and
" ideas "—clearness, beauty, force, and the rest—which

---

[1] Aristoph. fr. 231a (Dindorf).
[2] See A. Boulanger, *Aelius Aristide* (1923).

form the characteristics of the orator. In this morass, poetry flounders even worse than oratory. Homer may still be an example for the rhetorician, but he has ceased to be studied for his own sake. The poet's vision has been lost in the art of persuasive speaking. All that can be said for Hermogenes is that he can still admire— if he cannot fully understand—the language of poetry as minister of pleasure, whether in Homer or Sappho or Sophocles or—one is glad to note—in Theocritus.[1] But, even so, the impression that Hermogenes leaves is that the poets have no powers which the prose-writers do not share, or perhaps exceed. It is instructive that he nowhere quotes the poets at any length : in this respect he is a Quintilian rather than a Dionysius or Longinus. Dio, too, has some grasp on the texts, and so far may be reckoned among the critics. Such a claim can hardly hold for a sophist like Maximus of Tyre, whose standpoint is sufficiently indicated by his almost total identification of poetry and philosophy—a worse error than Plato's solution of their ancient quarrel.[2] To Maximus, the only difference lies in the concealment of the medicine by the honeyed cup of poetry.

The Stoics had won in the end. Homer had become no more than, at best, a riddling philosopher with a taste for pleasing symbolism ; at worst, a marvel-monger, with an eye on the gallery. Those who were not busied with philosophy could still read the poets for simple delight, and we owe much to Athenaeus and Stobaeus for their salvage from the wreck of ancient literature. But Greek criticism—itself the first chapter of a book which can never be completed, while poetry

---

[1] For Theocritus see e.g. Hermog. περὶ ἰδ. ii. ch. 3 (for the naïve-ness of his characters) ; for Sappho's sweetness, *ib.* ch. 4.

[2] Max. Tyr. iv. (Hobein, p. 41 f.). Maximus lived in the reign of Commodus.

exists—was fulfilled in Longinus. After that last Testament of Beauty, there was no one to recognise that Homer and Sophocles are not rivals or vassals of the philosopher, but great personalities whose mission, by expressing beautiful thoughts in fair words, is to heighten both the pleasure and the value of human life.

INDEX

245

PRINTED IN GREAT BRITAIN AT THE UNIVERSITY PRESS, ABERDEEN